The Kit Carson Campaign

Colonel Christopher Carson in military dress. Courtesy Navajo Community College, Tsaile, Arizona.

THE KIT CARSON CAMPAIGN

THE LAST GREAT NAVAJO WAR

CLIFFORD E. TRAFZER

University of Oklahoma Press
Norman and London

By Clifford E. Trafzer

The Judge: The Life of Robert A. Hefner (Norman, 1975)
Anza, Garcés, and the Yuma Frontier (Yuma, Arizona, 1975)
Diné and Bilagáana: The Navajo and the First Anglos (Tsaile, Arizona, 1978)
Navajos and Spaniards (Tsaile, Arizona, 1978)
Navajo Raiders and Anglo Expansionists: A Conflict of Interests (Tsaile, Arizona, 1978)
The Volga Germans: Pioneers of the Northwest (Moscow, Idaho, 1980)
Yuma: Frontier Crossing of the Far Southwest (Wichita, Kansas, 1980)
The Kit Carson Campaign: The Last Great Navajo War (Norman, 1982)

Library of Congress Cataloging-in-Publication Data

Trafzer, Clifford E.
  The Kit Carson campaign.

  Bibliography: p. 261
  Includes index.
  1. Navaho Indians—Wars. 2. Navaho Indians—Removal. 3. Carson, Kit, 1809–1868. 4. Indians of North America—Southwest, New—Wars. 5. Indians of North America—Southwest, New—Removal. I. Title.
E83.859.T7   979'.02   81–40283
                               AACR2
ISBN: 0–8061–2265–X (pbk.)

To the memory of my father

and

for all Wyandot Indians
who were removed from their
homeland and were never
permitted to return
to the Ohio country

Contents

Illustrations

Maps

Preface

Kit Carson stands as one of the most famous figures in the history of the American West. He was no less renowned than Davy Crockett, Wyatt Earp, and Billy the Kid. Indeed, many of the "infamous" people of the West had something in common—they were killers. That is not to imply that they were all cold-blooded murderers, but many killed other human beings and became famous for their exploits. Carson was considered a great "Indian fighter," which meant that he killed his share of Indians during his days as a trapper and scout. When most individuals picture Kit Carson, they conjure up a vision of a strong, fearless frontiersman, peering out from the tall trees to survey the lush valleys of the majestic mountains of the West. Kit became a hero in his own day and has maintained that high status to this very day.

There is a segment of the American population, however, that never viewed Carson as a hero. The Navajo Indians, who comprise the single largest tribe in the United States, were great warriors and were known as the "lords of New Mexico." The Navajos maintained their supremacy in the Southwest until the 1860s, when Kit Carson launched a decisive campaign against them. The purpose of this book is to present the history of the Kit Carson campaign and to interpret the events and personalities involved in the last Navajo war. It is a presentation of the ideas and decisions that shaped the policy of the United States and the New Mexico Territory toward the Navajos. As with most other scholarly studies of Indians, this work relies heavily on the primary sources left by white persons. Some of the oral history preserved and provided by Navajos is also presented. The Indians' view of their own history is too often ignored, and the attempt is made here to include both white and Navajo accounts of the war and its tragic aftermath.

The book was conceived in 1969, while I was a student at Northern Arizona University. A Navajo friend and I surveyed the literature on his people and determined that a full-length history of the Diné ("the People") was needed, and he suggested I write such a history someday. My graduate work focused on Navajo history, and I collected many documents on the Navajo Wars. My doctoral dissertation was to deal with the entire span of the wars from 1846 through 1866. While completing research in Santa Fe in 1973, I learned from Myra Ellen Jenkins, the New Mexico state archivist, that Frank McNitt had published his history of the wars. McNitt's book dealt with the Navajo wars from the Spanish era through the white period to 1861.

After McNitt's book appeared, Odie Faulk suggested that I do research on an Oklahoma topic, which became the essence of my thesis. I still had the mass of material that I had collected on the wars, but I could not decide how best to use these sources. The wise counsel of C. L. Sonnichsen proved very helpful. He suggested that I focus on that segment of Navajo history from 1862 to 1866 and write an interpretative narrative about the Kit Carson campaign. My work on the book was facilitated after I moved to the Navajo Reservation, where I chaired the Department of History and Navajo Culture in Navajo Community College. From Tsaile, Arizona, I traveled on foot, on horseback, and in my pickup the many trails once followed by Carson, and from my life on the reservation I learned even more about the people and their land. I wrote the first draft of this book in a hogan at Tsaile, "the place where the water enters the cañon."

Over the years several institutions graciously cooperated by providing me documents. They include the National Archives, the

Library of Congress, the Washington State University Library, Oklahoma State University, the Northern Arizona University Special Collections, the University of Oklahoma Western History Collections, the New Mexico State Records Center and Archives, the University of New Mexico Library, the Arizona Historical Society, the Kit Carson Museum, the Huntington Library, the Arizona Department of Library and Archives, the Bancroft Library, and the Navajo Community College Library. The primary and secondary works of several historians were of aid to me, including those of Frank McNitt, Lawrence Kelly, Frank D. Reeve, Gerald Thompson, and Lynn Bailey.

I owe a debt of gratitude to several individuals for making this work possible. Special appreciation goes to Susan Ruth Elrod, who rode with me along the many trails followed by Carson, edited the manuscript, and encouraged me throughout the writing of the book. Thanks are extended to Cindy De Grosse and Jill Wise who typed many drafts of this work, and to Dorothy Garceau, who proofread the final draft. Odie B. Faulk, C. L. Sonnichsen, and Jerry Crews are thanked for their kind encouragement and constructive criticism.

Several Indians and non-Indians at Navajo Community College helped me in my understanding of the Navajo way: Donald McCabe, John C. Martin, Howard and Carl Gorman, Mae K. Begay, Lawrence and Lena Smith, Ruth Roessel, Stanley Mitchell, Donald Curlovic, Kay Blosser, Marci and Jim Matlock, Alvin Amason, Darcy Dauble, Cindy Slivers, Atha Chee Yellowhair, Lynn and Martha Heunemann, Ken Beatty, Jerold Judd, Stanley Kedelty, and Mabel Myers. Great appreciation is extended to my former colleagues in the Department of History and Navajo Culture in Navajo Community College: Mike Mitchell; Vicki Morris; Teddy Draper, Sr.; Andrew Natonabah; Lorraine Begay; and Milton Chee. A special tribute is given to my friends Chancellor and Ella Damon, as well as to other Navajos who shared with me their oral traditions and history.

I have received enthusiastic support for my research endeavors from Native American Studies and the Department of History in Washington State University. In particular I wish to thank Ray Muse, Thomas Kennedy, William Willard, David Stratton, and Bob Harder. Finally, I express my thanks to my mother and father for their continuous support of my professional pursuits.

Pullman, Washington   CLIFFORD E. TRAFZER

The Kit Carson Campaign

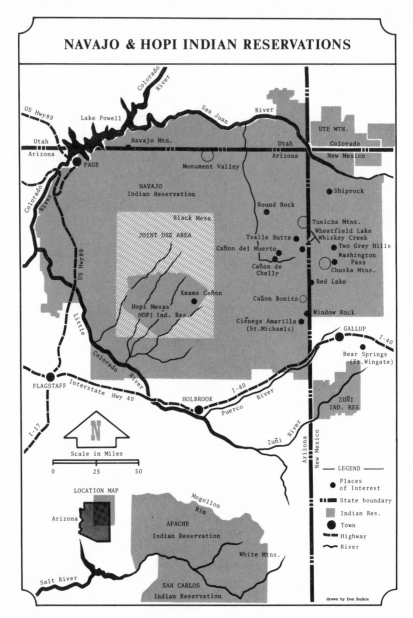

NAVAJO & HOPI INDIAN RESERVATIONS

Colorado River

US Hwy89

Lake Powell

San Juan River

Utah
Arizona

UTE MTN.

Navajo Mtn.

Utah
Arizona

Colorado
New Mexico

PAGE

Monument Valley

Colorado

NAVAJO
Indian Reservation

Shiprock

Round Rock

US Hwy89

Black Mesa

Tunicha Mtns.
Wheatfield Lake
Whiskey Creek

JOINT USE AREA

Tsaile Butte

Two Grey Hills

Cañon del Muerto

Washington
Pass
Chuska Mtns.

Cañon de
Chelly

Keams Cañon

Red Lake

Hopi Mesas
HOPI Ind. Res.

Cañon Bonito

Window Rock

Little

Ciénega Amarilla
(St.Michaels)

GALLUP

I-40

Colorado River

Bear Springs
(Ft.Wingate)

FLAGSTAFF

Interstate Hwy 40

I-40

River

HOLBROOK

Puerco River

ZUÑI
IND. RES.

I-17

Zuñi River

Arizona
New Mexico

N

Scale in Miles

0   25   50

LEGEND

Places
of Interest

State boundary

Indian Res.

LOCATION MAP

Mogollon
Rim

Town

Arizona

APACHE
Indian Reservation

Highway

River

White Mtns.

Salt River

SAN CARLOS
Indian Reservation

drawn by Don Bufkin

Navajo and Hopi reservations. Present boundaries and natural sites

CHAPTER 1

The Navajos Before Kit

B old streaks of yellow-and-orange sunlight have animated the wilderness of what is now northern New Mexico long before men traversed it. Stretching for miles in every direction is a land of great diversity, for encompassed in that vast region are towering mountains of sandstone as well as of volcanic ash. Below these massive monuments stand foothills that lead downward to the flat, hard plains with their grass, brush, and occasional trees. The high plains stretch for miles, to be interrupted only by arid desert lands. Glaciers, winds, and rains of years gone by created this beautiful and enchanting land, where cactus, piñons, and pines live in harmony. The San Juan River borders these lands on the north and flows westward until it reaches the Colorado River. South of the Colorado run many small arroyos that mark the Southwest like wrinkles of age.

Eons passed before men ventured into the region. These first Americans were followed by others of their own race, and still others followed in their wake. All was not peaceful among these first Americans as successive bands of people migrated into the area. At last a group of people came to these lands to rule the area as virtual lords. They came to be known as Navajos.

Thousands of years ago the forefathers of the Navajos and the Apaches began their migrations toward Navajo land. It took many years for these peoples to travel from the northern reaches of

Alaska and Canada to the great Southwest. Navajos and Apaches were not distinct tribes during those long, mysterious years of migration. They traveled in small bands, hunting, fishing, and gathering wild foods as they made their march. The many small bands that comprised the Navajos and Apaches were related to one another through their language, which in recent times has been labeled Athapascan, after Lake Athapasca of northwestern Canada. Some of these Athapascans migrated southward through Nevada and Utah, while others traveled along the eastern edge of the Rocky Mountains, arriving in the Southwest around 1500. According to anthropologists, the arrival of the Navajos and Apaches into the Southwest was late in comparison with the arrival of the Anasazi, the ancient Pueblo dwellers. The Navajos, however, do not agree, for they say that they have lived in the Southwest since creation. According to the Indians, First Man and First Woman entered the Fourth, or Glittering, World through a female reed that led them up from the underground to the world they know today.[1]

Francisco Vásquez de Coronado was the first European to make note of the ancestors of the Apaches and the Navajos when he made his historic jaunt into the Southwest in 1540. From Compostela, Coronado's army of 336 Spaniards and approximately 1,000 Indian allies made their way northward to Culiacán and onward to the San Pedro River, which crossed into what would become Arizona. The expedition continued its march up the San Pedro, through the White Mountains, and onto the high plains of northeastern Arizona. After engaging and finally defeating the Zuñi Indians at their pueblo Hawikúh, Coronado's army pressed eastward through central New Mexico. Continuing in an easterly direction, Coronado reached the Pecos River, which he crossed after building a bridge. Onward he traveled until he was confronted with a vast, sprawling plains. Grazing upon these great plains east of the Pecos were huge animals that resembled cattle but had beards that touched the ground and humps that were larger than the camels'. Other wonders met Coronado on the plains. Many of his men found strange parallel marks on the ground. Some of them followed the

4

tracks to discover by what means they had been created. The marks led them to an encampment of Indians; dogs dragged the poles that the Indians used to make magnificent tents. These people were Querechos, and they were the ancestors of the Navajos and the Apaches.

The Querechos were mobile hunters whom Coronado described as "the best . . . of any I have seen in the Indies." Like the plains tribes of later years, the Querechos subsisted "entirely on cattle [buffalo], for they neither plant nor harvest maize." The ancestors of the Navajos and Apaches used the skins of the buffalo to build their tipis, make their moccasins, and clothe their bodies. They used the sinew to string their bows and sew their garments. The dry dung of the great animals was used as fuel for their fires; the bones were used as awls. Water jugs were made from the bladders of the buffalo, and most other parts of the animal were consumed by the Indians. Coronado stated that the flesh of the buffalo was eaten "slightly roasted . . . and sometimes uncooked." The Querecho took a large hunk of meat in one hand and chewed it with his teeth, while his other hand grasped "a large flint knife with which he cut off mouthfuls, swallowing it half chewed, like birds." These people had no qualms about eating "raw fat without warming it, and drinking the blood just as it comes from the cattle." Indeed, after killing a buffalo, the Indians were known to "clean a large intestine, fill it with blood, and hang it around their necks, to drink when they were thirsty." The Querechos made use of every part of the buffalo, an animal that they revered, for it is remembered today in traditional Navajo ceremonies.

Coronado and his men were impressed by the Querechos; they found them to be inventive, intelligent, and courageous. The conquistadors were surprised that the Querechos were not in the least frightened by the approach of the Spanish army, even though they had never witnessed the movement of such a grand army, clad in armor and on horseback. One soldier wrote that when "they saw our army they did not move away nor disturb themselves in the least." "[On] the contrary, they came out of their tents and scrutinized us," he stated. The ancestors of the Navajos and the Apaches were not afraid of the Spaniards, perhaps because they felt themselves secure in their own land and superior in their warring ability, despite the awesome appearance of the strange force. The Querechos probably felt that they had more to fear from such enemies as the Comanches than they did from the Spaniards.[2]

During the late sixteenth and early seventeenth centuries a gradual accumulation of Athapascan-speaking peoples slowly became distinct from the other Apache groups of the Southwest. They called themselves the Diné (pronounced Din-á), or "The People," and they are known today as the Navajos. In 1626, Fray Gerónimo de Zárate Salmerón mentioned that there existed a tribe of Indians in New Mexico called the "Apaches de Nabaju." Salmerón was the first man to record this distinction, but he had little else to say about the tribe. Four years later another priest, Fray Alonso de Benavides, revealed that northwest of the Río Grande was a "Province of the Apaches of Navajo." He maintained that, "although they are of the same Apache nation as the foregoing, they are subject and subordinate to another chief captain, and have a distinct mode of living." This distinct mode of living to which Benavides referred was that the Navajo Apaches were farmers as well as hunters and gatherers. Indeed, the Spaniards learned that the name of these Indians was derived from the Tewan and Zuñi words *apachu,* "strangers" or "enemies," and *nabaju,* "planted fields." Hence, the name Navajo Apache indicated that these people were of an enemy group that planted crops as one means of livelihood.[3]

Although the Navajo Apaches cultivated the soil, they were more than agriculturalists; they were valiant raiders as well. Preying first on the Pueblo Indians and later on the Spaniards, the Navajos, like their Apache cousins, became skilled marauders. At least by the mid-seventeenth century and possibly before, the Navajos raided the Spaniards and Pueblos to obtain horses, cattle, and sheep. Farming as a major means of procuring food gradually gave way to the raising of livestock. To increase their stock, the Navajos increasingly turned to raiding (ironically, their economic dependence on livestock and wheat led to their ultimate defeat in the

Navajo Indians in traditional dress. Courtesy Navajo Community College.

mid-nineteenth century).

The pattern of Navajo raiding was established very early during the Spanish occupation of New Mexico. Even Juan de Oñate, the first colonial governor, captain general, and *adelantado* of New Mexico, was plagued by the Navajos during the early 1600s. The Indians would swoop down out of the mountains and raid the Spanish settlements along the Río Grande. With lightning speed the Navajo Apaches raided the Spanish town San Gabriel del Yunque at the confluence of that river and the Chama. San Gabriel, Oñate's capital, was situated at a precarious point, for it was on the trail used by the Navajos as they moved from Dinetah ("Land of the People," or "Navajo land") to the pueblos along the Río Grande. Navajo power in warfare was great. The Indians could have stung the Spanish so severely that they would have had to withdraw. Indeed, the Navajos were capable of driving the Spaniards from northern New Mexico had they desired to do so, pri-

7

Navajo pictographs illustrating a Spanish raid into the Cañon de Chelly. Courtesy of Navajo Community College.

marily because of the weak position of the first Spanish colonists. Increased depredations on San Gabriel by the Navajos prompted Pedro de Peralta, Oñate's successor, to move the capital of New Mexico about thirty miles south, to the foothills of the Sangre de Cristo Mountains. The new capital was called Santa Fe de Granada, a name later shortened to Santa Fe.

Navajo attacks on the upper Río Grande were not limited to Spanish settlements. Many missions and pueblos were raided by Apaches, possibly the Navajo Apaches, who not only raided stock but killed a few Catholic priests as well. Fray Diego de San Lucas and Fray Pedro de Arvila y Ayala were killed by Indians who may have been Navajos. Hopis, Zuñis, and other Pueblo people were attacked by the Navajos who raided their herds, ravaged their crops, and sometimes rode away with their women and children. A significant pattern was established during this era of Navajo-Spanish contact: the Navajos raided Spanish and Pueblo settlements for livestock and slaves, and the Europeans and their Indian allies reciprocated by stealing stock and enslaving Navajo prisoners captured on their campaigns to Dinetah. The enslavement of Indians had been forbidden by Spanish law for many years, but few settlers on the farthest edge of the Spanish Empire obeyed the law. Thus, while the Navajos raided and took captives, so did the Spaniards and the Pueblos. Through a Spanish system known as the *repartimiento,* Indian labor was exploited in New Mexico.

8

Under the system the Indians—Navajos, Pueblos, and Apaches alike—were forced to work for a pittance. The Spaniards believed that such a system was just, for, although the Indians did not receive just payment for their labor, they were given the opportunity to be "Christianized" and "civilized."[4]

Spanish leaders in New Mexico offered poor examples for the Hispanic people to follow in their relations with the Navajos. Most of the prominent leaders, including many governors, forced Indians to work for them and their associates without pay. They openly organized slaving expeditions against the Navajos, and they either sold their captives for a profit or gave them away to gain favors. Indeed, at one point in his career one governor of New Mexico, Don Bernardo López de Mendizabal, sent more than seventy Navajos and Apaches to the mines in New Spain to be sold as slaves. López actively worked to collect as many Navajo slaves as possible, seeking to accumulate a fortune from the inhumane institution while he was governor of the province. He also worked to set Indian against Indian in order to reap even more slaves. He once arranged a ruthless and unprovoked attack by the Pueblo Indians at Jemez on a band of Navajos who had gone there to trade. Fifteen Navajos were murdered in the treachery, and over forty were taken captive and sold. Other Spanish officials encouraged the Pueblos to aid them in their continual campaign against the Navajos. In retaliation the Navajos increased their raids on the Río Grande settlements after the mid-1600s.[5]

The hand of the Spanish crown was so heavy that the Pueblos organized a successful revolt in August, 1680. The Spaniards were driven from New Mexico to near present-day El Paso, where they stayed for twelve years, finally returning to northern New Mexico in 1692 and 1693 under the leadership of Governor Diego de Vargas. This was an important event in the history of the Navajos, for many Pueblos escaped the wrath of the returning Spaniards by fleeing to Dinetah. Side by side the Navajos and the Pueblos fought a series of campaigns against the Spanish colonists. Their efforts, however, were in vain, for the Spanish "resettled" Indian lands and forced New Mexico's native peoples into submission

Ashtishkiel, Navajo, in traditional dress, Fort Wingate, New Mexico, 1879. Courtesy Smithsonian Institution, Washington, D.C.

and slavery. The alliance with the Pueblos served the Navajos well. They learned many innovations from their Pueblo friends, such as loom weaving, farming, and some religious traditions. Ironically, the Reconquista of the Spaniards also benefited the Navajos, who acquired more horses, sheep, and cattle from their oppressors. The Navajo-Apaches, wrote Governor Francisco Cuervo y Valdez, demonstrated their audacity with "their reckless depredations upon the frontiers and pueblos." Navajo warriors swooped down on the Spanish ranches along the Río Grande and seized the livestock that would become the basis for their lifeway—and

10

the source of their ultimate defeat nearly two centuries later.

The Spaniards recognized the power of the Navajos all too well and, after they had secured their old settlements, launched a campaign that they hoped and prayed would bring the Navajos to their knees. In the summer of 1705, Captain Roque de Madrid moved against the Indians with utmost speed, surprising the Navajos in a forceful foray. At least thirty-nine Navajos, and possibly more, were killed by the king's soldiers, and this show of force was sufficient for some Navajos to desire peace. A delegation of Indians tried to visit Governor Cuervo to talk peace, but the arrogant governor was not disposed toward peace; instead, he ordered another campaign to subdue the Navajos. The governor's campaign against the "dreaded" Navajos proved to be a failure, for the Indians learned of the army's advance and took refuge on the red mesas and forested mountains of Dinetah. This expedition accomplished little, but some Navajos made overtures of peace to the soldiers as an act of good faith, bringing with them captive women and children, stolen stock, and trade articles.

A truce was arranged in 1705, and peace reigned in Navajo country for three years. However, the agreement for peace was made with only a segment of the Navajos, because no one leader or small group of leaders could speak for the entire people or the "Navajo Tribe." In 1705 peace was made with some eastern bands of Navajos, and not all the Indians identified with these bands. It is not surprising, then, that western bands of Navajos broke the peace in 1708 by raiding some Hopi villages and pueblos along the Río Grande. The Spaniards, unfortunately, did not understand that the Navajo tribe was a conglomerate of several bands of Indians under the direction of local headmen, or *naat' aani,* who were not responsible to a single chief. According to the Spaniards, the treaty agreement of 1705 was made between themselves and the "Navajo Tribe," and, when the agreement was broken by the western bands of Navajos in 1708, they blamed all Navajos. Once the peace was broken, the Spaniards attempted to punish all Navajos they could find, without distinguishing between those who had kept the agreement and those who had not.[6]

11

This circumstance recurred time and again until the final defeat of the Navajos, and it was a significant contributor to hostilities in New Mexico for over a century. Thus the war of 1705 and the subsequent peace serve as an excellent example of the intermittent war and peace in New Mexico between the Navajos and the Spaniards, Mexicans, and Anglos, until the final military destruction of the Diné. Repeated campaigns were launched against the mighty raiders, until at least some of the Navajos sued for peace. Treaty after treaty was composed and agreed upon by the Spaniards and certain bands of Navajos, who, of course, did not represent the entire tribe. Either the invaders did not understand the political makeup of the Navajos, or they chose to ignore it. In either case, the result was war, then peace; war, then peace. It was a vicious cycle, and neither side was the victor. The Navajo lifeway came to be tied to taking Spanish horses, cattle, and sheep, for the Diné became skilled fighters and raiders who were proud of their exploits as warriors. Yet first and foremost they were intelligent individuals who realized from time to time that it was to their advantage to seek the path of peace. These circumstances permeated the entire history of the Southwest from 1700 to 1864. The Navajos were not pawns being manipulated by the invaders but rather clever, intelligent, and wise warriors who held the upper hand in their relationships with whites for many years. They were, in fact, the virtual "Lords of New Mexico."[7]

The Navajos were never a united nation, but, by and large, the various bands held a common negative attitude toward the whites who had invaded and settled New Mexico, a land inhabited by Indians for thousands of years. A significant split occurred in the loose-knit nation in the early nineteenth century that drastically influenced the future course of the Navajo Wars and ultimately aided in the final defeat of the Diné. This schism occurred in 1818, when a Navajo chief named Joaquín rode into the Pueblo of Jémez and announced that a segment of the Navajo people desired peace with the Spaniards. Joaquín reasoned that the Spaniards were much too strong a force to be reckoned with, and thus the Navajos would ultimately lose any war prosecuted against them by the king's men. Joaquín tried to convince his fellow tribesmen that peace, not war, was the best policy to pursue. When his pleas proved fruitless, he withdrew his band from the tribe so that they could negotiate separately with the Spaniards. Approximately two hundred Navajos followed Joaquín when he severed his relationship with the other Navajos. The split proved to be permanent as well as harmful to the Navajo people as a whole, who faced an ever-increasing flow of immigrants into northern New Spain. Joaquín informed on other Navajos by warning Spanish soldiers that warriors were in the Carrizo Mountains preparing to spring upon the settlers at the earliest opportunity. To show their good faith, Joaquín's Navajos agreed to accompany a detachment of soldiers into the field against their own people.

Reaction to the defection of Joaquín's band was immediate, for the other Navajos were enraged over the treasonous actions of this segment of their own people. In fact, the reaction to these "traitors" was so strong that the other Navajos labeled Joaquín's band the Diné Ana'aii, or Enemy Navajos. The effect of this defection was permanent: the Diné Ana'aii thereafter were considered foes of the other members of the Navajo Tribe. From this time forward the Enemy Navajos acted periodically as scouts and soldiers for the Spaniards, Mexicans, and Anglo-Americans, until their own brothers were decisively defeated by the Anglo-Americans.

Perhaps Joaquín and the other leaders who followed him sincerely believed that continual war against the white men was fruitless. A better explanation for the permanence of this defection, however, was that the Indians had much to gain by their alliance with the whites. Not only had they gained a worthy ally against hostile Utes, Apaches, Pueblos, Comanches, and other Navajos, but they would usually be secure from the attacks of the white men. For the most part the Diné Ana'aii would be secure from civilian and military expeditions organized to capture slaves and stock from the Navajo people. Moreover, the Indians would have ample opportunity to trade with the white men and procure from them many useful trade items, such as weapons, metal utensils, and food.[8]

13

*Peshlakai, Slender Silver Maker, ca. 1885. Courtesy Smithsonian
Institution.*

While these events were occurring on the northern frontier of New Spain, great changes were developing throughout Latin America. Most important, the first two decades of the nineteenth century were marked by a number of wars for independence in the Latin-American countries, including Mexico, where Agustín de Iturbide had successfully concluded a war that gave Mexico its independence from Spain. The effect of the war and the subsequent independence was minimal in New Mexico, where leaders were much more concerned with the threat of Indians than they were with Spanish loyalists or soldiers of the crown. According to one observer, the news of Mexico's independence did not even send a ripple of excitement to the northern interior. As usual, the soldiers in New Mexico were busy chasing Navajos in hope of subduing them once and for all. Likewise, the Navajos were little concerned about the change of government in Mexico City, for their war with the settlers and soldiers of New Mexico would continue regardless of the flag flying over the capital of the province. In 1822 the Navajos pressed their war with the Mexicans with increased vengeance, reportedly causing the deaths of more than twenty-five New Mexicans that year.

Thomas James, an American trader who was in Santa Fe during this era, argued that the fierce Navajos were killing men, women, and children indiscriminately and were leaving a path of destruction throughout New Mexico. With great fervor Navajos were attacking south of Santa Fe and north of Taos as well. Cattle, horses, mules, and sheep were swept from their grazing lands and driven off to the mountain haunts of the Navajo country. In the midst of all this marauding, Governor Facundo Melgares was unable to muster a spirited militia. James reported that the militia at Santa Fe was nothing more than "a gang of tatteredemalions" whose members carried "every species of arms." Many of the soldiers were armed with bows and arrows, and only "a few had guns that looked as if they had been imported by Cortez." The "courageous" Governor Melgares, who stood five feet tall and was "as thick as he was long," waddled to dinner while his troops were sent out to fight the "blood thirsty Navajos." James maintained that, by the time the Mexican troops were organized, the Navajos

15

"had returned in safety to their own country with all their plunder." Melgares was not successful in his military campaigns against the Navajos, but he did arrange a council with a delegation of Indians, who signed a treaty of peace at Zía Pueblo.[9] James's report should be taken with a grain of salt because of his strong personal biases against the Navajos and the Mexicans. He had little love, and less use, for either; and he probably hoped that the United States would someday acquire New Mexico and subdue the "savage Indian menace."

Late in 1822, Governor Melgares was replaced by "a man of commanding appearance." His name was José Antonio Vizcarra. The new governor was portrayed not only as a man of dignity and grace but also as an excellent horseman and a fine soldier. While winter still whispered its cool graces over the clear landscape of northern New Mexico, Vizcarra and a detachment of soldiers proceeded to the Laguna Pueblo of Paguate (four miles south of Cebolleta), where they met a few Navajo leaders. Among the chiefs Vizcarra met in that cold February of 1823 was Chief Juanico, one of the most important headmen of the era. Negotiations began almost immediately, with Vizcarra demanding the return of all Mexicans held captive by the Indians. In return, he agreed to order the release of all Navajos held captive by the Mexicans, "but only if they wish to go, for if they should wish to receive the beneficial waters of baptism it does not seem proper for Catholics to deny them."[10] The Indians were told to return all livestock stolen from Mexicans and were instructed to surrender their lifeway as mobile warriors and accept the life of pueblo dwellers. Navajos were proud of their lifeway as herders and horsemen and would not easily accept life as communal farmers. They could no more be confined to pueblo living during this era than the southwestern winds could be made still.

Chief Juanico was not silent during the council with Vizcarra. The chief explained that many of his people were going hungry that winter and, therefore, could ill afford to surrender stock that the Mexicans claimed was stolen. To do so would mean starvation and possibly increased raiding. Nonetheless, Juanico gave his word

Mariano Martínez, Navajo chief. Sketch by R. H. Kern, September 8, 1849. Courtesy National Archives, Washington, D.C.

that he would attempt to end further marauding, and he asked the Mexican commandant to give him and other leaders four months to consider the treaty. Juanico wanted time to approach the other bands of Navajos about accepting the peace agreement. The chief well understood that he could not sign a treaty that would bind all Navajos, for he was the leader of only a segment of the tribe. Juanico and Vizcarra were not impressed by the council, and possibly neither leader believed that the proposed treaty would work. Vizcarra almost immediately launched an expedition against the Indians, while the Navajos continued to raid the ranches of New Mexico. The governor's determination to defeat the hostiles led him to launch the grandest army that had ever been organized in this region of the Southwest.[11]

Vizcarra's command numbered fifteen hundred men, and at least one, and probably more, Diné Ana'aii went along as scouts. In June, 1823, Vizcarra's troops moved out from Santa Fe, marching through Jémez Pueblo and Chaco Cañon before heading into a pass through the Chuska Mountains. The route of Vizcarra's command took them up past the red rim of the Cañon de Chelly and westward down into the tall mesas of the Hopi country before turning northward into Utah. Vizcarra did not face an enemy in a regimented battle; his foe was continually on the move and knew when to retreat, scatter, or attack. The Navajos proved to be an elusive and clever enemy, but on August 9, 1823, Vizcarra overtook a small party of warriors. Juanico was one of the Indians in the band, and, upon seeing Vizcarra and the other New Mexicans, the chief called to the captain and asked to talk peace. Vizcarra's voice was arrogant and determined as he defiantly shouted to Juanico that he had come not to talk but to fight. At that moment Vizcarra shouted to his men, "Adelante!" The soldiers charged the Navajos, who were positioned above the soldiers on a mesa. Shooting began almost immediately as the soldiers scampered up the mesa. Some of the Navajos left the scene of battle to attend to their livestock, which they hoped to drive safely from the mesa. As Vizcarra's men pressed forward, the warriors withdrew, taking up positions that were more advantageous, thus aiding their cohorts in their effort to drive off the livestock.

The air was filled with the pungent odor of discharged powder as the soldiers fired at the Indians, who fought back with their bows and arrows. The firearms gave the soldiers the advantage as the Nakai, as the Navajos called the Mexican troops, pressed forward, driving the Indians into a retreat. The warriors were forced to flee, but they took as many animals as they could drive at a rapid pace. Vizcarra pursued the Indians and actually overtook many head of livestock. When it appeared that the soldiers had routed their enemy, Vizcarra instructed his men to gather up the animals abandoned by the Indians. While the dust was settling, he ordered Lieutenant Manuel Sánchez and three soldiers "to round up a few cattle that were seen near there." Sánchez had just begun herding the animals when his small detachment was attacked by Indians. On two occasions Navajo warriors gallantly attempted to retrieve their lost stock. The second encounter resulted in fierce hand-to-hand combat, but Vizcarra and five soldiers "had the satisfaction, with the aid of God, of aiding them, dismounting quickly and charging the Indians." Although no one was killed in this skirmish, many Indians and soldiers were wounded.[12]

While Vizcarra was preoccupied with chasing a few Navajos and their stock across the far reaches of Navajo country, another detachment of his command was likewise pursuing the Indians. The smaller troop was under the command of Colonel Francisco Salazar, who had scouted northward into Utah. The Navajos eluded Salazar as effectively as they had Vizcarra, for they proved ghostlike in their ability to disappear from the vast landscape. Like Vizcarra, Salazar briefly engaged the Navajos, but without much consequence. At one point 8 daring warriors attacked Salazar's command, which was much superior, numbering a total of 250 soldiers. The clash occurred in an instant, and the effect was negligible, but one of the Mexicans chose to pursue the Navajo warriors once they had withdrawn.

Salazar was surprised again the next morning by a large band of Navajos, who had stealthily encircled their enemy from all sides. The troops decided to retreat rather than face their foe, and the results proved dangerous as well as embarrassing. The retreat turned into a rout as Navajos, skilled in the art of horsemanship,

Chapaton, leader of the San Juan band of Navajos. Kern, September 8, 1849. Courtesy National Archives, Washington, D.C.

divided the soldiers and forced them to run. The agile horsemen rode between the soldiers, causing so much havoc that they managed to capture several horses as well as the superior weapons of the command. Four troopers were dead by the end of the day, and the soldiers suffered additional attacks the next morning. Salazar's soldiers fell into disarray, for they were again and again divided by the vengeful warriors. The Indians pressed the invaders unmercifully until the sun showed straight above them, and then they withdrew, leaving the Mexicans in confusion. Salazar regrouped his men and was fortunate not to be attacked again, for if the warriors had wanted it so, they could have dogged the Nakai to death.

Salazar withdrew from the area the next day, finally rejoining Vizcarra at the mouth of Cañon de Chelly. Vizcarra's command returned to Santa Fe without incident. The commander reported that thirty-three Navajos, including eight women, were killed on the expedition and thirty more were captured. Over nine hundred head of sheep, goats, cattle, mules, and horses had been seized. Five Mexicans were killed, thirteen were wounded, and four others died of sickness while on the march. All in all the campaign accomplished little for the Mexicans, for it had not brought the Navajos to their knees. Nor did Vizcarra's campaign end Navajo raids against the Mexicans or the theft of Navajo stock and captives by the Nakai. In short, the predatory war in the Southwest continued despite intermittent peace.[13]

A short, precarious peace reigned in New Mexico during 1824, but, as the next year opened, warfare was renewed. The Navajos intensified their raids against the Mexicans, largely in response to furious attacks against them by the civilian population of New Mexico, whose main objective was to steal Navajo stock and slaves. Although the enslavement of Indians had been illegal for many generations, the laws had always been ignored. Indeed, it was not uncommon for Hispanos and the Diné Ana'aii to raid Navajo rancherias to capture women and children who were sold as chattel. New Mexican hacendados purchased Navajo slaves and forced them to work in their homes, stables, and fields. They reasoned that slavery was sanctioned by God, who had commissioned Christians to spread his word to the "savage heathens" of this world. What better way, they reasoned, than to place Indians under the civilized, Christian influence of the Hispanic people. Slavery forced Indians into a condition of servitude in which they received the word of God, thereby making it possible for the souls of these "barbarians" to enter the eternal bliss of heaven. Most New Mexicans cared little that the Indian slaves were forced to live a life of hell, robbed of their freedom and their spirit.

While the civilians successfully stole from the Navajos, they did not defeat them. Vizcarra's term of office was about to end in the early cold, clear months of 1825, and the colonel reasoned that, before he was replaced, he would lead another expedition against the Navajos to crush his old foe before his successor arrived. Thus, in March, 1825, he organized a command to chastise the Navajos. His efforts were in vain, however, for his expedition into Dinetah failed to locate the Indians. Jaded animals and lack of supplies led Vizcarra to abandon his plans and return to Santa Fe. Accompanying him on the expedition were members of the Diné Ana'aii, who informed the colonel that, although his detachment had not found their tribesmen in the field, the Indians could be found gathering near the little New Mexican pueblo Abiquiu. Vizcarra sent word of this to Governor Bartolomé Baca, who ordered his troops to attack. The Mexican force surrounded and surprised the peaceful Navajos, capturing forty-one men and women. All but three of the captives were set free, but before they gained their freedom, they informed the colonel of the location of a large concentration of their own people who were hostile to the Hispanos. With this information Vizcarra ordered Captain José Caballero, thirty soldiers, one hundred militiamen, and seven Navajo scouts to locate and attack the Indians. An encampment of Navajos was surprised by the captain and his troops on April 7, 1825, and eleven prisoners were secured by the Navajo scouts, who handed over the captives to Baca. He either sold the Indians into slavery or gave them away as gifts, a common practice among the Hispanic gentry. The encounter accomplished little, except to inflame hostilities further. It certainly did not end the warfare.

Navajo hogans, made of logs, stones, and adobe. Courtesy Navajo Community College.

Antonio Narbona became the military and political governor of New Mexico in 1825. He was described by one Anglo-American as "a Gentleman of pretty good talents, quite a man of business."[14] Early in Narbona's career as governor an important event occurred among the Diné Ana'aii. For unknown reasons Joaquín, the leader of the Enemy Navajos, lost power, or perhaps died, and in his place emerged Francisco Baca, a literate half-blood who took control of the Enemy Navajos. Baca's power was soon disputed by another prominent leader, who eventually emerged and overshadowed the first two leaders of the Diné Ana'aii in intelligence, ambition, and cunning. His name was Antonio Sandoval. This chief and his band of Enemy Navajos, as well as the Mexican citizenry, contributed significantly to the unstable conditions in New Mexico during the early nineteenth century. All these parties carried on a predatory war with the Navajos, the Navajos swooping down out of their mountain haunts to pillage the surrounding rancheros, and the Mexicans and their Indian allies raiding rancherias in Dinetah. Thus the 1830s and 1840s were filled with continual fighting between the Navajos and the Mexicans. Slaving, raiding, and fighting characterized Mexican New Mexico, and little changed after Anglo-Americans arrived in the arid Southwest in the middle of the century.[15]

Far removed from the Navajo frontier were fevered stirrings in 1846 that would greatly influence the course of the Navajo Wars and the lifeways of all Indians in the American Southwest. Since the opening of Mexico to American trappers, traders, and emigrants in the 1820s, there had been suspicion and conflict between the Mexicans and the Americans. The successful revolt of the Texans in 1836 only added fuel to the flames of the hostilities. The boundary dispute between Texas and Mexico had never been fully resolved, even when Texas was annexed into the Union. Four days after President John Tyler signed the joint resolution to Congress to annex Texas, a new president, James Knox Polk, was inaugurated. "Young Hickory," as he had been dubbed, had campaigned on an expansionist platform, and it was his intention from the outset to settle the boundary question with Mexico. Efforts to do so diplomatically were thwarted, primarily because of internal difficulties in Mexico. Military forces from both sides of the Río Grande began a movement toward each other that resulted in a clash of arms. Blood was shed by Mexicans and Americans along the southernmost end of the Río Grande, and these events ultimately influenced the lives of all inhabitants residing along the northern reaches of the Río del Norte, particularly the Navajos.

The first shots of the Mexican War were fired on April 25, 1846, as General Zachary Taylor commenced a series of engagements against the Mexicans. In his message before Congress, President Polk proclaimed that Mexican troops had "invaded our territory and shed American blood upon the American soil."[16] While "Old Rough and Ready" marched against his adversaries in Texas and Chihuahua, another army was forming on the Great Plains. At Fort Leavenworth, Kansas, a large expedition was organized to secure New Mexico and California for the United States. The com-

24

mand was styled the "Army of the West," and Colonel Stephen Watts Kearny was chosen to lead it.

Born in 1794, the fifteenth child of a New Jersey family, Kearny grew up in Newark, attended Columbia College, and entered the army as a first lieutenant during the War of 1812. Known for his courage and fortitude, Kearny remained in the army following the war and served on the frontiers of Iowa, Nebraska, Missouri, and Indian Territory. He was commander of the Third Military Department of Missouri and was a very seasoned soldier at the time of his appointment as head of the Army of the West. Kearny had little difficulty recruiting men; eager lads seeking adventure abounded in the West. His largest group of recruits came from the First Regiment of Missouri Volunteers, who chose as their leader an articulate attorney named Alexander William Doniphan. The thirty-eight-year-old native of Maysville, Kentucky, was a strapping fellow of six feet, four inches, and a graduate of Augusta College. He would become the first Anglo-American to form a treaty with the powerful Navajo people.

Little did Kearny or Doniphan realize that their mightiest foe in New Mexico would be the Navajos and the Apaches, not the Mexicans. Without difficulty the Americans secured Santa Fe, and Kearny promised the inhabitants of New Mexico that he had come as a protector, not as a conqueror. He proclaimed that "the Apaches and Navajos come down from the mountains and carry off your sheep and your women whenever they please." Kearny boasted: "My government will correct all this." A pompous promise indeed, for a man who little understood that the Indians were more than a match for the American troops. To fulfill his promise, Kearny ordered Doniphan to send his volunteers to key positions on the frontier. This, however, had little effect on the Navajos, who struck with lightning speed, despite the presence of American soldiers. Doniphan was then commissioned to lead a decisive expedition against this "numerous, and warlike tribe who dwell in fastnesses of the mountains west of Del Norte." It was the commander's hope to end all depredations by these "naked, thin, and savage looking fellows."[17]

The autumn air was brisk in Santa Fe when Colonel Doniphan began preparations for the first Navajo expedition. Doniphan directed his men to stations on the New Mexican frontier, ordering Major William Gilpin to Abiquiu with two companies, and Lieutenant Colonel Charles Ruff to Cebolleta with three companies. Lieutenant Congreve Jackson, who replaced Ruff as commander, traveled down the Río Grande to Albuquerque, where he crossed the river. Jackson's men moved west across a high prairie and low sandstone mountains to Laguna Pueblo, all the while hearing rumors of Navajo raids. At Laguna the soldiers witnessed a ceremony performed by the Indians over the scalps of four Navajo warriors. The scalps were said to have been those of four warriors who had raided Laguna, driving off a number of sheep and killing a man and two children. The Lagunas had been victorious over their enemies and celebrated the victory with a ceremony.

Eighteen-year-old Private Marcellus Edwards later recalled that the celebration commenced with the deep beat of the drum until the quiet was broken by the emergence of thirty Indians, who walked into the plaza in two columns and faced each other. Each Indian wore a single eagle feather in his hair, and a tuft of feathers hung down his back. The Lagunas painted their foreheads black, but, from their eyebrows to their chins, they were colored with red paint. Their throats were painted white. Forward and backward the two lines of warriors moved as the tempo of the drumbeat increased. The women joined in the dance to show their support of the men, and soon the streaming scalps were presented to the group on long poles. Fierce shouts of victory and contempt followed as the Lagunas celebrated the defeat of their old enemy. Long into the night the dance continued, as an occasional shot shattered the night whenever a warrior felt the urge to send a bullet whizzing by the scalps.

Not only were the Americans and New Mexicans interested in the defeat of the Navajos, but so were many Pueblo Indians of the Río Grande. Kearny, however, was particularly eager to defeat the Diné. On October 2, 1846, Kearny ordered Doniphan and his volunteers to march into Navajo land and "secure a peace and better conduct" from the Navajos. Directives were sent to Major Gilpin and Colonel Jackson to penetrate Navajo country and make terms of peace with the Indians. When word reached Jackson near Cebolleta, Captain John W. Reid asked Jackson for permission to take "a small body of troops, to make an excursion into the country, and learn more certainly whether the Navajos were disposed for peace or war." Accompanying Reid and his thirty soldiers was Sandoval, the leader of the Enemy Navajos. This branch of the tribe was then residing near Mount Taylor at Cañoncito, just west of Albuquerque. Sandoval and his people scouted for Captain Reid in 1846, and their service proved to be of great aid to Reid as it would for Anglos who invaded Navajo land during the next twenty years.[18]

Sunlight was barely showing over the Chuska Mountains when Reid's soldiers were awakened by the crisp morning air. They had encamped near the rusty waters of Red Lake (present-day Navajo, New Mexico), and it was there that the Navajos first encountered the Americans or Bilagáana, as the Navajos called the white Americans. Accompanied by several Navajos, the soldiers made their way north toward the camp of the famed Chief Narbona. The Diné were "dressed in splendid Indian attire, having fine figured blankets and panther-skin caps, plumed with eagle feathers."[19] One soldier found the Navajos to be "of good stature" and "the most enlightened tribe of wild Indians inhabiting this continent." The Navajos, he explained, were "a mounted tribe; living on their horses." Indeed, he commented, "the Arab cannot excel the Navajo in horsemanship; and better horses can hardly be found."[20] When Reid's soldiers met a large band of Indians, "the plain was covered with these mounted warriors, with their feathers streaming in the wind, their arms raised as for conflict; some riding one way and some another; and in the midst of these exciting scenes they indulge in the wild Indian yell, or shout of triumph." Armed with bows, arrows, and lances, the Navajos were imposing warriors, and their "bold and fearless character" earned them the title the "supreme lords of this mountain country."[21]

Reid was the first American soldier to parley with the Navajos, and it was his good fortune to meet the famed, aged Narbona. The arthritis-ridden chief was much respected by his people. In his youth he had been a fierce and gallant warrior. His years had given him wisdom and cunning, and he was inclined toward peace with the "new men." His wishes prevailed over those of warriors with him who favored war. Reid succeeded in securing an agreement with Narbona's band, but, again, it did not bind all Navajos to the peace pact. Many subchiefs would continue to favor open hostility against their enemy, the Nakai. Thus, although Reid had succeeded in meeting with Narbona, his council with the chief did not end all Navajo depredations in New Mexico.

Colonel Doniphan, confident that he could end the Navajo Wars within thirty days, went to work implementing his plan of attack. On October 22, 1846, he ordered Major Gilpin and 255 men to journey up the Río de Chama into the San Juan Mountains. The major followed the Río San Juan westward until he met a party of Navajos, and, after receiving a directive from Doniphan, he asked the Indians to gather their people together for a grand council at Shash Bito, as the Navajos called Bear Springs (east of Gallup, New Mexico). Doniphan's council commenced on the cold, windy day November 21. Many Navajo headmen were present, but certainly not, as Doniphan claimed, "all the head chiefs of each of the cantons, comprising the powerful tribe of Mountain Lords and scourgers of New Mexico." The colonel erroneously believed that a lasting peace could be concluded, since all parties were present "to whom power was delegated . . . the Navajos, Mexicans, and Americans."[22]

Zarcillos Largos, a "very bold and intellectual" man, emerged as the principal spokesman for the Navajos. After the Anglos stated their position, Largos replied that "he was gratified to learn the views of the Americans" and that "he admired the spirit and enterprise" of the soldiers. He added, however, that he "detested the Mexicans" and would not treat on this matter. Negotiations continued all that day and the next. Doniphan stressed that "the United States had taken military possession of New Mexico," and that, therefore, it was the duty of his country to protect the New

28

Mexicans "against violence and invasion." Although the United States had invaded Navajo land, Doniphan said that the hope of his country was to "enter into a treaty of peace and lasting friendship with her red children." If, however, the Indians refused the "olive branch," his country would offer the Navajos nothing less than "powder, bullets, and the steel."

Bold Largos stood and said: "Americans! you have a strange cause of war against the Navajos. We have waged war against the New Mexicans for several years. We have plundered their villages and killed many of their people, and made many prisoners. We have just cause for all this." He pointed out that the Americans had "lately commenced a war against the same people" and that the soldiers had "conquered them, the very thing we have been attempting to do for so many years." Largos could not understand how the soldiers could "turn upon us for attempting to do what you have done yourselves." He could not understand why they had "cause of quarrel" with the Americans "for fighting the New Mexicans on the west" while the Americans continued to fight in the south. "Look how matters stand," explained the chief. "This is our war. We have more right to complain of you for interfering in our war, than you have to quarrel with us for continuing a war we had begun long before you got here. If you will act justly, you will allow us to settle our own differences."[23]

Doniphan diplomatically responded that, since "the New Mexicans had surrendered" and since "they desired no more fighting . . . it was a custom with the Americans when a people gave up, to treat them as friends." The colonel argued "that it would be greatly to their [the Indians'] advantage for the Americans to settle in New Mexico," for the Navajos could "open a valuable trade" with the United States.

Largos reportedly agreed that, if the United States truly had possession of New Mexico and was going to hold it, the Indians would cease their "depredations and refrain from future wars." A treaty was drawn, calling for "a firm and lasting peace . . . between the American people and the Navajo tribe of Indians." The treaty was signed, but the peace was not to be a lasting one. Many

Navajos did not sign the document and were not bound by its provisions. Blood was shed before the ink dried on Doniphan's treaty, and the Navajo Wars would continue for nearly twenty years.[24]

Doniphan's meeting with the Navajos at Bear Springs marked a significant change in Navajo history. The Indian policies pursued by the Spanish and Mexican governments gave way to those of the American government. By the time of the American invasion of the Southwest, the United States had developed an Indian policy designed to benefit the government, not the Indians. Government agents like Doniphan were bent on demanding a policy based on treaties of peace, trade, and territorial limits. The Indians were asked to sign peace treaties and were threatened with war if they did not adhere to the terms dictated by government officials. By so doing, Doniphan and the Americans who followed assumed superiority over the Indians and denied them their traditional sovereignty. A handful of whites would ultimately determine the fate of the Navajos and of all their neighbors. Of this the Navajos foresaw nothing. They would not have believed that the Bilagáana would one day defeat them in battle and force them into exile far from their beloved Dinetah.

The years 1846 to 1849 were filled with increased numbers of raids against the Hispanos and Anglos by the powerful Navajos. The Indians simply continued their traditional way of life, plundering the New Mexico ranches and pueblos for livestock and foodstuffs. The army made two efforts to end depredations on the frontier, but both were in vain. In September, 1847, Major Robert Walker and a battalion of Missouri volunteers left Santa Fe for the Navajo country. The troops moved south along the Río Grande to Albuquerque before crossing the river, heading west to Bear Springs. It was reported that "nearly every man left drunk" on his way from Albuquerque to Navajo country. Walker's detachment marched past Laguna Pueblo and Mount Taylor, following a route that took them near present-day Interstate 40. They followed the trail to Bear Springs before moving northwest to Red Lake, where the soldiers established their base of operations. Small groups penetrated the surrounding area in hopes of engaging the Indians. This activity did little to bring a halt to Navajo raids, and Walker determined to march to the purported stronghold of the Indians at the Cañon de Chelly. For approximately six miles the soldiers crept cautiously into the canyon, where the red sandstone walls became higher and higher with each turn of a bend. Fearing an ambush in the narrow and dangerous passage, Walker decided to retreat from the forbidding gorge. He returned to Santa Fe with little to show for his effort, except to report that he was the first American soldier to penetrate the narrow path leading into the Cañon de Chelly.[25]

Few Navajos followed the path of peace during this era, and raids actually increased in the spring of 1848. Colonel Edward W. B. Newby, the commander of the newly formed Ninth Military District of New Mexico, was alarmed by the "frequent outrages, committed upon the persons and property of the peaceful inhabitants . . . by the Navajos, Apaches and other tribes." He lamented that most of his force were infantry, and as such were "powerless against the rapid movements of mounted men . . . familiar with every inch of the country." According to Newby, his men were "compelled to sit still while murder and robbery" were "committed under their very eyes." For that reason he followed the advice of the civilian population of the territory and authorized the Mexican inhabitants "to arm and equip themselves—organize in parties or bands and hold themselves in readiness to repel all incursions and to recover the property that may have been taken from them by the Indians." By allowing more civilians to raid into Navajo country, the commander sanctioned the continuation of predatory warfare that had too long plagued New Mexico.[26]

Like Doniphan and Walker before him, Newby decided to put an end to the Navajo Wars by marching into Dinetah. The colonel skirmished with the Navajos on a number of occasions, but he never fought a pitched battle with his foes or brought them to their knees. When he offered the Navajos a peace agreement, they accepted. Those headmen present scrawled their marks on the treaty, but, like the treaty of 1846 and like those to be signed in the future, it was a worthless scrap of paper. The Indians simply signed the document to appease the white men, for they knew that, once the accord was signed, the Bilagáana (Anglos) would leave their land. Indeed, it was to their benefit to sign the paper, because they would be rid of the invaders, at least for a while.[27]

Newby's treaty did nothing to end hostilities. Not all Navajos signed it. Those clans that did not, and even, perhaps, some of those that did, continued to attack New Mexican ranches. To cope with the "Indian problem," a full Indian agency was established at Santa Fe by order of the secretary of war in 1849. James S. Calhoun received the first commission as Indian agent in the Territory of New Mexico, which then included Arizona as well. Calhoun was a poor choice, because he knew nothing about Indians or New Mexico. What was worse, Commissioner of Indian Affairs William Medill was ill-informed about the Navajos and general conditions in New Mexico: "so little is known here of the condition and situation of the Indians in that region that no specific instructions, relative to them can be given at present." When Calhoun arrived in the West, he merely accepted the prevailing white view that the Indians had to be either properly chastised or exterminated and definitely had to be shown the power of the American army. The greenhorn agent, uninformed as he was, set out to accomplish the wishes of the New Mexicans by working in cooperation with Colonel John M. Washington, the military governor of the territory. Together they planned an expedition against the Navajos that they naïvely believed would end hostilities forever.[28]

With companies of infantrymen, artillerymen, and dragoons, together with a handful of Indian scouts and many New Mexican volunteers, Calhoun and Washington set out to awe the Navajos into submission. The two officials of the United States must have been impressed by their column of 348 men as they marched westward to the broad, sandy basin of the Tunicha Valley on the eastern side of the rough Chuska Mountains. As they approached present-day Two Grey Hills, they were joined by a large delega-

Narbona, respected leader of the Navajos, killed by the soldiers of John M. Washington. Sketch by R. H. Kern, August 31, 1849. Courtesy National Archives.

tion of Navajos led by José Largo, Archuleta, and Narbona. Of the three the aged Narbona, who had signed Doniphan's treaty, was the most respected. All the chiefs listened as the government officials outlined a new, comprehensive treaty. All were receptive to the idea that the treaty should be enacted at the Cañon de Chelly. In the wake of casual negotiations, Sandoval, of the Diné Ana'aii, rode forward and spiritedly addressed several hundred Navajos, who sat on their mounts and listened to the scout. Patiently they remained silent, clutching their weapons. The proceedings were marred, however, when, in the midst of this haranguing, a New Mexican volunteer stepped forward and claimed that one of the Indians was riding a pony that had been stolen from him some months earlier. When Washington heard about this, he ordered the Indians to hand over the horse immediately. The Navajos did not comply, and the colonel directed Lieutenant Lorenzo Tórez to seize the animal and the rider. Washington ordered the warriors not to resist, warning that, if they did, they would be fired upon.

Three or four hundred Indians were gathered at the scene, and the entire camp was thrown into confusion by Washington's arrogant and careless demand. Sensing the calamity, the Indians decided to make a break for it, whereupon Washington ordered his men to open fire. The mountain howitzer (a cannon that shoots six-pound balls), was quickly made ready, swung into position, and fired into the frenzy of fleeing warriors. Three rounds exploded, and, when the thick, gray smoke and the sand cleared from the air, the soldiers saw seven Indians lying dead or wounded on the ground. For a brief moment the soldiers silently viewed the bloody scene before realizing that among the dead was Chief Narbona, whose body lay lifeless from four or five deep wounds. No honor was displayed by the soldiers that day. They desecrated the chief's body and cut his long white hair from his scalp to display as a trophy of their great victory. Although the parley was ruined by this senseless massacre, neither Washington nor Calhoun faltered in his mission. The army traveled over the Chuska Mountains through the piñon-, ponderosa-, and aspen-lined passage now known as Washington's Pass and continued toward the Cañon de Chelly. There without much difficulty they concluded a peace treaty with Chiefs Chapitan and Mariano on September 7, 1849. Like the treaties of Doniphan and Newby, Washington's treaty was little more than a paper agreement between the United States and a small segment of the tribe. It would not bring lasting peace.[29]

Most inhabitants of New Mexico—including the Indians—were pessimistic about the results of Washington's treaty. Calhoun himself had little hope that the treaty would bring peace. The Indian agent despised his charges, stating that the "Navajos commit their wrongs from pure love of rapine and plunder." Accordingly he felt that, with four companies of dragoons and some Indian allies, he could "in less than six months . . . so tame the Navajos and Utahs that you will scarcely hear from them again." Calhoun favored the use of New Mexican volunteers and Indian allies against the Navajos, and he adhered to this opinion throughout his years in the territory. Time and time again he would appeal to the federal government for funds to be used for a militia as well as for weapons and ammunition. The agent believed that the regular army was ineffective as a deterrent to Indian raids and that the officers in the army were inept. Oftentimes he encouraged volunteers—New Mexicans and Indians—to launch punitive expeditions against those he called "the savage Indians who are daily murdering and robbing the people of New Mexico." He argued, with more than a trace of racism in his words, that the Navajos "must be exterminated or so chastised" so as to stop their marauding. Thus he appealed to the volunteers "to pursue the Navajo Nation to their extermination or complete surrender." Calhoun called for an Indian policy that had unfortunately been a part of American history from the beginning. The agent rationalized that the Navajos were either to be tamed, confined, and civilized or to be exterminated from the face of the earth.[30]

The use of "volunteers" served to heighten hostilities, primarily because these privateers launched campaigns against the Navajos for personal gain—for sheep, cattle, and horses. Most important, however, these civilians stole more and more Navajo women and children and sold them into bondage. Thousands of Indian slaves were taken by New Mexicans and sold into servitude for great profits. Children between five and fifteen years of age brought as much as two hundred dollars on the auction block in Santa Fe. Sandoval and his band of Diné Ana'aii were notorious for taking women and children from other Navajo bands and selling them as slaves. After a raid in 1851 in the region surrounding Red Lake, two Navajos from the vicinity went to Colonel Daniel T. Chandler and sorrowfully stated that "Sandoval in his last campaign against us, stole everything we had, our horses, wives, children, and even the sheep skins we slept on." That same year the Reverend Hiram Read commented that the "famous half-tamed Navajo Chief named Sandoval . . . came into town today to sell some captives." He observed that Sandoval's captives were "of his own nation which he recently took prisoner." As Indian agent, superintendent of Indian affairs, and, later, governor of the New Mexican Territory, Calhoun sanctioned the slave trade and even encouraged it. In a letter to the commissioner of Indian affairs, Calhoun casually commented that "Sandoval, our Navajo friend near Cebolleta, returned . . . from a visit to his Navajo brethren with eighteen captives, a quantity of stock and several scalps." From the time the Spaniards first colonized New Mexico, slaving had been a most significant source of hostility between the Indians and the white men. Americans who permitted such practices contributed catastrophically to the continuation of the Navajo Wars.[31]

After Narbona's death Navajo raids increased daily, while the efficiency of the army rapidly decreased. In 1850, Calhoun reported to President Zachary Taylor that "our Indian troubles at this moment are of a more terrible, and alarming character, than we have ever known them before." Hostilities in New Mexico were extremely explosive as Navajos preyed upon the pueblos, towns, and ranches of northern New Mexico, and civilians robbed, captured, and murdered Navajos in Dinetah. The civil government of New Mexico was disgusted with the United States military and demanded that something be done about "the savage Indians who are daily murdering and robbing the people." The feud between the

Fort Defiance, Arizona, nestled in Cañon Bonito, 1855. Courtesy Southwest Museum, Los Angeles, California.

territorial and the federal governments was matched only by the strife among the different branches of the federal government in New Mexico. Authorities in Washington, D.C., reacted to conditions in New Mexico by reorganizing the territory into the Ninth Military District and assigning Colonel Edwin Vose Sumner to run the new department. A graduate of West Point and a veteran of the tragic Black Hawk War and the Mexican War, Sumner was well prepared for his duty in New Mexico. The colonel arrived in Santa Fe in July, 1851, and immediately made plans to campaign against the Navajos.[32]

With four companies of dragoons, two companies of infantry, and one company of artillery—about 350 men in all—Sumner and his men marched against the Navajos. Westward they traveled to Zuñi Pueblo before turning north toward the great Window Rock, at the southwestern end of the Chuska Mountains. Through the Chuska Valley they marched seven miles until they arrived at the

37

entrance to Cañon Bonito, a well-watered cañon. There the troops met a lone Indian rider. Sumner tried through the rider to persuade the Indians to meet with him; however, memories of Narbona's murder were still fresh, and the chiefs refused.

Leaving some of his men at Cañon Bonito to build a log fort, the colonel continued his journey to the west end of the Cañon de Chelly, at the present site of Chinle, Arizona. The mouth of the cañon was sandy and broad, stretching onto a plain about two hundred yards wide. Soon the red sides of the cañon wall began to reach skyward, and no doubt Sumner began to worry about a possible ambush. Desiring to take the offensive against the Navajos, he ordered his men to shoot Navajos on sight. Much to his dismay, the Indians dogged his troops, cautiously keeping out of rifle range. The expedition moved into the Cañon de Chelly, protected by a detachment of soldiers who skirted the southern rim of the cañon. About thirteen miles into the cañon the colonel found it "prudent and proper to leave." Before returning to Santa Fe, Sumner went to Cañon Bonito, where he placed Major Electus Backus in charge of the new fort, standing defiantly in the heart of Navajo country. Fittingly, the post was named Fort Defiance.[33]

While the colonel was in the field, the Navajos were reportedly raiding "in every direction through this Territory, committing murders and depredations." In fact, it was said that warriors were committing "depredations within seven miles and a half of this city [Santa Fe]." Again civil authorities demanded the use of volunteer troops, but the army under Sumner's command stood steadfast in its belief that this action would only increase hostilities. He observed that "this predatory war has been carried on for two hundred years, between the Mexicans and the Indians, . . . quite time enough to prove, that unless some change is made the war will be interminable." Mexicans and Indians alike, he claimed, "steal women and children and cattle from each other, and in fact carry on the war . . . like two Indian nations."[34] He asserted that a continuation of such "warfare will interfere very much with my measures." This policy brought a degree of peace to the frontier during the winter of 1851 and 1852. A few Navajo chiefs pledged themselves to peace, but were much disturbed when Indian Agent John Greiner complained that "the Navajos have captured their children—stolen their stock." Chief Armijo responded with anger and passion that "my people are all crying in the same way" and that "three of our Chiefs now sitting before you . . . mourn for their children—who have been taken from their homes by the Mexicans. More than 200 of our children have been carried off and we know not where they are." The Navajo headman insisted that "the Mexicans have lost but few children in comparison with what they have stolen from us." The Indians asked for justice, and the agent made a vague promise that justice would be done—a promise that he failed to keep.[35]

The storm followed the calm as the wars commenced again in the spring of 1853, when Navajos allegedly swept down upon the ranch of Ramón Martín near the little town of Chama. On the night of May 3 a shot rang out near a corral, and Martín was mortally wounded. The Navajos took his horses and roped five captives, driving them for about a quarter of a mile. The Indians released three of the captives and told them to tell the Mexicans that, "when a paint horse and a mule, stolen from the Navajos, were given up, then the two boys would be delivered."[36] Calhoun's successor, Governor William Carr Lane, acted by sending Donaciaro Vigil and a detachment to Navajo land. Vigil met with a few Navajo chiefs, who decided to release the two captives and meet with the governor in Santa Fe soon afterward. The Indians met with Governor Lane but refused to hand over the warrior responsible for shooting Martín, whereupon the new commander of Fort Defiance, Captain Henry L. Kendrick, was asked to investigate. The entire matter was dropped when Lane lost his bid as the New Mexico delegate to the United States Congress and turned over the governorship to William Messervy. The new governor was replaced when President Franklin Pierce chose David Meriwether, a seasoned frontiersman and former Indian trader, to fill the post.

The new governor promptly decided that "the government must either feed and clothe these Indians to a certain extent, or chastise them in a decisive manner." He wanted to create a "buffer zone" between the civilian inhabitants and the Navajos, in hope of halting the predatory war between the two. Most important, however, Meriwether chose an excellent man as Indian agent to the Navajos. He was Henry Lafayette Dodge, one of thirteen children born to the famed dragoon Colonel Henry Dodge. Like Meriwether, Dodge was familiar with the Navajo people, whom he admired and respected.[37]

Dodge was an impressive figure, though he stood a mere five feet seven inches tall. His skin was dark and tough from long exposure to the sun, and his face bore a stern but pleasant countenance that revealed wit and intelligence. His gray eyes were piercing and reflected a sincerity that was rare in men in his position. Not only did he understand the Navajos and their position, but many Indians understood him. Dodge was interested in their welfare, and he worked long and hard for their benefit. Unlike agents before him and many after him, Henry Dodge spent a good deal of time in Navajo land, living and working among the people. The agent took up residence in the Chuska Mountains on the eastern approach to Washington Pass, due west of Sheep Springs. There he built a cabin that served him as an agency site as well as a home.

Even before he moved out to the Navajo country, Dodge made preparations for a tour of Dinetah. Without military escort he traveled throughout Navajo country from the Cañon de Chelly to the Río San Juan, explaining his policy and gaining the confidence of the Indians. On August 31, 1853, he arrived in Santa Fe with a delegation of 104 Navajos, including the famed chiefs Zarcillos Largos and Barboncito. The Indians parleyed with Dodge and Meriwether for five days and heard the words of the Americans, who demanded that the Navajos cease their raids and that they obey the treaty of 1849. Dressed in their best buckskins and finest blankets, the Indians faced the Americans and explained their grievances against the Mexican slavers. In a most friendly atmosphere the Americans agreed for the first time to work with the Navajos in preventing such atrocities. Between 1853 and 1856, Dodge worked diligently with Major Henry Lane Kendrick to keep the peace in Navajo land. Together they opposed encroachment into Navajo country by New Mexican stockmen, thieves, and murderers.

Dodge became something of a legend among the Navajos, who found him honest and just in his dealings with them—rare qualities, it seemed to them, in a Bilagáana. They named him "Red Shirt" because of the red-flannel shirt that he often wore. Dodge introduced the Navajos to iron working and silversmithing, which the proud Diné readily learned and for which they became famous. The Navajo frontier was relatively peaceful during Dodge's term of office, though isolated incidents of fighting occurred from time to time. The presence of Agent Dodge, however, prevented a full-scale war. In October, 1856, Apaches made a raid on Zuñi, and Major Kendrick decided to scout the pueblo in an attempt to thwart future attacks. The major asked Dodge to accompany the party, and he agreed. The detachment arrived at Zuñi in mid-November and moved south about thirty miles. On the morning of the nineteenth, Dodge and Armijo rose before sunup and set out to hunt deer. As the two neared a prominent mesa, they saw a deer, which Dodge killed with his first shot. The Navajos remained with the deer to dress it while the agent continued the hunt for more game. Dodge never returned, however. A party of Kendrick's men picked up his trail and followed it to a spot where he had been captured by Mogollon and Coyotero Apaches. Even with the aid of the famed Apache chief Mangus Coloradas, it was difficult to determine the whereabouts of the Navajo agent. Finally, on January 2, 1857, José Mangus, the brother of Coloradas, informed the army that Dodge had been shot and scalped by Apaches soon after he was captured. His naked remains had been left in the snow for the wolves, buzzards, and coyotes. The Navajos had lost the only agent they had ever known who was sincerely interested in their lifeway and well-being. Dodge had helped prevent an outbreak of war during his years with the Diné; as Charles W. Wentz of the First Cavalry of New Mexico Volunteers put it, Dodge "possessed unbounded influence over the Navajo Chiefs, and was fairly worshipped by them." Wentz speculated that, "had he lived, I am of the opinion that the subsequent Navajo Wars would never have occurred."[38]

Of course, there is no way of knowing whether Dodge could have prevented the years of fighting that followed his death, but without his presence the wars continued, and much blood was shed before the end of the last great Navajo War. Greedy land encroachment by the New Mexicans, raids conducted into Navajo land by Utes, and a drought that destroyed Diné crops contributed in stirring the embers of hostilities smoldering in New Mexico after Dodge's death. Intermittent fighting occurred until 1858, when a full-scale war broke out. When Major Thomas H. Brooks, the new commander of Fort Defiance, arrived in New Mexico, trouble was already brewing. The source of the trouble was the army. For some time the soldiers at Fort Defiance had grazed their horses and cattle near Red Lake, twelve miles north of the fort. Traditionally these lands had belonged to the most renowned of all Navajo war chiefs, Manuelito, and his family. Manuelito did not take lightly the government's use of his lands, especially during this time of drought. It was bad enough that the army had taken Cañon Bonito without permission and established a fort in Navajo land. To steal the finest grazing lands in the region and exclude Navajos from grazing their animals on them was too much for Manuelito to endure. In protest the war chief herded his stock onto the land the army claimed, and in response soldiers charged his herd, shooting nearly sixty head of his stock. The situation burst into flames after a Navajo warrior killed a black slave named Jim, who was owned by Major Brooks. Probably the Navajo was a relative of Manuelito's who killed Brooks's slave in retaliation for the slaughter of the chief's stock. A demand went out from the fort for the murderer—the Indians were told to turn over the culprit or face grave reprisals. The Indians tried to placate the army by bringing in the body of a man who they said had committed the deed. An autopsy allegedly proved that the body was that of a Mexican, not an Indian, whereupon Colonel Dixon S. Miles launched a campaign against the Navajos. He marched through Navajo land and even traversed the southern branch of the Cañon de Chelly; however, he was not able to confront the Navajos, who were far too clever to face such a large force.[39]

The Miles campaign continued after the arrival of the new department commander of New Mexico, Colonel Benjamin L. E. Bonneville. It was Bonneville's hope to launch so decisive a campaign that he would crush the power of the Diné. Several "scouts" and expeditions were conducted between September and November, on which livestock was captured, crops and hogans (Navajo homes) were destroyed, and a few Navajos were killed. Yet Bonneville was unable to deliver the decisive blow against the Navajos that he had hoped for. Instead, the army accepted the peace overtures of the Navajos who felt it to their advantage to sue for peace. On November 20 a council of peace was held at Fort Defiance, and agreements were reached on an armistice. Neither Bonneville nor Superintendent James Collins approved of the treaty, and both men went to Fort Defiance to parley with the Navajos themselves. On Christmas Day, 1858, the final draft of Bonneville's treaty was concluded. The most significant article of the treaty called for a change in the eastern boundary of Navajo land, which was moved far to the west. The Diné were cheated out of much of their traditional land, land that had been recognized as theirs in 1855 by Governor David Meriwether. Chances are that they did not fully understand the details of the treaty, particularly those provisions outlining the new boundaries of Dinetah. It is highly unlikely that they would have signed away a huge portion of their land if they had known the full contents of the treaty.[40]

Samuel Yost, the Navajo Indian agent, was strongly opposed to the treaty, saying that its provisions were of "such a character that they cannot be endorsed by any enlightened mind." The treaty, he argued, would "transpose the Navajos from the pursuits of industry and agriculture . . . to robbers and plunderers." Yost believed that the treaty deprived the Indians of some of their very best land, which they cultivated and used for grazing. By stealing their land, the government was inviting trouble because the treaty compelled "them to abandon cultivating the soil and stock raising." Yost was correct, for the Navajos once again were forced into a lifeway of raiding. The Diné tried to abide by the treaty for a few months, returning livestock and captives to the government. Then Ute attacks on the Navajos caused warfare to ignite again on the New Mexican frontier. Ute agent Albert H. Pfeiffer reported that the Navajos were striking the Utes in retaliation within three miles of his agency. One Ute chief told Pfeiffer that by "the beginning of the other moon he would have his people ready to invade Navajo country, together with the soldiers and New Mexicans." The war commenced again after a short period of peace.[41]

In May, 1859, Major John Smith Simonson was ordered to the Navajo country to demonstrate the power of the United States. His arrival did little to halt the war, though he met a few Navajo leaders and tried to bring peace to the territory. He was aided by an agent of the Interior Department, who was soon replaced by a new Navajo agent. His name was Silas F. Kendrick, and he worked tirelessly to prevent further warfare. Kendrick traveled among the Navajos collecting stock that the Indians allegedly had stolen from the Río Grande valley. These animals were gathered together at Fort Defiance and in November were herded onto a trail that led to Albuquerque, where they were to be sold. The first night on the trail, however, the herd was stampeded by Navajos, who escaped with all but eighteen horses. The soldiers were rightfully embarrassed, and the next day they took out their anger on a lone Navajo warrior, who was lured into camp, stripped of his clothing, tied to a post, and viciously whipped, reportedly for carrying firearms. When word of this deed reached the various Navajo chiefs, they were outraged and promised retaliation.[42]

Two hundred Navajos attacked the military herd grazing near Fort Defiance in January, 1860. Had the soldiers not been reinforced, the Navajos would have succeeded in taking the army's entire herd. The Navajos' raid failed, but as they were returning to their mountain haunts, they surprised four soldiers who were cutting wood and killed three of them.[43] In addition, on several occasions Navajo warriors struck the military wagon trains that carried supplies from Albuquerque to Fort Defiance.[44] The army did little to foster good relations in order to bring about an end to these attacks, and, more often than not, the commander at Fort Defiance, Major Oliver L. Shepherd, deepened hostilities through his bad faith. For example, on January 20, a headman named Agua Chiquito was persuaded to enter the fort. He refused to confer with Shepherd but instead asked to see Kendrick. As the Indian and the agent were talking, Shepherd interrupted the conversation and ordered that from then on no agent of the Indian Department was permitted to talk with Navajos without his permission. At that, Chiquito was ordered to leave, but as he moved toward the gate, the major told the sentries to shoot him. Fortunately, the agile Indian made his escape uninjured. The underhanded incident only heightened hostilities.[45]

In 1860 most of the Navajos joined in all-out war. It was their hope to rid themselves of the Bilagáana once and for all. Navajo raids increased to such an extent that Governor Abraham Rencher called out the militia and asked the Utes to strike the Navajos with the "greatest vigor." Meanwhile, the regular army, under Colonel Thomas T. Fauntleroy, remained inactive and did not strike at the Navajo warriors. Fauntleroy ordered another fort constructed in Navajo land, this one near Bear Springs (southeast of Gallup, New Mexico). The fort would soon come to bear the colonel's name and would be the scene of a most unforgiveable incident. Meanwhile, the Navajos were raiding in every direction, and several chiefs decided to launch a decisive attack on Fort Defiance. In the predawn hours of April 30, a force of approximately one thousand warriors gathered about the fort and launched a three-pronged attack. For two hours the fighting blazed, but the warriors were unsuccessful in their attempt to overwhelm the soldiers and take control of the fort. With better weapons the Navajos could easily have defeated the unsuspecting army, but bows and arrows were not sufficient to overwhelm the soldiers.[46]

The war continued throughout the summer of 1860, and, because Fauntleroy was unable to launch a campaign against the Navajos, he was replaced as field commander with Colonel Edward Sprigg Canby. The colonel was an experienced soldier; he had fought the Seminoles and the Mexicans following his gradua-

Colonel Edward R. S. Canby. Courtesy Navajo Community College.

tion from West Point in 1839. In September, an army of Ute, Pueblo, and Mexican volunteers combined forces with the regular army to campaign against "the common enemy of both white men and Indian." In October, Canby began his scout against the Navajo Indians, directing his brother-in-law, Major Henry Hopkins Sibley, to march from Fort Defiance west toward Ganado and then north to the mouth of the Cañon de Chelly. Canby headed the second column north toward the northern rim of the Cañon de Chelly (known as the Cañon del Muerto) and then southwest to the mouth of the gorge. The two columns were reunited there and moved out together toward Black Mesa. A third column, under Captain Lafayette McLaws, moved north of Fort Defiance to cut off any Navajos trying to flee east away from the two larger columns.[47]

With great difficulty the columns made their way to the mouth of the Cañon de Chelly. Canby's command cut its way northward through "a most picturesque region of red sandstone formations" before heading west toward Black Mesa. At first Sibley encountered no Navajos, but early one morning he discovered, surprised, and attacked a band of Navajos who were driving a large herd of horses and sheep. Five warriors were killed in the encounter, three women and two children were taken captive, and two hundred horses and two thousand sheep were seized.

Sibley's soldiers continued their trek. After rejoining Canby, they returned to Fort Defiance. Minor operations were conducted against the Diné on the eastern edge of Navajo land along the Chuska Mountains and on the north along the San Juan River. In this campaign thirty-four Navajos were killed, and eight thousand head of livestock were taken (a relatively small number of animals compared with what the Indians actually owned).

The Navajos were intelligent warriors who wisely chose not to face a superior army unless forced to do so. They knew their homeland, and they could evade the soldiers in their beloved Dinetah. Thus Canby decided that the only way to defeat the Lords of New Mexico was to pursue them relentlessly in all seasons of the year and destroy their means of existence. The colonel reasoned that a series of campaigns must be organized by troops stationed throughout Navajo country and that forays had to be conducted in the "Navajo way," surprising the Indians, destroying their homes, and burning their crops. Canby planned to extinguish every means of livelihood, particularly the sheep, cattle, and horses. Then, and only then, Canby declared, could the Navajos be defeated.

Six companies of soldiers were transferred to Fort Fauntleroy and operations commenced along the Zuñi Mountains as well as in the northern reaches of Dinetah. Utes, Pueblos, and New Mexicans were used in small scouting parties to search out the Navajos in their hiding places. The Navajos were kept on the alert and were in continual dread of being surprised and attacked. Throughout the fall and winter of 1860 the Indians were pursued so relentlessly that they became divided into small bands that were "destitute of stock and resources of any kind." Starvation and a heavy winter hurt the Navajos greatly, and various chiefs slowly became convinced that they should sue for peace. Even the great warriors like Manuelito, Herrero, Barboncito, Delgadito, Armijo, and Ganado Mucho made overtures to Canby, who became convinced that the Navajos definitely desired peace. By February, 1861, approximately two thousand Navajos were camped near Fort Fauntleroy, where a council of peace was to commence. At a meeting on February 15, at which twenty-four chiefs were present, Canby presented the Navajos with his peace plan. The Navajos' acts of aggression against Pueblos and New Mexicans were to stop, and the chiefs were to accept the authority of the United States government. The headmen were to make war on other Navajos who continued to raid, and they were not to permit these *ladrones* ("rogues") to live in their country. Finally, all Navajos desiring peace were to assemble west of the fort and live there until the fighting ended. The United States agreed "to render them assistance that may be necessary to place them in the same condition with other nations under the protection of the government." That may have been a shallow concession, but at least there were no provisions calling for the removal of the Navajos from their traditional homelands.[48]

Canby and Fauntleroy were so confident that a lasting peace had been secured that they began ordering substantial withdrawals of troops from the Navajo country. Within two weeks after Canby's treaty was presented, thirty-four chiefs had signed the document. Peace seemed to be on the horizon, for the Navajo War had ceased. On April 25, 1861, the last soldiers were withdrawn from Fort Defiance, and the troop strength in Navajo land was substantially reduced. The withdrawal of troops was unfortunate for the Navajos and for the Bilagáana: some unscrupulous New Mexicans took advantage of the situation to begin raiding the Indians again. The Navajos were in a very weakened state and could not properly defend themselves from their traditional enemy, the Nakai of the Río Grande. Too few bluecoat soldiers were available to protect the Diné, and hostilities broke out once again. New Mexicans made slave raids into Navajo land, taking advantage of the peace to steal women and children and kill the Navajo warriors who stood in their way. One raiding party "openly avowed their intentions to disregard the treaty made with the Navajos, and on their return to home, to organize a new expedition to capture Navajos and sell them." Unfortunately, there was no provision in Canby's treaty about the punishment of slave raiders, horse thieves, and murderers who preyed on the Navajos, though Canby promised to "have no hesitation in treating as enemies of the United States any parties of Mexicans or Pueblo Indians who may be found in the country assigned to the Navajos." He could not prevent these incursions because of developments beyond his control. His attention was drawn away from the Navajos to new enemies who were invading the Territory of New Mexico—Confederate soldiers from Texas.[49]

When Canby's troops withdrew from Dinetah to meet the Confederate invasion, the Navajos were faced with many pressing problems of survival. Their crops and homes had been destroyed in Canby's campaign, and they were destitute, cold, and hungry.

Their security was constantly threatened by raids into their homeland by Utes, Pueblos, and New Mexicans. The world seemed to be closing in on them, as the food, clothing, and protection promised by the American government were not forthcoming. It seemed to the Navajos that the Bilagáana had lied once again and that their words, as thick as smoke when spoken, vanished into the air. The Indians were in the worst of conditions, for they had to choose between life and death. The Diné could either submit to starvation, cold, and attack or fight as they had for generations. Their choice was simple. Like the great warriors they were, they proudly refused to die without a fight.

To support their families and in retaliation for the attacks on them, many Navajos once again mounted their horses and rode into New Mexico to raid the ranches of the Hispanos and Anglos. At first renewed warfare proved successful for the Navajo warriors because the army and the civilians were busy warding off the invasion from Texas. The raids did not, however, defeat the Nakai or the Bilagáana but only caused more troubles for the Diné. Although the renewed raiding temporarily ended their hunger and brought renewed prosperity to Dinetah, it soon generated a new force in New Mexico that would present a terrible dilemma to the Navajos. The events about to begin would radically change the lives of all Navajos from that time forward. The man who would be responsible for the changing course of events was Kit Carson.

CHAPTER 2

Carson, Confederates, and Indians

At a glance Kit Carson was not an impressive figure of a man. He was about five and a half feet tall with broad, somewhat stooped shoulders and a deep barrel chest. His frame was well knit and symmetrically proportioned, while his full face was suggestive of his plain, simple manner. Kit's auburn hair was usually worn down the back of his neck, "a la Franklin mode." Off and on throughout his life he sported a distinguished reddish mustache which drooped over the sides of his lips. The key to his character was found in his blue-gray eyes, which were quick and piercing.

Carson had a modest, straightforward personality and was known to be self-reliant but not ambitious, aggressive, or domineering. Kit was nearly illiterate and could write little more than his own name. His lack of "book learnin'" was always an embarrassment to him. He was much impressed and even awed by figures of authority, like his friend John C. Frémont, whom he considered well educated, well spoken, and well bred. Although Kit became a hero in his own day as a hunter, trapper, scout, and soldier, he was not a great leader. Nonetheless, he was admired and liked by most people who knew him, except for the many Indians who hated and despised the great "Indian fighter."

Christopher Carson was born in Madison County, Kentucky, on

A romanticized sketch of Kit Carson and his horse, Apache. From Dewitt C. Peters, Kit Carson's Life and Adventures *(1893).*

December 24, 1809, and grew up in Boon's Lick, Missouri. Kit was apprenticed as a saddlemaker, but, dissatisfied with his lot as a saddler, he ran away at the age of sixteen to join a wagon train heading for Santa Fe. His ardent thirst for adventure was a significant element of Carson's makeup, and it remained a part of him throughout his life. He loved excitement, and he thrived on the hardship, danger, and challenge of the big-sky country. These particulars of his character were important in influencing Kit's decision in the 1860s, to leave his family and his home in Taos, New Mexico, to fight Confederates, Apaches, and Navajos.

Just as important was his commitment to his superiors, who were oftentimes his friends. He was stubbornly devoted to his duty and fiercely loyal to his country. When Abraham Lincoln was elected president, for example, Carson and seven other prominent citizens of Taos went to the town plaza and raised the Stars and Stripes to signify their support for the Union. When the Civil War erupted, Kit remained loyal to the United States, though many of his associates returned to the South to fight for the Confederacy. Kit would soon stand and fight the southerners who would threaten the Territory of New Mexico.[1]

Part of the southern war strategy was to capture the American Southwest, where the Confederacy hoped to secure gold, ports, and commercial alliances. Henry Hopkins Sibley, having resigned his commission in the United States Army, had joined the Confederate cause and led the South's attack into New Mexico. Sibley organized a volunteer force which some Texans said was composed of the fiercest fighting men who "ever threw a leg over a horse or that had ever sworn allegiance to any cause." Some of these Texans were former Rangers while others were outlaws. All of them sought adventure and hoped to "whup" the Yankees in an offensive fight. With approximately 2,600 Lone Star volunteers, Sibley marched up the Río Grande toward Fort Craig, where his brother-in-law, Edward Canby, lay in wait for the arrival of the southern forces.[2]

When the Civil War broke out, Colonel Canby's attention was drawn away from the Navajos, with terribly unfortunate results for the Indians and the army. Had the forces of the United States remained in the Navajo country at full strength, it is probable that Kit Carson's campaign would not have been necessary. As it was, when Canby's regulars were withdrawn from Dinetah, the region was open to attack by traditional enemies of the Navajos.

In June, 1861, some of the snow was still on the rugged mountains northeast of Taos, and the winds carried the sweet scent of sagebrush. But the tranquillity of the scene surrounding Carson's home was not typical of the rest of the country at the outbreak of the Civil War. Kit resigned his appointment as Ute Indian agent to enlist as lieutenant colonel of the First New Mexico Volunteers, a detachment which he led after September, 1861. In January of the next year Kit was ordered down the Río Grande to Fort Craig, south of present Socorro, New Mexico. There Carson's volunteers waited with Canby for the arrival of the Confederate Army.

Carson's only action against the Confederates came during the Battle of Valverde on February 21, 1862. Although Kit's regiment was enthusiastic, it was unseasoned and untried. Most of the volunteers were New Mexican paisanos, country folk and farmers unskilled in combat. Half of Canby's troops at Valverde were inexperienced New Mexicans, a definite advantage to the outnumbered Confederate soldiers who marched north to meet Carson's men at Fort Craig. Carson's regiment struck out north from the fort toward 'he crossing at Valverde before sunrise on that fateful February morning of 1862.[3]

Fighting was fierce at Valverde as rifle and artillery fire raged back and forth across the river. Knives, sabers, and pistols were drawn and used in hand-to-hand combat, while the heavier weapons from both sides spewed their deadly leaden spray across the field of battle.[4] During the day-long battle Carson's troops were kept mostly in reserve because they were green, unseasoned soldiers. Kit's company, therefore, had "remained on the west side of the river and had taken no part in the battle" during the morning hours of February 21. Carson reported, however, that around "1 o'clock in the afternoon I received from Colonel Canby the order to cross the river, which I immediately did." The volunteers formed on the right side of the battlefield and fought their way toward a number

Kit Carson, loyal Unionist. Courtesy Arizona Historical Society, Tucson.

of small sandy hills. After moving about four hundred yards, Kit's company met between four and five hundred Confederate soldiers, who charged toward the front of his line. The volunteers prepared for battle, and, when "the head of the enemy's column came within some 80 yards of my right, a volley from the whole column was poured into them, and the firing being kept up caused them to break in every direction." Carson's troops were between the rebels and a 24-pound artillery piece that the southerners were attempting to capture at the time of the charge. At the very time Carson's troops concentrated a steady fire at the Confederates, "a shell from the 24-pound was thrown among them [the Confederates] with fatal effect." The Confederates chose not to regroup, and the Union troops chose not to charge. Carson was ordered "to retreat and recross the river." Under Kit's direction the volunteers executed this movement in good fashion and returned to Fort Craig that evening.[5]

Colonel Carson and his volunteers were cited for their valiant efforts against the Confederates, but it was not their lot to continue the fight against the invading Texans. That job would be left to others, particularly the Colorado Volunteers, who would defeat Sibley's soldiers in the Battle of Glorieta Pass in late March, 1862. Carson and his soldiers were left in charge of Fort Craig, and there they remained until the Confederates were defeated.

The colonel was relieved of his command for a time to visit his wife, Josefa, and his family, but his days with the army had not ended. The guardianship of the territory was assumed by the New Mexico Volunteers as the regular army headed east to continue the fight against the southerners. Colonel Canby was ordered to the East as well, and in his stead came the new commander of the Department of New Mexico, James Henry Carleton. More than any other individual in New Mexico, Carleton would influence the future course of American policy toward the Mescalero Apaches and the Navajo Indians.[6]

Born and reared in Maine, Carleton joined the First Dragoons in 1839. He had fought with General Zachary Taylor ("Old Rough and Ready") at the Battle of Buena Vista during the Mexican War.

General James H. Carleton. Courtesy Museum of New Mexico, Santa Fe.

When the War Between the States erupted, Carleton was colonel of the First California Infantry. Appointed brigadier general of the California Volunteers, the forty-eight-year-old commander led his California Column into New Mexico, where this "Great Mogul" assumed command on September 18, 1862.

There was much in Carleton's features that hinted at his character. He had an aggressive, jutting chin, and his eyes were wide, dark, and piercing. His flowing sideburns and thick, heavy mustache added to the arrogance of his countenance. Most of the army regulars who served under him found him arbitrary and sometimes cruel in his dealings with others. He was an unscrupulous, ambitious, selfish man, whose bearing radiated an abrasive, tyrannical personality.

Carleton was called a "humanitarian" in his day, however, for he believed it his duty and destiny as a good Christian gentleman to tame the "savages" and to make civilized beings of these "barbarians." The general's roots in a Calvinistic tradition had a great deal to do with his attitude toward the "uncivilized" Indians, whom he considered in need of the white man's culture, religion, and economic lifeways. Moreover, like Carson, the general was greatly influenced by the aggressive doctrines of Manifest Destiny, which expanded the territorial limits of the United States into lands occupied by Indians. Carleton would become the director of a severe and unmerciful campaign against two of the most powerful and warlike tribes in the American Southwest.[7]

Defeating the Mescaleros and the Navajos was only one of Carleton's objectives after assuming command of New Mexico Territory. More important was his wish to demonstrate to the policymakers of the United States that "wild" Indians like the Navajos could be "tamed." Carleton planned to destroy the lifeway of the Navajos by defeating them in battle, removing them from their homeland, and concentrating them on a reservation. There he envisioned that the Navajos would be "civilized" in the ways of whites and Christianized. He was particularly interested in changing the economic life of the Navajos from that of ranchers and raiders to that of farmers. Like the Mescaleros, the Navajos were to be removed to the Bosque Redondo, where Carleton could launch his grand experiment to make civilized human beings out of "savages." His reservation system at the Bosque Redondo would soon be called Fair Carletonia, in honor of the architect of this innovation in American Indian policy. Before Carleton could put his ideas into effect, however, he had to find a soldier who would carry out his plans to campaign against the Indians. Carleton turned to Kit Carson to direct his war against the Mescaleros and the Navajos.

Carleton knew Kit Carson from their days of fighting the Jicarilla Apaches in 1855, and the general believed that the colonel was just the man he needed to implement his field tactics against the Indians. Kit was a simple man of "sound" character (except that he killed people from time to time, particularly Indians). He was not formally educated, but he knew the American West better than most other white men of his day. Kit was easily impressed by people like Carleton who were formally educated and had social "upbringing" and rank. He often yielded to casual adulation and could be persuaded and maneuvered through words of praise, flattery, and commendation. Kit envied such frontier figures as Carleton and usually showed them the utmost respect, admiration, and loyalty. Indeed, despite Carleton's paternalistic lectures, scoldings, and directives during Kit's campaign against the Navajos, the colonel never wavered in his feelings about his commander. Carleton was Kit's superior, and Kit never questioned the wisdom or necessity of the general's orders and policies. In short, Carson was Carleton's tool, and he permitted himself to be used by the general. Because of his loyalty to his country and his friend, his thirst for adventure, and his innate sense of duty, Carson would agree to launch an all-out campaign against the most hostile Indians of New Mexico. The campaigns against the Apaches and Navajos were conceived and planned by Carleton, but they were executed by Carson.

Commissioner of Indian Affairs William P. Dole argued that it was up to the War Department and not the Interior Department to deal with "the wild and warlike" tribes of New Mexico. Military forces, he maintained, should be launched against these Indians, who were "actively hostile, and, on account of their numerical strength . . . truly formidable." The army had an obligation "not only to preserve the lives and possessions of our resident citizens, but also to reduce the hostile tribes to subjection, [and] punish them for the barbarous atrocities they are continually committing." According to the commissioner, the two "most formidable of the tribes thus arrayed in hostility towards our people are the Apaches and the Navajos." The Navajos, he claimed, were the "most insidious, but it is believed no less dangerous" than the Apaches.

The commissioner stated that in 1861 these two tribes were "leading a wild and predatory life, gaining a scanty subsistence by the chase and an irregular and imperfect cultivation of the soil." Apaches and Navajos thus were "a constant source of irritation and vexation to the whites." He recommended that they be defeated and placed on reservations, and he wanted the War Department to execute a crushing campaign against the Apaches and Navajos. The cry for war came loud and clear not only from the Interior and War departments but from New Mexican civilians as well. Their view of a campaign was somewhat different, however, from that of the departments, for they favored the complete extermination of the tribes. They could then, without interference, take over the traditional lands of the Indians.

The Navajos and other tribes faced grave problems in dealing with the United States. Conflicting policies were forwarded by the different branches and levels of government. The Interior Department demanded that the War Department defeat the Navajos, but the Interior Department refused the responsibility of providing for the Diné after Carson's campaign. The bickering among the different government agencies contributed greatly to the plight of the Indians, who were caught in the unmerciful bureaucracy of the federal government. The territorial government was no better, for the New Mexicans would settle for nothing less than the total surrender of the Mescaleros and Navajos. Territorial officials, newspaper editors, and the New Mexican Citizenry complained about the inefficiency and ineffectiveness of the United States Army and the Indian Bureau. All levels and departments of government could agree on one thing, however. They all wanted to see the defeat of the "wild tribes" of New Mexico, and to this end Carleton commenced the first stages of his "Indian policy" in the fall of 1862.[8] The Mescaleros were the first to feel the force of his personality.

The heart of Mescalero Apache country was nestled in the Capitan Mountains of south-central New Mexico. Along the Bonito River, one of many small rivers that snake through the Capitans, the army had built Fort Stanton before the Civil War. The fresh-smelling piñon and juniper trees of the area provided wood for the soldiers, and the fort was constructed on a relatively flat plain in the midst of these trees on the high side of the river. The scene surrounding the post provided a spectacular view, especially to the west, where Sierra Blanca towered above the other peaks, displaying its snow-capped grandeur most of the year. It was here that Kit Carson was ordered to begin an all-out campaign against the Mescaleros.

By special order Carleton instructed Carson to reoccupy Fort Stanton and to commence his campaign against the Apaches. On October 12, 1862, Kit received this order from Carleton: "All Indian men of that tribe are to be killed whenever and wherever you can find them. The women and children will not be harmed, but you will take them prisoners, and feed them at Fort Stanton until you receive other instructions about them." If the Indians attempted to sue for peace, Carson was instructed to say that "when the people of New Mexico were attacked by the Texans, the Mescalero broke their treaty of peace, and murdered innocent people, and ran off their stock." Carleton perhaps did not realize or cared not to consider that, when the American soldiers left Fort Stanton, the Indians were without any means of livelihood except their old practice of raiding.

When the soldiers left, the Apaches were at the mercy of New Mexican settlers and the Texan invaders. According to James Collins, superintendent of Indian affairs in New Mexico, before Sibley's army entered the territory, "the Mescaleros were receiving rations at Fort Stanton, and were conducting themselves well; but soon after the abandonment of the fort by the government troops

61

they became involved in a quarrel with the Texans that brought on a fight, in which several Indians and some of the Texans were killed." The Texans "left the Indians, smarting under the injuries they had received from the invaders." Within a short time the Apaches "assumed a hostile attitude towards the citizens on the Río Bonito."⁹ Indian Agent Lorenzo Labadie reported that the Apaches "have been in a continuous state of hostility, and have committed heavy depredations upon the people." He charged that the Mescaleros had "killed some forty men and six children, and carried a number of children into captivity" in August, 1862, alone. According to the agent, these "wild, hostile, barbarous" Indians had stolen "horses, mules, donkeys, and cattle, besides large numbers of sheep." The Apaches felt justified in seeking the path of war, for not only had the Texans harassed them, but the New Mexicans were guilty of raiding the Indians as well. In July, 1862, "a party of eighty men (Mexicans) made an expedition into the country of these Indians in pursuit of stolen property; they returned with four Indian children, captives, and about forty horses and mules." Whether it was the Apaches or the New Mexicans who made the first raid is hard to say, but all blame for the hostilities fell on the Apaches, who had taken up arms to protect and to feed themselves. This, unfortunately, mattered little to Carleton.¹⁰

Kit was instructed by Carleton to tell the Apaches that he had "been sent to punish them for their treachery and their crimes; that you have no power to make peace; that you are there to kill them wherever you can find them." Carleton stated that "if they beg for peace, their chiefs and twenty of their principal men must come to Santa Fe to have a talk here." Carson was to tell them that, even though they might ask for peace, he was to "keep after their people and slay them until" he received orders to end the hostilities. The savage-minded commander of New Mexico had no faith in the Apaches and believed that "if we kill some of their men in fair, open war, they will be apt to remember that it will be better for them to remain at peace than to be at war." The Christian gentleman from Maine convinced himself "that this severity, in the long run, will be the most humane course that could be pursued toward these Indians." The general summed up the duty of Kit Carson against the Apaches by stating, "The Indians are to be soundly whipped, without parleys or councils."[11]

No sooner was Fort Stanton reoccupied than Carson had his men in the field. Two companies were sent out on a scout and told that there was to be "no talk, no council, kill the men, capture the women and children." On one scout Captain James Graydon met a party of Mescaleros heading toward Santa Fe to parley a peace with Carleton. Their intentions were peaceful and honorable, but, when given the opportunity, Graydon opened fire on them, killing Manuelito and José Largo, two prominent chiefs of the Apaches. Four warriors and a woman were killed on the spot, and after a short chase, the blood of five more warriors was shed. An unreported number of other Apaches was wounded or killed in the treacherous and unwarranted conflict. Graydon returned to the fort with seventeen horses and mules to report his "victory" in the fight.

Carson cared little for this kind of warfare, and even Carleton, who had ordered that "all Indian men . . . are to be killed," was concerned enough over the event that he wrote Carson: "If you are satisfied that Graydon's attack on Manuelito and his people was not fair and open, see that all the horses and mules . . . are returned to the survivors of Manuelito's band." This was a minute concession to the families of those Indians who were murdered while seeking peace with the whites.[12]

Southwest of Fort Stanton, Captain William McCleave encountered several hundred Apaches at Dog Canyon, a wide, arid draw in the shadow of the Guadalupe Mountains on the New Mexico-Texas border. McCleave's forces clashed with about one hundred Apaches and reportedly "whipped them in a fair fight and drove them before him." Following this scrape, several Apaches went to Fort Stanton to surrender to Colonel Carson. As ordered, Carson told them that they would have to go to Santa Fe and make peace with Carleton, the "Big Captain." Five of them started north accompanied by a military escort and the Mescalero Indian agent, Lorenzo Labadie. Arriving on November 23, they soon parleyed with the New Mexican commander. "The Ready" spoke for the Apaches, stating that the Americans were stronger than the Indians and that the soldiers had better weapons. "Give us like weapons and turn us loose," he argued, and "we will fight you again." Their spirit was not lacking, but the Apaches were worn out and hungry and had "no more heart." He told Carleton, "Do with us as may seem good to you, but do not forget we are men and braves."[13]

Carleton had decided what to do with the Apaches before their arrival in Santa Fe. He planned to remove them from their old home and resettle them in southeastern New Mexico along the Pecos River. Carleton believed that the Indians, away from their traditional home, would forget their old ways and slowly come to live and think like whites. The general had previously ordered the establishment of a post in a desolate place called the Bosque Redondo, a circular wooded area that was to be the center of the new reservation. The meeting in Santa Fe was the first time the Mescaleros learned about the plans Carleton had made for them, and they were told to return to their people and tell them that peace could come only if they submitted to his wishes. They were told to move to the Bosque, where they would be fed and protected by the soldiers at Fort Sumner. If they chose to remain in their traditional homeland, Carson's troops would hunt them down like animals and kill them.

The Apaches had little choice, for they could fight and die or submit. They accepted their fate, and by March, 1863, approximately four hundred Mescaleros were living at the Bosque Redondo. Carleton was well pleased with the success of his campaign against the Indians of New Mexico. "Now that the Mescaleros are subdued," he wrote, "I shall send the whole of Colonel Carson's regiment against the Navajoes, who still continue to plunder and murder the people." Kit had a short visit with Josefa and his children before he began his preparations for a fight against the Navajos.[14]

At the outbreak of the Civil War most of the eastern bands of Navajos were inclined toward peace. Canby's campaign against

Barbas Hueros, Light Beard. Courtesy Smithsonian Institution.

them had taken its toll, and fifty-four chiefs had agreed to live in peace with the Bilagáana. It is quite probable that Canby's treaty with the Navajos would have ended most of the fighting between the Indians and the whites in New Mexico. True, the treaty had its deficiencies. It lacked a provision for return of captives held not only by the Navajos but also by the New Mexicans. It also lacked a provision to protect Navajos from the ruthless incursions of the New Mexicans, even though Canby recognized that "one of the gravest difficulties . . . in maintaining a peace with these people, is that resulting from the dangers of aggression from their neighbors." Another danger, Canby warned, was of a "most serious character," and that was starvation, which would force the Navajos to launch their forays again in order to feed their families.[15]

While some Navajo chiefs were away from their homes near Beautiful Mountain rounding up stolen stock to return to the army in compliance with the treaty, their homes were raided by a company of civilian marauders who ravaged their homes, stole their animals, and either killed or enslaved fifteen Navajos. Canby stated that he had "no doubt of the permanent settlement of these troubles if the inroads of Mexicans can be restrained." The Civil War prevented Canby from fulfilling his wish to halt raids on the Navajos by Hispanos, Utes, and Pueblos.[16] The New Mexicans were quick to indict all Navajos for any trouble. The Indians, they argued, "had murdered hundreds of our people, and carried our women and children into captivity." The entire Territory of New Mexico, they claimed, had been "invaded and overrun by these rapacious Indians" who were daily "murdering, robbing, and carrying off whatever may come in their way." Without any consideration for the loss of Indian families, the New Mexicans maintained that every *familia* "has to mourn the loss of some loved one who has been made to sacrifice his life to these bloodthirsty Navajoes." The New Mexicans further argued: "It belongs to the people to relieve themselves of the evils they are suffering and administer such chastisement to these marauders as they deserve." Henry Connelly, the governor of the territory, therefore ordered the militia to make "ready to march to the Navajo country." Authorization of such volunteer forces served only to heighten hostilities.[17]

Even before the governor's authorization to raise civilian troops, volunteer forces were raiding the Navajos from the New Mexican village of Cubero. In May the alcalde, or mayor, of the settlement reported that a "party of Mexicans (mostly composed of *Deserters* from the Volunteer Forces of the Territory) and some friendly Indians numbering about 100 persons, went out on a campaign party, as they said, against the Navajos." After a few days, two Navajos went "into Cubero under a flag of truce" and said that they were representing the major chiefs of the region—Cayentano,

Armijo, and Barboncito. They stated that "the Navajos did not wish to fight—that they were anxious for *Peace,* and wished this fact to be communicated to the Commanding Officer of Department Headquarters and the Superintendent of Indian Affairs at Santa Fe." Untrusting of the New Mexicans, "the Ambassadors . . . had three (3) horses saddled and bridled" ready for a break, if necessary. During their negotiations with the alcalde, three "Mexicans from Ceboyeta, surreptitiously mounted and ran them [the horses] off to parts unknown."[18]

The Indians complained to the alcalde: "For some time past, two months and more, parties of Mexicans from the Río Grande and Ceboyeta have been in the pursuit of Indians—'Kidnapping' Indian children and taking them to the River for Sale, several have been sold in this place for $2 or $300." The trade in Navajo slaves seemed to be "a thriving business to some persons." According to William Need, who was at Cubero, the slave trade "exasperates the Navajoes, and certainly tends to aggrevate [*sic*] and complicate affairs between them and the ranch owners on the Rio Grande: causing them to Rob and Steal cattle and sheep and horses and mules from innocent parties." Need was astute in his evaluation of the situation; slave raiding and stock stealing were important factors in perpetuating and aggravating hostilities.[19]

The prospect of a lasting peace with the Navajos was further jeopardized by Canby's choice of a new commander at Fort Fauntleroy. Manuel Chaves received his commission as lieutenant colonel on August 1, 1862, and it is hard to imagine that Canby could have chosen a worse person to fill the position. Chaves had spent his life fighting Indians, and he had little liking for the Navajos. On many occasions he had launched expeditions into Navajo land to steal stock and enslave captives. To the New Mexicans who lived along the Río Grande he was a hero, but to the Navajo Indians of Dinetah he was a scourge. He arrived at the fort on August 8 and continued Canby's policy of issuing rations to the starving Indians. At that time there were two thousand Navajos living near the post, but this number soon dwindled to approximately five hundred. Chaves was lax in disciplining his own men,

Manuel A. Chaves, noted Indian fighter and commanding officer at Fort Fauntleroy during the massacre. Courtesy Navajo Community College.

who, like so many other soldiers, passed their time drinking and gambling.

Such activities became volatile when, on September 13, horse racing commenced and betting became the order of the day. During the third race the finest of the Navajo ponies was matched against a thoroughbred owned by Finis E. Kavanaugh, an assistant surgeon. Several accounts of the race and the subsequent events have survived, and these are conflicting in detail.[20]

When the race began, the horses dashed like lightning toward the finish line. Down the track they went—and then the race exploded into controversy. One story has it that, sensing defeat, the Navajo pulled his pony into the path of Kavanaugh's mount, while another story says that the bridle broke on the Navajo pony. Regardless of the cause of the confusion, violence would result. The Navajos wanted another race, while the soldiers only wanted to take their "winnings" and make for the fort. Gathering in large numbers in front of the post to protest, the Navajos, some of whom were intoxicated, demanded a new race. When a few Indians approached the guardhouse, a shot rang out, and an Indian fell. No one was ever certain who fired the shot, but "squaws and children ran in all directions and were shot and bayoneted."

Sergeant Nicholas Hodt reported that, as he was leaving the fort in pursuit of the Indians, he "saw a soldier murdering two little children and a woman." The sergeant "hallooed immediately to the other soldier to stop," but he simply "looked up, but did not obey my order." Hodt ran up to the soldier, but he "could not get there soon enough to prevent him from killing the two innocent children and wounding severely the squaw." The sergeant placed the soldier under arrest, and, as he took his prisoner toward the fort, he was greeted by a Lieutenant Rafael Ortiz, who had "a pistol at full cock, saying, 'Give back this soldier his arms, or else I'll shoot you, God damn you.'"

Hodt did as he was ordered but reported the incident to Colonel Chaves. The colonel did nothing about the matter except give "credit to the soldier who murdered the children and wounded the squaw." Chaves had even ordered the artillery to open fire on the fleeing Indians, but fortunately the sergeant in charge of the mountain howitzers refused to obey, claiming that he did not hear the order.

The Fort Fauntleroy massacre ended all chance of a peaceful settlement with the Navajos. Colonel Canby was shocked to hear the news, for he had hoped to avoid another war with the Navajos. Canby relieved Chaves of his command and ordered him to Albuquerque to await a court-martial. Unfortunately, the court never convened, and the murderer went free. The massacre was ruthless and unnecessary, and there was no possible way to undo what Chaves and his soldiers had managed to do in one afternoon of treachery. The breach between the soldiers and the Indian was final, and all chance of a peaceful settlement ended with the unmerciful killing of 12 Indians and the enslavement of 112 more. The soldiers contributed significantly to starting a new Navajo war that would bring Kit Carson to Dinetah to begin his campaign in the summer of 1863.[21]

CHAPTER 3

The Summer Scout

The troops must be kept after the Indians," Carleton declared, "not in big bodies, with military noise and smokes, and the gleam of arms by day, and fires, and talk, and comfortable by night." Carleton—and—Carson believed that the soldiers should be kept "in small parties moving stealthily to their [the Indians'] haunts and lying patiently in wait for them." To defeat the Navajos, they reasoned, the troops had to fight, think, and act like the Indians themselves. Carson and his men were to follow "their tracks day after day with fixedness of purpose that never gives up." Carleton compared the duty of Carson's men with that of a hunter: "if a hunter goes after deer, he tries all sorts of wiles to get within gunshot of it. An Indian is a more watchful and more wary animal than a deer." Thus a Navajo had to be "hunted with skill; he cannot be blundered upon; nor will he allow his pursuers to come upon him when he knows it, unless he is stronger."[1] Carleton wanted to hunt the Navajos as if they were wild animals, an analogy that had racial overtones. Such was the perception of General Carleton, the man who directed the last Navajo war.

Before Carleton's ascendancy to department commander of New Mexico, Colonel Canby had put into motion the makings of another campaign against the Navajos. On May 10, 1862, Canby ordered the reorganization of the volunteer regiments of the territory. He

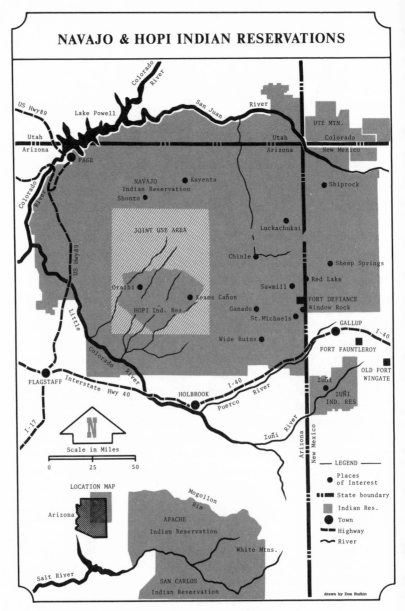

NAVAJO & HOPI INDIAN RESERVATIONS

Colorado River
San Juan River
US Hwy89
Lake Powell
UTE MTN.
Utah
Arizona
Utah
Colorado
PAGE
Arizona
New Mexico
NAVAJO
Indian Reservation
● Kayenta
● Shiprock
Shonto
Colorado River
JOINT USE AREA
● Luckachukai
Chinle ●
● Sheep Springs
US Hwy89
Oraibi ●
Sawmill ●
● Red Lake
● Keams Cañon
FORT DEFIANCE
HOPI Ind. Res.
Ganado ●
Window Rock
Little
St.Michaels ●
● GALLUP
Colorado River
Wide Ruins ●
I-40
FORT FAUNTLEROY
FLAGSTAFF
Interstate Hwy 40
I-40
OLD FORT
WINGATE
HOLBROOK
Puerco River
Zuñi ●
ZUÑI
IND. RES.
I-17
Zuñi River
Arizona
New Mexico

N
Scale in Miles
0   25   50

LOCATION MAP

Mogollon Rim
Arizona
APACHE
Indian Reservation
White Mtns.
Salt River
SAN CARLOS
Indian Reservation

— LEGEND —
● Places of Interest
State boundary
Indian Res.
● Town
Highway
River

drawn by Don Bufkin

Navajo and Hopi reservations

placed the finest soldiers he could find in Kit Carson's First New Mexico Volunteers and ordered them to perform "mounted service in the Indian country, in suppressing the bandits and in restoring law and order." Before Canby's departure for the East he laid the foundation for the Kit Carson campaign. Nonetheless, it was General Carleton who implemented the plan, directed the campaign, and demanded the removal of the Diné.[2]

Kit Carson was a reluctant campaigner against the Apaches and the Navajos. He had enlisted to fight the Confederates, not the Indians, and throughout his campaigns against the Indians he requested leave to visit his wife and children. Following the campaign against the Apaches, Carson wrote Carleton to explain that his "duty as well as happiness, directs me to my home & family and trust that the General will accept my resignation."[3] The commander, however, would not accept Kit's resignation and persuaded him to remain in the army to fight the Navajos. Carleton was able to convince Carson that he was the only man in New Mexico capable of directing the campaign against them. The general probably reminded Kit that, as a soldier, he had an obligation to his superior and his country. These factors and Carson's own penchant for adventure convinced Kit that he must lead the Navajo campaign.

Carleton decided that, since "the Mescaleros are subdued, I shall send the whole of Col. Carson's regiment against the Navajos, who continue to plunder and murder the people." Plans for a campaign against the Navajos were formulated in Carleton's mind before Carson agreed to lead it, and even before he waged his war against the Mescaleros. On September 27, 1862, Carleton ordered Lieutenant Colonel J. Francisco Chávez to construct Fort Wingate, near the present town of San Rafael, New Mexico, on the eastern border of the Navajo country. Inquisitive Navajos noted the construction of the fort, and some went to Santa Fe to confer with Carleton regarding the purpose of the fort and the intent of the new commander. These Navajos favored peace and had lived according to Canby's treaty of 1861. Nevertheless, Carleton told them that there would be no peace for Navajos unless they surrendered and accepted removal to the Bosque Redondo. For the Navajos this

Navajo medicine man who practiced the traditional beliefs of the
Diné. Courtesy Smithsonian Institution.

was an impossible choice, for they would not emigrate from their traditional lands without a fight. Like many other Native Americans, they held their land sacred. Since the creation of the world, the Navajos said, Dinetah had been theirs and was given to them by the Holy People of the First World. They could not surrender their land and move from it, for to do so would be a violation of their deepest religious beliefs. They chose to fight for what they knew to be theirs.[4]

In April, 1863, the general ordered Carson to begin preparations for the Navajo campaign. Kit was told to select some "Ute Indians from the neighborhood of Abiquiu . . . to be employed as trailers." He was told to hire about "ten of the best Ute warriors—and say four of the best Mexican guides." These New Mexicans and Indians were to serve "as spies and guides for the contemplated campaign against the Navajoes." Carson was to choose "none but the best," for his work was "to be thorough, and we must have *men* to do it." Carleton did not officially open the campaign against the Navajos until June 15, 1863, when he decreed "that Colonel CHRISTO-PHER CARSON, with a proper military force proceed without delay to a point in the Navajoe country known as *Pueblo Colorado*, and there establish a defensible Depot for his supplies and Hospital." From this point near present-day Ganado, Arizona, Carson was "to prosecute a vigorous war upon the men of this tribe until it is considered at these Head Quarters that they have been effectually punished for their long continued atrocities."[5]

On July 7, 1863, Kit Carson and 221 men left Los Lunas, New Mexico, and headed west toward the Navajo country. This was just a portion of Carson's command, which eventually numbered 736 men and was supported by an additional 326 soldiers under the command of Colonel Chávez at Fort Wingate. Kit's expedition was the largest ever assembled to fight the Diné, and Carleton tried to ensure the success of the expedition by sending Carson out with a large body of men and a competent military staff. Officers serving with Kit were hand-picked by Carleton and included Captains Francisco P. Abreu, Francis McCabe, José D. Sena, John Thompson, Eben Everett, Joseph Berney, Charles Deus, Asa B. Carey, and

75

Albert H. Pfeiffer. These officers, all experienced fighting men, were charged with the responsibility of defeating the people Carleton characterized as "the aggressive, perfidious, butchering Navajos." The general further told his officers to chastise the Navajos severely because they only "understand the direct application of force as a law" and when that force was withdrawn in 1861 they had become "lawless." Since he felt that the Navajos were the most powerful and hostile tribe in the territory, Carleton told Carson's men "never to lax the application of force with a people that can no more be trusted than the wolves that run through the mountains."[6] No doubt the Navajos had similar views about the Bilagáana who had invaded their lands, killed their people, and failed to abide by their own treaty obligations.

Navajo attitudes were of no concern to Carson, however, and he rode off with instructions from Carleton that "the war be vigorously prosecuted against the Navajoes." When Carson left Los Lunas on July 7, Captain Albert Pfeiffer was absent from the command; he had been wounded in an Apache attack that had resulted in his wife's death. Because of this event, Pfeiffer joined Carson's command late, after it had reached Pueblo Colorado on August 2. Pfeiffer had a reputation as "the most desperately courageous and successful Indian fighter in the West," and he was among Carson's most trusted officers.[7] Even though his command was not at full strength, Carson made his way toward Dinetah without difficulty. From the Río Grande, Carson's troops moved northwesterly along a portion of the Río San José across a broad golden plain that gradually climbed toward Laguna Pueblo. Passing south of Mount Taylor, one of the sacred mountains of the Navajos, Carson made his way through the sharp, black volcanic rocks and reached Fort Wingate on July 10. He remained at the post for three days to rest and to supply himself with provisions for his upcoming campaign.

Carson continued his journey, making his next stop at Fort Lyon, a post formerly called Fort Fauntleroy, but renamed after the defection of Colonel Thomas Fauntleroy to the Confederacy. Although the fort had been abandoned, Kit stopped there because of its location, next to Bear Springs. Owing to the lack of food and

Kit Carson about the time he began his campaign against the Navajos.
Courtesy Library of Congress, Washington, D.C.

water along the trail, Kit's horses and "mules were completely broken down and unable to travel." Therefore, he decided to give them a rest at the site of Doniphan's first negotiations with the Diné in 1846. Many Navajos lived in this region and raised their crops near the spring, which they called Shush Bito. Carson took advantage of the fields of wheat that he found in the area by feeding the produce to his animals. This was an extremely significant act, for it inaugurated and symbolized the Kit Carson campaign against the Navajos, for the success of the campaign was due in large part to his destruction of Navajo crops. More than any other factor, the burning, consuming, and trampling of wheat and corn on which the Navajo depended would lead to the defeat of the Lords of New Mexico.[8]

At Bear Springs, Carson was joined by Captain Asa B. Carey and Lieutenant Franklin Cook. The twenty-seven-year-old Carey would become the colonel's most trusted officer during the campaign and contribute greatly to the defeat of the Navajos. Leaving Carey and Cook at Bear Springs to rest, Carson headed northwest again on his journey to old Fort Defiance. His march took him across a hilly country that gradually rose to elevations that supported occasional junipers and piñons. The rolling country slowly gave way to a small mountainous cañon whose face was strikingly vertical and deeply colored in tones from red to yellow. Carson passed through the narrow cañon, which opened into a small valley, and continued his journey north along the western edge of the sandstone cliffs. He passed by Window Rock, which exposed the deepblue sky accentuated by the rusty red of the vaulting arch. He followed these cliffs, which distinguish the southern end of the Chuska Mountains, for about six miles, until he entered Cañon Bonito, the site of Fort Defiance.

When Colonel Carson arrived at the fort on July 20, his animals were again in poor condition from lack of food and water. This problem would remain with the old scout throughout the campaign because of the vast distances the animals would have to travel in the Navajo country. When Carson's mounts reached Fort Defiance, however, they were sated by the cool waters of the stream flowing

Hasteen Belody. Courtesy Smithsonian Institution.

through the cañon, and their hunger was satisfied by a large quantity of Navajo wheat. Kit estimated that he found "say one hundred thousand pounds" of wheat that the Navajos had planted for their own consumption in the spring of 1863. By using Navajo crops, Carson provided for his men and his animals and deprived the Navajos of much-needed food. This procedure established the pattern that would result in the starvation of thousands of men, women, and children of the Navajo tribe.

Before Carson's arrival at Fort Defiance, Ute Indian scouts had arrived and found a few Navajos peacefully farming the region of Cañon Bonito. According to Kit's report to Carleton, the Utes attacked the Navajo farmers and their families without provocation, killing one man and capturing twenty head of sheep. When Kit arrived at the fort, he "was joined by nineteen Ute warriors, who had been operating against the Navajoes." Carson's Ute scouts had not seen any Navajos, but they reported having met another "party" of Utes returning to their country having eleven captives (women and children), and that there are two other parties now in this country." The colonel, convinced that the Ute warriors would be useful in his upcoming campaign against the Navajos, "hired five of this party as spies." The former Ute agent followed Carleton's instructions when he hired the Utes, but it was unfortunate that he did not demand an end to their age-old practice of enslaving Navajos. Instead, he condoned their actions.

Three days after arriving at Fort Defiance, Carson led a detachment of Ute scouts and seventy soldiers on their first survey of the Navajo country. Kit retraced his trail south past Window Rock before swinging west past the yellow meadow called Ciénega Amarilla. His troops moved gradually up toward the southern end of Fort Defiance Mesa before descending into a sparsely wooded valley near present-day Ganado, Arizona, a place that was then called Pueblo Colorado. Carleton had ordered Carson to build a post, to be called Fort Canby at this location.

Kit and his Ute scouts rode ahead of the command along the Río de Pueblo Colorado (Ganado Wash), and, as they neared their destination, they "came on a small party of Navajoes, and killed

80

three men." A Paiute woman who had been a captive of the Diné was found with these Navajos, and she eagerly reported to Carson that "a small party of Navajoes, with a large herd of sheep, cattle and horses, were at a pond of water about 35 miles West." Carson could not pass up this opportunity to engage more Navajos, and he immediately decided to "pursue them with the command as soon as possible after its arrival."[9]

Kit waited two and a half hours after his troops arrived before starting out to chase the Navajos. The patrol had traveled all night, fighting hunger, thirst, and fatigue, and "arrived at the water, only to find that the Navajos with their stock had left the previous evening." The Navajos were uncanny in their ability to know when troops were behind them and when to move before they were attacked by the Bilagáana. Carson was no doubt disappointed at not finding the Navajos camped where he thought they would be, but he decided not to end the search for his elusive enemy. For more than two hours he followed their trail before deciding to give up and return to Pueblo Colorado.

As Carson rode back to rejoin the main body of troops, his scouts scoured the area in search of Navajos. Their efforts proved unfortunate for eight Navajos, who met their deaths at the hands of the Utes, raising the total number killed by New Mexicans and Indians operating independently of Carson. It is known, however, that Kit was extremely pleased with the performance of the Utes, who, in Carson's opinion, "*more* than come up to the expectations I had formed of their efficiency as spies." The Utes had no compassion for their Navajo neighbors and, consequently, killed, captured, and sold them whenever and wherever they could. According to Kit, no "small straggling parties of Navajoes" could possibly "hope to escape them."

The Utes cooperated with Carson not only because the Navajos were their traditional enemies but, more important, because they reaped a profit from their activities. They enslaved the women and children captured in their campaigns against the Navajos. Carson was in favor of allowing the Utes to enslave the Navajos because it had been "customary" throughout the history of these

Colonel James H. Carleton, ca. 1861. Courtesy Huntington Library, Los Angeles, California.

two peoples, and, besides, he argued, the slaves were usually sold in New Mexico, "where they are fed and taken care of and thus cease to require any further attention on the part of the government." He was "satisfied that the future of the captives disposed of in this manner would be much better than if sent even to the Bosque Redondo."

Carleton, however, was violently opposed to permitting the Utes to make slaves of the Navajos, not because it was "most humane and proper" as he put it, but because it would interfere with his plan to Christianize and "civilize" his ignorant, "savage" charges.[10] Carleton had long planned to collect the Navajos at the Bosque Redondo, "away from their haunts and hills, and hiding places of their country; there be kind to them; there teach their children how to read and write; teach them the arts of peace; teach them the truths of Christianity,"[11] This was Carleton's primary concern, and therefore he wrote Carson demanding that "*all* prisoners which are captured by the troops or employes of your command will be sent to Santa Fe." He emphatically told Carson that: "*There must be no exception to this rule.*"[12]

While Kit was at the Pueblo Colorado, he reported that the Navajos had "planted a large quantity of grain this year." The Navajos were not farming on a large scale, but agricultural products, particularly flour for fry bread, were an important part of their daily diet. Along the stream that meanders through the golden hillsides of the Pueblo Colorado, the Navajos were cultivating wheat and corn. The wheat crop was one of the best Carson had ever seen, but the corn was "rather backward and not so plentiful." The colonel ordered his soldiers to collect the crops along Ganado Wash. There was a large amount of corn and "over seventy five thousand pounds of wheat," which Kit dried and used for fodder during the upcoming winter. Although these crops were growing in abundance in the area, Carson did not feel that Pueblo Colorado was a fit site for the proposed post. Five days after he arrived in the area, he made a formal request to Carleton to establish Fort Canby at the site of old Fort Defiance. The choice of Pueblo Colorado was not a good one; food, water, wood, and forage were lacking. Carleton accepted

Sketch of Fort Canby, Arizona, 1863, by Private George L. Fellner, First New Mexico Volunteers. Courtesy National Archives.

the opinion of the colonel and ordered him to select the site for Fort Canby at his own discretion.[13]

Carson moved his troops east of Pueblo Colorado and across the foothills that lead into the southern end of Fort Defiance Mesa. As the soldiers climbed out of the hills and into the mountains, they entered a thick forest of bushy piñon pine, which abruptly gave way to the taller ponderosas. The hooves of the horses were silenced by the soft carpet of pine needles that cushioned the earth. The soldiers must have been very careful as they wove their way through the wooded mesa. They had to dodge branches here and there, and they were constantly on guard against possible attack. As the soldiers dropped down on the eastern side of the mesa, they beheld the yellow valley before them and the rust-red cliffs near Window Rock in the distance. Carson's command moved into the valley and edged north along the sandstone mountains, which totally blocked the eastern sky and threw huge shadows over the valley. About five miles north of Window Rock, Carson found the site of Fort Defiance. He failed to comment about the old post's condition, but it can be assumed that the Navajos had destroyed what to them was a symbol of the Bilagáana. Here at Cañon Bonito, Carson constructed Fort Canby and began preparations for his summer scout against the Diné.

Kit was delayed in beginning his campaign because he was dogged by distracting personnel problems. Among the troops who reinforced Carson's soldiers in July, 1863, was Major Arthur Morrison. The major was in trouble before he arrived in the Navajo country. Charges had been filed against him by a subordinate, Lieutenant David McAllister, who claimed that the major had delayed leaving Los Pinos on the journey west to join Carson's campaign. Morrison was allegedly so drunk that he could not stand up, but not too drunk to declare in a "loud and vulgar" tone that he would be glad to find some prostitutes for his *compadres*. "I am the damdest best pimp in New Mexico," the major proclaimed— at least according to McAllister. Morrison was given the choice of resigning his commission or facing a court-martial. He chose to resign. As for McAllister, he, too, had his problems. While serving as officer of the day at Fort Canby, he was caught committing an indiscreet carnal act. He was found drunk that day and in bed with an enlisted man. No further details were given, but McAllister was also forced to resign his commission in December, 1863.[14]

Although his men were causing Carson embarrassment and trouble, he decided to take to the field in pursuit of the Navajos. In early August he was once again scouting the mountains and cañons near Pueblo Colorado when some Indians were spotted. Kit and Captain Charles Deus headed in one direction, while another part of the command moved to scour some hills close by. Major Joseph Cummings very foolishly "left the command alone and proceeded up the cañon." As he moved up the draw, it became narrower, and, "when entering its narrowest point about four miles from where he left the command he was killed." The Navajos who scored this kill made their escape without being detected. The warriors had shot Cummings in the stomach, and the bullet had passed through his body, lodging in his spine. Cummings bled profusely because the bullet had severed an artery, and he finally died from loss of blood. Carson was "melancholy" about the major's death, one of the few casualties suffered by Carson's command during the entire war. The Navajos were not so fortunate.[15]

After Cummings's death Kit began his first major march against

Sketch of Zuñi Pueblo. Courtesy Southwest Museum.

the Navajos. Leaving the Ciénega Amarilla (near present-day Saint Michaels, Arizona) on August 5, the colonel headed south toward Zuñi with 16 officers and 333 men. Carson's route from the well-watered valley of the Ciénega Amarilla took him east and south near Window Rock. The troops moved onto a rolling, open plain that stretched southeast toward the region where present-day Gallup stands. The command moved south through a broken piñon forest that led to the rocky cliffs towering above Zuñi Pueblo.

Carson's objective was "to visit that village, procure some guides, then to scour the country to the Moqui and Oribi villages." The first day out, Kit's command encountered several fields of corn and wheat and took some of the grain for their animals and destroyed the rest to prevent Navajos from harvesting the precious foodstuff. Hundreds of acres of Navajo crops were destroyed in this manner throughout the expedition and those that followed. Within a few days Carson had destroyed other fields and had taken thirteen women and children prisoner. Only seven of the prisoners

86

were sent to Fort Defiance; the other six were given to Ute scouts as slaves for their "services," since Carson had yet to receive Carleton's communication directing him to send all captives to Santa Fe. More than one thousand head of goats and sheep, as well as some horses, were captured early in this scout. The soldiers responsible for stealing Navajo livestock were given a bounty of one dollar for every sheep or goat and twenty dollars for each horse.[16]

Carson's men took a westerly trail from Zuñi and swung northwest to the Hopi mesas before heading east again to Pueblo Colorado. While Carson was on this scout, he was attacked by a small band of Navajos, who tried to escape with his horse herd. Their efforts failed, but no one was reported wounded or killed in the scrape.[17]

On the bright morning of August 20, Carson and his command left Pueblo Colorado, moving north toward the Cañon de Chelly. Before them lay a long grade that rose steadily through the valley of tumbleweeds and sagebrush between Fort Defiance Mesa and Black Mesa (which Carson called Mesa de la Vaca). In a small sandstone cañon south of Chelly the soldiers discovered large fields of corn, pumpkins, and beans, which they consumed, packed or destroyed. Carson, sensing that the Indians who cultivated these fields were watching his action, decided to set an ambush for them. As the main command was leaving the cañon, Kit secreted twenty-five men under Captain Pfeiffer in two parties, believing that the Indians would return as soon as the troops left. Two Navajo men returned as Carson had predicted and were allowed to pass through the first party lying in ambush. As soon as they were between the soldiers, however, an order was given to open fire on them and kill them. The colonel was disappointed by the results, for, "although badly wounded, I am sorry to say the Indians escaped." Such comments demonstrate how Carson's campaign failed to distinguish between "hostiles and friendlies"; his war was pursued against all Navajos—men, women, and children—indiscriminately.

Not far up the trail, as Kit later reported, he "discovered the bodies of two Indians killed by a party of Utes." An advance guard of Kit's command saw a Navajo warrior that day and, after pursuing him, managed to kill him. The colonel encountered very few Navajos as he and his troops moved through the low, sandy valley. Those they found they killed, enslaved, or captured for forced removal. Word spread throughout the valley that Carson's command of death and destruction was moving north toward the sacred Cañon de Chelly. Before reaching the west end of the cañon, Kit's command "arrived at a large bottom containing not less than one hundred acres of as fine corn as I have ever seen." Some was fed to the animals, but most of the crop was trampled and burned. Carson commenced a "scorched-earth policy" that would characterize his entire campaign. He would keep the Navajos on the run, always in fear of attack by his troops, and he would destroy their means of livelihood. Whenever Kit happened upon a Navajo rancheriá, he destroyed the hogans, crops, and animals that were the basis of their economy. His policy would leave the Indians psychologically shaken and physically ruined. Without the security of their homes the Navajos would freeze in the cold, snow, and ice, and without their food supply they would starve during the lean winter months ahead. Carson would ultimately defeat the Diné not through the barrel of a gun but through his scorched-earth campaign.[18]

At eight o'clock on the sunny morning of August 23, Carson and his men arrived at the west entrance of the Cañon de Chelly for the second time during the campaign. On his first scout in August, Kit had passed by the entrance to the cañon but had not penetrated it. Tsegi, or Rock Canyon, as the Navajos called it, is near Chinle, Arizona, and has three branches. The past home of the Anasazi people (ancient Pueblo Indians), the cañon had long been inhabited by Navajos, probably from the early eighteenth century. Neither Carson nor Carleton was aware that, in 1859, Captain John G. Walker had explored the cañon. They assumed in their communications that white men had penetrated the gorge only a short distance and had always retreated because of the threat of ambush. The colonel did not realize that the cañon was divided into two major branches. Such information, gained by Walker, would have been most helpful to Kit and, as will be seen, would have saved the Indian fighter a good deal of concern and anxiety.

At the western end of the Cañon de Chelly, Kit and his men faced a sandy entrance that stretched about two hundred yards. The cañon walls were colored with shades of red, brown, and tan, which were set off by black vertical streaks. Despite the striking natural beauty of the cañon, Carson probably perceived its depth only as a dangerous tactical obstacle. Kit at last determined that there were not enough Navajos living in the cañon to warrant entering it, and he ordered his men to move on, telling Carleton "that there are very few Indians in the Cañon, and these are the very poorest." The colonel also concluded that the Navajos living in the Cañon de Chelly had few animals and therefore depended "entirely for subsistence on the corn destroyed by my command." The loss of this food, he argued, "will cause actual starvation" and further "oblige them either to come in and accept emigration to the Bosque Redondo, or to fly south." Carson was convinced that "they will adopt the first of these courses."

After leaving the cañon, Kit's command rode north about twelve miles to a region where they "found an abundance of running water and good grass." Carson made "a careful examination of the country" but could not find any Navajos. Like the Navajos in other regions, those living around the towering red buttes knew of Carson's presence and chose not to reveal themselves to him. They rightfully feared that they would be murdered as the Navajo farmers south of the cañon had been. Thus Carson saw no Navajos, and he reported that there was "not one to be seen, nor has there been any seen in this vicinity for a long time."[19]

The command continued its march eastward, passing within view of the spectacular sandstone monuments known as Round Rock and Los Gigantes Buttes. The trail that Carson followed took him across a sandy plateau and down into a small valley that skirted the edge of the Lukachukais. The bright rust-red colors of the cliffs flow out into the valley from the mountains like fingers from a hand. The ride through this region was difficult for the horses and the men because of the sand and dust. Some relief was gained as the party rode slowly upward into the higher reaches of the valley. The forest of piñon pine became thicker as the soldiers moved toward an impressive square-headed butte that dominated the region, which was known to the Navajos as Tsaile (pronounced *sail-ee*).

Carson's troops watered their horses in a small creek that flowed out of the mountains and entered what appeared to be a small, gently sloping cañon. *Tsaile* is the Navajo word for "place where the water enters the canon," and Kit correctly determined that the small stream runs through the eastern opening of the Cañon de Chelly. He did not, however, realize that there is more than one eastern opening into the cañon. Tsaile Creek, which Carson and his troops crossed, flows the length of the northern branch of the Cañon de Chelly, known as the Cañon del Muerto, or the Cañon of the Dead One. Kit continued his march through the sweet-smelling pine forests as the piñons slowly gave way to the larger ponderosas. Although several Navajo families were living in this region of Dinetah, Carson was unable to locate a single Indian. He traveled only four miles past Tsaile Creek before reaching another small stream, known today as Whiskey Creek. Kit camped in the cool shadow of the towering ponderosas along the banks of the creek.

While encamped in the pines, Carson surmised that the two creeks could be of advantage to him in his campaign against the Navajos. The colonel believed that "both of these streams could be turned off," preventing water from entering the Cañon del Muerto. He maintained that, by cutting off the water supply into the thirsty bottomlands of the cañon, he would compel the Indians to abandon this "stronghold" and "refuge." Kit never took this action, which certainly would have been difficult to engineer and to protect, because the Navajos would have fought tenaciously to destroy any dam system built by the army.

With the splendid array of mountainous buttes and imposing cañons on his left, Carson marched along the western edge of the Chuskas. As he moved south, the landscape changed from the pine forests to a valley of low-lying brush and occasional trees. Behind

Fort Defiance in 1900, in the heart of Navajo land, renamed Fort Canby during Carson's campaign. Courtesy Western History Collections, University of Oklahoma Library, Norman.

his troops stood the faint images of Tsaile Butte and White Cone Mountain, and before him lay the valley that led into Cañon Bonito. Carson had not engaged the Navajos in any great military action and he reported killing only one man and wounding another — certainly far from the decisive blow that the colonel had hoped to deliver to the Navajos. Kit's summer scout was, however, extremely harmful to the Navajo people because of the severe damage he did to the crops. Acres upon acres of corn and wheat were destroyed by the relentless campaigner, to say nothing of the many hogans (log-and-adobe houses) that Navajos later claimed were burned by the soldiers.[20]

Carson's command arrived at Fort Canby on the last day of August, 1863. Although the results of his scout were minimal as far as military engagements with the Indians were concerned, the colonel believed that much had been gained on the expedition, for not only were the crops destroyed, but knowledge was gained about the Navajo country as well as the possible location of many Navajos. The trek convinced Kit that several bands of Navajos had fled south and west toward the San Francisco Mountains, near present-day Flagstaff, Arizona. He suggested to Carleton that the general order troops north from central Arizona to operate against these Navajos. It was Carson's opinion that such "a force operating against them from that point, would greatly facilitate the entire subjugation of the Navajo Nation."

When Carson returned to Fort Canby from his first scout, he learned of the many problems that had plagued the post during his absence, including homosexuality, drunkenness, and whoring. When he returned from his second scout at the end of August, he was greeted by even more disturbing news. Drinking, fighting, and frolicking with prostitutes were the least of the infractions. The most severe problems centered around the post commander, Major Thomas J. Blakeney. Born in California, Blakeney had enlisted in the Seventy-first Pennsylvania Volunteers and had served in the East during the early part of the Civil War. In February, 1863, he received a commission in the California Volunteers and became a protégé of General Carleton. The Californian did not get along with his fellow officers or the enlisted men of the New Mexico Volunteers. He had been eager to avail himself of "the advantage of experience in the Indian Campaigning under the leadership of so distinguished a frontiersman" as Kit Carson. After a small diet of hardship and travel with the veteran scout in the Navajo country, however, Blakeney formally requested a release from his duties with Kit.[21]

According to an officer at Fort Canby during Carson's recent expedition, Blakeney's conduct was "overbearing and unbecoming to an officer." Even worse than his actions toward his own men was his treatment of Indians. On August 6 "an old-Bald-headed Indian came into campe [sic] and gave himself up," saying that he had come in "to have a talk with his white bretheren [sic]." The Navajo was placed under guard and confined to quarters. Six days later he was shot dead by soldiers, who claimed that he was killed while trying to escape. Then, on August 26, four Navajos arrived at the fort. Three of them entered the post to talk peace. They entered in good faith and "under a flag of truce." As soon

92

as they were within the fort and within reach of the guards, they were seized and dragged off to prison. It was a treacherous act, indeed, particularly since the Indians had "represented that they came to sue for peace and that their tribe or band, numbering from seventy-five to one hundred souls, was outside the Fort and wanted to come in as friends." The day after their capture two of the Navajos managed to escape. They had been ordered by Blakeney to police the parade ground of Fort Canby and bury "offal and dead dogs" outside the post. While they were engaged in this degrading assignment, they made their escape. They were hunted down by the soldiers, who murdered one of them as soon as he was found. The other warrior was wounded, and he died from his wound on the evening of August 27.

Charges were brought against Blakeney by his men, who argued that he had intended to murder the Navajos from the outset. One soldier reported that the major had forced the Indians to bury the dogs without the aid of shovels. The commander forced these proud warriors and leaders of their people to handle the dead dogs and fecal material with their bare hands and to dig holes in the same manner. Blakeney's order to the Indians to do this labor was given "in such a manner" as to "convey the idea to the Provost-Sergeant that he was not to bury dogs, but was to shoot and kill the . . . Indians." Blakeney set up the entire incident so that the Indians could be murdered. At first Carson was greatly angered by Blakeney's actions. Eventually, however the charges against Carleton's friend were dropped. The major's treatment of Navajos who came in to surrender served only to heighten hostilities and prolong the war, for the Navajos soon came to fear that the policy of the Bilagáana was to execute all Indians regardless of their intentions. Word spread throughout Dinetah that the whites were eager to exterminate them.[22]

As if this were not enough, Carson also had to contend with minor incidents of drunkenness and whoring. Lieutenant Nicholas Hodt, who had tried to prevent the murder of two Navajo children during the massacre of Fort Fauntleroy, was found "beastly intoxicated" and "in bed with a woman of bad character" during Kit's

Navajos at Fort Defiance. Courtesy Navajo Community College.

summer campaign. Hodt had a great contempt for the commander of the post and reportedly exclaimed "God dam Major Blakeney,— God dam all these California Officers." One such California officer who had come to New Mexico with Carleton was James H. Prentiss, a surgeon. Hodt hated Prentiss and relished the fact that the surgeon got himself into trouble through his drunkenness. Dr. Prentiss had access to the hospital supplies, and, toward the end of August, he helped himself to the "Hospital Whiskey and Wine," which he "applied to his own use." When Allen F. Peck, head surgeon of Fort Canby during the Navajo campaign, found Prentiss in a drunken state, he pressed charges against him. Dr. Prentiss was enraged and very much intoxicated when he heard about the charges. To the officers and men of the fort he publicly proclaimed: "Goddamn the son of a bitch who prefered charges against me; he is a coward, God-damn him; and I will bet he will not fight." Carleton saw to it that the charges were dropped against Blakeney, and he set Prentiss free after he made restitution for the wine and whiskey he had stolen.[23]

Carson had little concern for solving the problems arising from garrison duty at Fort Canby, for his interest was in the war against the Navajos, not his unruly men. Under orders from Carleton, the command of the post was turned over to a competent officer, Captain Asa B. Carey. Following a brawl at the fort "between a woman known by the name of 'Mountain Cal' and a Mexican Heroine, in which both were severely scratched and bruised," Carey ordered both prostitutes to leave the fort. The incident had been caused by "bad liquor and intoxication," so Carey was overjoyed to learn that the commissary department had run out of whiskey. Many of Carson's men were alcoholics, "so addicted to the use of stimulating beverages, that when they get a *taste* of the ardent spirits, they cannot restrain themselves." Carey prohibited the post sutler from selling liquor to the officers and men under his command without his permission. Much of the chaos that had plagued the post was ended by this order. Carey continued to run the fort, while Kit pursued his campaign against the Navajos into the fall of 1863.[24]

CHAPTER 4

The Fall Campaign

G o to the Bosque Redondo, or we will pursue and destroy you. We will not make peace with you on any other terms." This was the ultimatum Carleton told Carson to give to the Navajos early in the fall of 1863. The general argued that the Navajos had "deceived us too often and robbed and murdered our people too long—to trust you again at large in your own country." Carson was ordered to tell the Indians that the war would be pursued against them, even if it took years, until they ceased "to exist or move." According to Carleton, "there can be no other talk on the subject." The unbending general had formulated his "Indian policy" over many years and was influenced by the past policies of the United States and his own feelings toward the Indians. Removal was certainly not a new policy in the United States, and Carleton had lived during the era of the mass removal of thousands of Indians from the East in the 1830s and 1840s. Also, he saw Navajos as most white Americans had traditionally viewed Indians. To Carleton, Navajos were uncivilized savages who lived in a barbaric manner. Carleton reflected a changing, "progressive" mood in the nation, arguing that the "heathens" should be Christianized and "civilized" in the white man's ways. To accomplish these "humanistic" goals, however, Carleton first had to defeat the Navajos. To this end he encouraged Carson to break the spirit of the Navajo Indians in the fall of 1863.

Navajo women spinning and weaving wool. Courtesy Navajo Community College.

Between September 9 and October 5, Kit Carson would continue the war against the Diné in a fall campaign. Like his other scouts of the Indian country, this campaign would fail to engage militarily a large number of Navajos. Yet he would continue to harass them, regardless of whether individual Navajos were inclined toward peace or war. During Carson's fall campaign he was ordered by Carleton to capture as many Navajos as possible so that they could be relocated at the Bosque Redondo, where they would be "tamed" and "educated" by the white men. "No Navajoe Indians of either sex, or of any age," he told Carson, "will be retained at Fort Canby as servants, or in any capacity whatever." Carleton insisted that "all must go to the Bosque Redondo." Neither Carleton nor Carson condoned the killing of Navajos who had surrendered, and the general explicitly ordered the colonel not to "permit an Indian

97

prisoner once fairly in our custody to be killed unless he be en-
deavoring to make his escape." Carleton not only was concerned
about waging a "just" war, but also wanted as many Navajos as
possible to go to the Bosque Redondo, where they could be "civilized" in the ways of the white society.[1]

Before the fall campaign opened, Carleton instructed Carson to
"seize six of the principal men of the Zuñi Indians and hold them
as hostages until all Navajoes in and near their village are given up,
and all stolen stock surrendered." The general appears to have
had information that linked the Zuñis to the Navajos, but that
is unlikely, because traditionally the two tribes were enemies. Indeed, the Zuñis had aided the Americans against the Navajos on
several occasions. Carleton went so far as to threaten the Zuñis,
stating that he would "certainly destroy their village as sure as the
sun shines" if he heard "that they help or harbor Navajoes, or
steal stock from any white men, or injure the person of any white
man." Such statements and instructions were not only ill-conceived
but racist as well. Perhaps Carleton had forgotten that the Zuñis
had been friendly with whites for many years before the Navajo
campaign of 1863. Perhaps he did not care.[2]

With 10 officers and 395 men, Kit Carson began his fall scout
on September 9, 1863. Leaving Fort Canby, the colonel moved
south to the Ciénega Amarilla, where the army had a hay camp.
There he procured some alfalfa for his 192 horses before heading
southeast to Zuñi Pueblo. At Zuñi, Carson met a Captain Pishon
of the First Cavalry of California Volunteers, who was heading
east from Fort Mojave. The captain reported to the colonel that
"he had seen no fresh trails of Navajoes on the Little Colorado."
Nevertheless, Carson was "determined to examine that section of
country with a view to future operations." Before leaving Zuñi,
Carson had to comply with Carleton's instructions to deal with the
Zuñi Indians who had allegedly aided the Navajos. It took him but
a short time to determine that the Zuñis were not helping the
Diné in any way and, in fact, were at war with their traditional
enemies at the time of his arrival. In an attempt "to show their
friendliness to the Whites and the enmity to the Navajoes," the

Kit Carson, ca. 1868. Courtesy Smithsonian Institution.

governor of Zuñi provided Carson with three scouts. Twenty other Zuñis joined the expedition, which headed in a southwesterly direction. Carson was convinced that the Zuñis were "not on friendly terms with the Navajoes." He was much impressed by their sincerity after "having seen the dead bodies of some Navajoes whom they had recently killed in an engagement."[3]

Kit made camp about thirty-five miles southwest of Zuñi at a place called Jacob's Springs, which was "situated in the midst of an extensive plain." A small lake afforded the mules and horses drinking water, even though the water was slightly salty. In an attempt to familiarize himself and his troops with the region west of Zuñi, Carson dispatched a party of infantrymen and Indian scouts "to examine the Mountains South and East of our Route." Since no Navajos were discovered, the troops continued their march westward toward the Little Colorado River. About fifteen miles from the river Kit decided to push on rapidly with his "Mounted Men" in hopes of surprising "some party who calculating upon the fact that no previous expedition had penetrated that portion of the country, would be there with their herds in fancied security." At this point Kit left the supply packs and the infantry troops with Captain Francis McCabe and ordered him "to proceed to the River next day . . . while I proceed with the Mounted Men of my command to examine the country Northwest of our line of march."

Carson left McCabe at sundown one evening and traveled west by the light of the moon. He was guided by an enlisted man, who told Carson that he was familiar with the area. By ten o'clock, however, Kit became convinced that the scout "who professed knowing the country" was actually very "ignorant of our whereabouts." Therefore, Kit camped and continued his journey the next morning. The colonel was discouraged, not only because his guide had failed him but also because he "saw no indications of Indians." The Navajos were elusive and clever. Kit's enemies were aware of his scout and chose not to engage his force. Most Navajos were safe in their mountains and cañons, terrain which they alone knew.[4]

McCabe and Carson reunited the command on the Little Colorado River, where the captain informed the colonel that the Zuñis "had

Navajo headmen inside a Navajo summer lodge. Photograph by C. Wharton James. Courtesy Navajo Community College.

returned to their village, having taken about fifty head of sheep and goats from the Navajoes." On September 22 the soldiers discovered "fresh sign" of Navajos, so Kit ordered five officers and over one hundred men to pursue the Indians. After traveling two days, Captain Pfeiffer and his soldiers came upon seven unsuspecting Navajos who were driving fifteen horses upriver. Although Carson's men pursued the Indians, they were not able to overtake and engage them "owing to the broken-down condition" of their own horses. All the Navajos escaped except for a small child, who was captured and, in all probability, sent off to the Bosque Redondo. Kit examined the Little Colorado for an estimated distance of eighty-five miles and determined to his own satisfaction that "no Indians have been on the River within this distance since

101

last Spring, excepting this party of seven seen by Captain Pfeiffer."

On September 27, Carson ordered Captain John Thompson to return to Fort Canby on the same route by which they had come. With 128 men and the best horses and mules, Kit and seven of his officers continued their scout. They traveled along the sandy banks of the river another fifteen miles before turning east. For sixty miles the soldiers traveled through Navajo land, but they discovered no Indians. In fact, they saw no "Indian sign" until they reached a small cañon, where they halted to have breakfast one morning. The colonel ordered his men to examine the region, and they "discovered a small village which had just been abandoned." His men put a torch to the village, burning all the hogans and destroying saddles, bridles, blankets, and a rifle. Nineteen animals were captured, including some mares that later escaped. The destruction of fields and hogans demoralized the proud Diné, who had felt secure in their homeland. True, they had suffered the attacks of Utes, New Mexicans, Pueblos, and Anglos, but nothing as devastating as Carson's war. The Navajos fled their homes in fear of being killed and, when they returned, found their homes, crops, and animals destroyed or stolen by Carson's command. Their lives were in total disarray.

Kit's men failed to find any Navajos around the hogans, either because they had fled the region or because they had successfully hid from the soldiers. In all probability the warriors watched Carson burn their hogans and fields, and then followed his men as they rode toward Fort Canby. When some horses of Carson's herd bolted, three soldiers spurred their mounts and chased them. Navajo warriors, who had probably watched the entire scene, took advantage of the opportunity for revenge. They attacked the three soldiers, letting fly their deadly arrows, killing one of the bluecoats and wounding another. No doubt Carson and his men were angry and vengeful about the killing of their comrade. Eight miles south of Pueblo Colorado, at a place called Jarra, six soldiers encountered a lone warrior. As soon as they sighted the Navajo the chase was on, and the soldiers were soon able to overtake the Indian. The blood of many warriors flowed through that Navajo's veins, and he

Largo, Navajo scout. Courtesy Arizona Historical Society.

fought fiercely for his life against bad odds. He was wounded three times, but managed his escape nonetheless. Only one soldier was wounded, but all six suffered from embarrassment.[5]

In his report to Carleton, Kit stated that he was "sorry to say" that his scout "was a failure as regards any positive injury inflicted on the Navajoes." He argued, however, that "the fatigues and hardships undergone by my command are fully compensated for by the increased knowledge of the country and of the haunts of the Navajoes and their Stock." The result of this campaign was the same as the first. Few Navajos were found, and few were killed. Little property was destroyed, but the movement of the troops through Dinetah was an ever-present concern of the Navajos, who well knew of Carson's campaign and his presence in their homeland. No doubt the Navajo people were aware of the relentless campaigner, who was often seen "reeling in his saddle from fatigue and loss of sleep, still pushing forward and hoping to come upon them." The lack of water and forage for his mounts led Kit to decide that a winter campaign was impossible. He reported that he could not "take the field with a mounted force" because his animals were much "too poor to stand the rigors of Winter at this place." All in all, his scout was a failure, although one observer reported that he had done "all that man could do under the circumstances."[6]

Colonel Carson believed that a major reason for the failure of the expedition was that the Hopis were acting in concert with the Navajos, who were "continually advised of the movements of any body of troops operating in the vicinity of the Moquies [Hopis]." To correct what Carson considered to be a problem, he told Carleton that there was a great "necessity of removing them [the Hopis] to some more hospitable section of the country . . . where they would be out of the power and influence of the Navajoes." He stated that "until they *are* removed I am satisfied that there will always be a barrier opposed to the removal of the Navajoes." It is doubtful that many, if any, Hopis were aiding the Navajos. Like the Zuñis and other Pueblo Indians, the Hopis were traditional enemies of the Diné, and they had little to gain from helping their red neighbors and much to gain from a defeat of the Navajos. The

Hopis may have done little to help Carson in his expeditions, but they also did little to stop the campaign launched against the Diné. Perhaps Carson was searching for a scapegoat so that he could explain his own failures.[7]

From October 5 to November 15, 1863, Kit was at Fort Canby. While the colonel rested, he continued his campaign, dispatching Captain Francis McCabe and seventy-six men to scout the region below Fort Canby along the Río Puerco. On October 5 the expedition left the fort "for the purpose of proceeding to and examining the *Mesa del Puerco.*" McCabe moved south across the gradual rolling plain toward the Río Puerco and the first evening camped approximately twenty-five miles from the post. He was guided to this point by a Zuñi scout named Pedro Pino and was later joined by six other Zuñis, who served as guides for a portion of the expedition. The captain operated at night so that "the darkness would conceal my movements."

Thus, during the evening and early morning hours, McCabe advanced toward an unidentified mesa, which he reached around 2:00 A.M. on October 7. He immediately ordered sixty of his soldiers to climb the mesa, a task that "occupied one hour and was laborious in the extreme." When the command reached the top of the mesa, McCabe divided his men into three groups and ordered them to scour the "growth of cedar brake and pinons." No fresh signs were found, so the troops returned to the base of the mesa before moving on to another section of the rise eight miles down the trail.

Again McCabe dispatched three groups, and again they found no recent signs of Navajos. After scouring the region for some time, McCabe was "satisfied that that place has not been resorted by indians for a long time." It had been the captain's anxious "hope of finding an indian camp but did not succeed in finding any." With great disappointment he reported that he "was not fortunate enough to meet the indians and punish them." Like the other fall expedition, McCabe's was a failure, even though the captain was "satisfied that the knowledge gained by myself and my men of the part of the country . . . may be very useful on some future occasion." McCabe returned to Fort Defiance on October 11 without having even seen one Navajo, let alone a large encampment.[8]

Two days after Captain McCabe's arrival at the post, Carson ordered another expedition to take the field north of Fort Defiance in search of the elusive Indians. With a command of 260 men Captain John Thompson left Fort Canby on October 13 "en route for the Laguna Negra for the purpose of Establishing a Grazing Camp for the Quarter Masters animals and Company horses." With the Chuska Mountains on his immediate right Thompson moved north, moving in the deep shadow of the red sandstone and passing by Red Lake. The second day out the command reached its destination near present-day Crystal and there built a corral for stock.

On the morning of October 17, Thompson began his scout for Navajos, dispatching Captain Jules Barbey and fifty men "for a scout of six days near the mouth of Cañon de Chelly." On the evening of the same day Thompson ordered Lieutenant Paul Dowlin and sixty men on a scout for six days in the Chuska Valley. Both of these commands returned to the grazing camp at Laguna Negra on October 21, and, although both commanders filed reports of their activities during the scout, Barbey's has yet to come to light. Dowlin's results, however, are known, for he reported killing two Navajos and wounding another in the Chuska Valley. Dowlin's report is lacking in detail, and thus the conditions surrounding the engagement of these Navajos are not known.[9]

Captain Thompson was relieved of his field command on October 21 and was replaced by Major José D. Sena. It would become increasingly apparent to Carson that Major Sena was a fairly incompetent field commander who would bumble in his attempts to perform his duties. When he arrived at Laguna Negra, he obeyed Carson's instructions and continued sending out search parties in pursuit of the Navajos. On the day after he assumed command, Sena ordered Captain Charles Deus to take sixty men of Company M and scout in a northwesterly direction from Laguna Negra toward the Cañon de Chelly. For six days Deus hunted for the Navajos, but he ultimately reported that he had seen no "fresh

106

Navajo scout. Courtesy Arizona Historical Society.

signs" of the Indians. Before Deus returned, Sena sent out another command to search north along the Chuska Mountains. On October 23 still another expedition, led by Lieutenant Peter Bishop, left the grazing camp for a four-day scout of the Chuska Valley. Unfortunately, Bishop's report has not come to light, but it can be assumed that he failed to engage any sizable number of Navajos, for, had he done so, Carson would have reported Bishop's success.

While these troops were operating in the field, the Indians successfully raided the army herd at Laguna Negra. "On the night of the 25th of October 1863" Sena reported, "the Navajo Indians drove off a Herd Consisting of Eighty Nine Sheep (Rations of the Command) from the Corral." Sena and his soldiers were not even aware until later that the Indians had entered the area and driven off their stock. When Sena discovered the theft, he sent out a detachment to recover the animals. This patrol was inept; although the men tracked the horse herd, they returned empty-handed the same day they went out. Captain Deus picked up the trail and followed it to the eastern entrance to the Cañon de Chelly, but he chose not to follow the Indians, probably from fear of being attacked. He returned to report his findings to Major Sena, who also chose not to pursue the Indians. Instead he ordered his men to return to Fort Canby, where they arrived at 1:00 on the afternoon of October 29.

While Sena's troops were operating north of Fort Canby at Laguna Negra, Lieutenant Charles Fitch was scouting thirty-five miles southeast of the post. He reported having killed a number of Navajos, but his statements were unsubstantiated, and it was later learned that his report was filled with lies. He was charged with filing a false report and was forced to resign on November 25, 1863. The attempts by Thompson, Sena, and Fitch to engage the Navajos were fruitless, and little was gained from these expeditions, except, perhaps, for "additional knowledge." Indeed, that was about all that Carson and his troops had gained since the beginning of the Navajo campaign, and it was not enough to satisfy General Carleton.[10]

The loss of stock from the government's grazing camp was an embarrassment to Carson and Carleton. It was not the first time

The Chase. *Sketch from R. Glisan,* Journal of Army Life *(1874).*

Carson's herds were attacked, nor would it be the last. Throughout the fall of 1863 the Navajos attacked the army herds at will, which, of course, was a supreme embarrassment to Carson. What is most interesting and somewhat amazing, in light of Carson's great acclaim as an "Indian fighter," is that, although the old scout could not even find the Navajos, the Indians had little trouble finding him and raiding his herds. The Navajos were daring warriors. They attacked Fort Canby while Carson was peacefully resting from his scout of Dinetah. On another occasion a detachment commanded by Major Francis P. Abreu enroute from Santa Fe to Fort Canby was surprised by a party of eight Navajos. Abreu reported that, while the detachment was encamped at Fort Lyon (old Fort Fauntleroy), a party of fifteen soldiers was sent to drive the mule herd to water. On the night of October 12, less than one mile from camp, "they were attacked by a party of Indians . . . who run through the Herd." Confusion reigned for a few minutes until the soldiers fired a few rounds at the Navajos, who made their escape but without seizing a single mule. The troops rounded up the scattered herd and spent a sleepless night under the stars.

The next day Navajos attacked another group of soldiers, this time near Fort Canby. On the morning of October 13 "two wagons which had been sent about a mile from the Post for wood, were attacked by Indians." The Navajos laid an ambush for the teamsters and the escort of six soldiers. At the first blast of rifle fire the soldiers fled with great haste, "leaving the wagons and teams in the possession of the Indians." All told, the army lost ten mules, for the Indians left two of the weakest animals for the soldiers. Captain Carey tried to find the stolen animals with thirty infantry-men but was unable to follow the Indians for he had "no mounted force." Carey was embarrassed about the flight of his men at the first crack of a weapon. His men could not even accurately report the number of Indians who had attacked them, the number of warriors reported ranging anywhere from ten to fifty. The captain felt that "had proper vigilance been used by the Non. Com. Officer in charge, the Party would not have been surprised." Carey commented with "regret" that one of his men "in his hurry left his Musket at the wagons and the Indians got it."

The next night the Navajos struck again, attacking the wagon train of Miguel Romero, who was hauling alfalfa to Fort Canby. As the hay wagons made their way north from the Ciénega Amarilla, the Navajos attacked the train despite the military escort accompanying it. Romero and four soldiers were riding well ahead of the wagon train "when some ten or twelve Indians, mounted made a dash at them, and succeeded in taking from them 5 mules and one Poney." The attack was not without casualties: one of Romero's teamsters was severely wounded, and a noncommissioned officer attached to the escort was shot through the wrist with an arrow.

While the Navajo won several skirmishes, they were of little help to the tribe. The warriors were not able to take enough food to feed their hungry people, and the loss of stock did not dampen Carleton's hopes of defeating the Diné. Thus the Navajo attacks had very little influence on the course of the war, for the Bilagáana would continue the fight. Indeed, the attacks affected Carson's campaign very little, except to embarrass the army with the loss of stock, "which was the result of carelessness."

The forays of the Navajos demonstrated the strong spirit of at

110

least a portion of the Navajo Nation.[11] Nevertheless, by the late months of 1863, some Navajos were feeling the effects of Carson's campaign. On November 22, for example, Carleton reported that 188 "men, women, and children of the Navajoe tribe of Indians, leave Santa Fe for the Bosque Redondo." Most of the Indians had surrendered at Fort Wingate. They included Delgadito, a noted Navajo headman, who was permitted to remain at the fort to help the soldiers persuade other Indians to surrender.

Carson's efforts to secure Navajo prisoners had been fairly fruitless, and Carleton was not at all pleased by the colonel's performance. Indeed, when Carson asked for a leave of absence to begin on December 15, Carleton responded, "I have not authority to grant you a leave." However, the general enticed the colonel by stating that it was "important before long [that] we have a consultation about further operations against the Navajoes." He told Kit that "*as soon as you have secured one hundred captive Navajoe men, women, and children,* you will turn over the command of the troops and post of Fort Canby to Captain Carey, U.S.A. and come with those captives to Santa Fe." It had been six months since Carson had seen Josefa, and he was very eager to be with his wife, who was expecting their sixth child. Kit would have to wait until January 26, 1864, however, before he could start for Santa Fe.[12]

Carleton was eager to conclude the Navajo campaign at the earliest possible date, and he wrote General Lorenzo Thomas in Washington, "I can count confidently on getting the bulk of the tribe before Spring opens." Carleton commanded Carson to continue to press his war against the Diné in the late fall and early winter of 1863. Kit viewed another foray as futile but decided to comply with the wishes of his friend and superior by launching still another scout. Kit's hope was to find the Indians in the western reaches of Navajo country near the Hopi villages. He pondered his last campaign of the fall with great apprehension and reluctance; he looked upon the trek and the forthcoming campaign in a mood that was not enthusiastic. Kit was particularly concerned about his animals, which were in very poor condition: ". . . many . . . are now dying daily."[13] Because of the state of his mounts, Carson informed Carleton, "the operations of the Command will necessarily be Confined to short distances from this post, and in small parties." Carson's last expedition of 1863 was to begin on November 1, but, because of the arrival of the paymaster at Fort Canby, he delayed until the fifteenth of that month, probably to allow his men time to sober up.

A cold breeze was sweeping the parade ground on that November morning when Carson and his officers mounted up to begin their twenty-two-day "scout in the vicinity of the Moqui Villages." All the rest of the men of his five companies had to march on foot over the snow-covered mesas and mountains of Dinetah. Accompanying the troops were eleven Zuñi scouts whom Kit believed would "be useful as Spies." Carson was thankful, however, that "considerable snow" had fallen, for it would help him "follow the trail without fear of my men and animals suffering for water." The cold and snowy weather worked in Carson's favor in another way, for nature's hand would help defeat the native people of Dinetah. American troops rarely campaigned when winter came and the snow fell, primarily because of the lack of forage for the animals. Thus it is not surprising that numerous Navajos were not aware of Kit's movement toward the Hopi mesas.[14]

Carson's route to the Hopi villages was by now a familiar one: he rode south to the Ciénega Amarilla, climbed Fort Defiance Mesa, and descended into the valley surrounding Pueblo Colorado. From there he headed due west across a high plateau of yellowish sand until he reached a cañon known today as Keams Cañon. The First Mesa was fourteen miles from Keams Cañon and just west of Polacca Wash. As Carson moved toward the mesas, he continued his operations against the Navajos. The second day out, he detached thirty men under the command of Sergeant Andrés Herrera to follow "a fresh trail which intersected our route." While following the trail, Herrera's "party came on a village lately deserted which they destroyed." About twenty miles after leaving the main command, the sergeant "overtook a small party of Navajoes, two of whom he killed, wounded two, and captured fifty head of sheep and one horse." Kit was delighted to hear of Herrera's "success"

Navajo woman weaving a rug. Courtesy Navajo Community College.

and felt that the occasion merited his "warmest approbation" for the "energy and zeal displayed." These were the only Indians that the troops saw until they reached the Hopi villages on November 21.

Kit's journey to the Hopi villages was long and tiring, each day a repetition of the day before. The colonel and his men were probably stiff and sore from many hours in the saddle, despite the fact that all of them were toughened to the saddle. Perhaps, however, they derived some pleasure from the brown-and-purple cañons, mesas, and mountains, whose shadows and tones changed with changing sun. When Carson arrived in Hopi country, he was encouraged for the second time during this expedition. He learned from the Hopis that "the inhabitants of all the villages except the Oribis [*sic*] had a misunderstanding with the Navajoes, owing to

113

some injustice perpetuated by the latter." The colonel determined to take "advantage of this feeling, and succeeded in obtaining representatives from all the villages—Oribi [*sic*] excepted—to accompany" him on the warpath. His objective "was simply to involve them so far that they could not retract—to bind them to us, and place them in antagonism to the Navajoes." Although Carson felt that he had the upper hand, the Hopis were using him as an ally as well. They had little love for their traditional enemies, which partly accounts for their "great desire to aid" the Americans "in every respect."[15]

There were other reasons why the Hopis demonstrated an eagerness to aid the Anglos. Before Carson arrived at their villages, he "was credibly informed that the people of that village [Oraibi] had formed an alliance with the Navajoes, and on reaching there I caused to be bound their Governor and another of their principal men." Kit kidnapped these chiefs and took them with him as "prisoners" to force the Hopis into helping him. The high-handedness did little to endear him to the proud Pueblos of Arizona. After completing the first day's ride from the Hopi mesas, Carson had his hostages untied but forced them to accompany him on much of his expedition against the Navajos. This was certainly unfair behavior toward a people who Carson himself maintained were "a peaceable people" who had "never robbed or murdered the people of New Mexico."

The party traveled northwest for about sixty-five miles with only two hours' rest. They finally halted on a tributary of the Little Colorado River on November 24. The next day Carson's command surprised a village of Navajos. Upon seeing the soldiers, the Navajos fled, and all of them made their escape, except for a small boy who was left behind in the confusion. No doubt a Navajo mother wept tears of sorrow over the loss of her child, but the Indians were not strong enough to make a stand against Carson and his soldiers. The troops destroyed the hogans in the small village, and any crops or animals in the area were also destroyed. Carson's men rounded up seven horses before leaving, and the little boy was slung behind the saddle of one of the soldiers and taken away from his family and his home.

114

Minky Pinky, Navajo woman, ca. 1860s. Courtesy Smithsonian Institution.

The same day a party of mounted soldiers rode out to scout the outlying area. Two of their horses gave out, and the detachment was forced to return to camp. While en route, the soldiers were surprised by three concealed Indians, one of whom fired a shot into the air and bravely rode right at the bluecoats. At first "the soldiers were going to shoot him, but owing to his gesticulating they allowed him to draw nigh." The warrior approached the soldiers probably hoping to find Carson, so that they might have a talk. The soldiers took two rifles from the Indian and sent him on his way. A few of the Hopis recognized one of the rifles and said that it belonged to the famed war chief Manuelito. Carson's soldiers did not recognize the great chief, and they missed their only opportunity to capture one of the most renowned of all Navajo headmen.[16]

The soldiers spent the next few days scouring the mesas and cañons north of the sacred mountains of the Navajos and Hopis, known as the San Francisco Peaks. These beautiful volcano-shaped mountains lie north of present-day Flagstaff and dominate the region of northern Arizona. In the fall of the year it is not uncommon for snow to cover the upper reaches of the cone of Mount Humphreys. Carson's men could easily view this scene as they scouted the high, rolling plateau north of the peaks. As the soldiers rode farther north, they lost sight of the occasional juniper and piñon that seemed to fight for survival on the plateau. Soon the terrain turned more desertlike, with wonderful mixtures of sand ranging in colors from white to yellow and from orange to purple. The soldiers saw sandstone figures etched by the passing of time as they rode across the flat, clear plain. Then, as they moved even farther north, they encountered a great cañon, which they were unable to see until they were upon it. The sides of the chasm dropped straight down to a small, muddy river and rose immediately in the same manner on the other side. This was the cañon of the Little Colorado River, which snakes its way west across a desert painted with pageantry. The river travels slightly north until it reaches its larger brother, the Colorado.

While scouting the region of the Coconino Plateau north of the San Francisco Peaks, Kit saw only a few Navajos. At one small ranchería he captured a child and a woman and took both of them prisoner. As was his general practice, Kit probably destroyed their hogans and took any food he found. In addition, he took five hundred head of Navajo sheep and goats, along with seventy valuable horses. Other Navajos were sighted in the cañons cut by the Little Colorado River, but, owing to the poor condition of the army's mounts, the soldiers were unable to pursue them. Carson lamented, "Had our horses been in a fit condition, there is no doubt but that we would have been enabled to overhaul these Indians." His troops, however, failed to strike the Indians because their horses "were unable to travel sufficiently quick, owing to the fact that they had been the three days previous without sufficient rest, and with but little grass." The men encountered additional Navajo "signs" but were not able to engage the Indians, who wisely retreated in the face of this superior force. Carson "was reluctantly obliged to let them go unmolested."

On his return to the Hopi villages the colonel "discovered at a distance the smoke of an Indian Encampment." He gathered a mounted party as well as fifty foot soldiers and marched toward the camp "with the hope of being able to surprise them." For eight miles the soldiers marched as rapidly as possible until they came to a valley. As the soldiers descended a steep hill into the valley, they were detected by the watchful warriors. Upon seeing over fifty soldiers charging down into the valley, the five Indians turned and fled. They escaped unharmed but were forced to leave behind some weapons and clothing, which the troops captured along with a horse and four oxen. This was the last Carson saw of the Navajos as he returned to Fort Canby by way of the Hopi mesas.

In the meantime, the soldiers at Fort Canby had seen some Navajos. While Carson was making his return to the fort, Captain Carey informed Carleton that about "sixty Navajoes attacked our herd." The Indians had been "whipped off by the guard and herders." When the Navajos attacked this time, the guard was ready for them, perhaps because the soldiers had been embarrassed by their previous losses. The bows and arrows of the Navajo raiders were not as efficient as the firearms the soldiers used, and this time the whizzing arrows did not put the soldiers on the run. They stood firm, and the air around them cracked with the reports of their rifles. The warriors were forced to retreat from the grazing grounds without their prey. No one was reported hurt in the brief fight. When Carey learned of the skirmish, he dispatched a detachment to chase the Navajos, who easily outraced the soldiers. The bluecoats were unable to track the Diné and returned to the fort without engaging them.[17]

Horses were of extreme importance to the Navajo warriors, who fought most effectively when mounted. For them, as for their brothers on the plains, having a horse oftentimes meant the difference between life and death. The soldiers needed horses as well, but they were not fighting for their lives. Thus it is not surprising that both the soldiers and the Indians coveted each other's mounts, and Carson was particularly concerned about his animals, especially after his last scout, which was conducted primarily on foot. On December 13, Kit's adjutant wrote that should the animals "fall into the hands of the Navajoes, the operations of the 'Expedition' would be effectively Crippled." On December 13, two days after this communication, a Navajo band surprised the herd and made off with forty-eight mules and seven oxen, which were needed by the command as pack animals. With great audacity the Indians attacked a herd that was lazily grazing south of the black rocks near Fort Canby. The attack came in the afternoon, when "a party of Navajo Indians consisting of about one hundred and thirty, twenty of which were mounted, atacted [sic] the Government herd." Those warriors who were dismounted attacked ten soldiers stationed on a hill on the west, while the mounted braves surprised five soldiers stationed south of the herd. Major Sena, who was in command of the fort at the time of the attack, reported that the soldiers who had been surprised put up "a very hard fight which lasted about a half an hour." The Navajos easily outnumbered the soldiers, but most of them were armed with bows and arrows, while Sena's soldiers enjoyed the superior firepower. The crack of rifles and handguns could be heard for miles, echoing through the rocks and crevices of Cañon Bonito. The Navajos held firm against the

An elderly Navajo warrior with traditional fighting weapons. Courtesy
Smithsonian Institution.

rifle fire and made off with a good portion of the herd without a reported injury. Only two soldiers were wounded in the fight, but all the bluecoats suffered once again from embarrassment.[18]

Colonel Carson was enraged by the loss of his herd, and he was particularly irate at Major Sena for his usual incompetence. Kit was disappointed in the performance of the officer, and he was humiliated about the attack. He told Carleton that he and his men responded rapidly once the attack was reported: "Five minutes after it was reported that the Herd was attacked, every officer and man at the Post who could be mounted were in pursuit of the Indians." Carson's command chased the Navajos for "about seven miles, when it was found that the Indians had divided into several small parties, and knowing that they had a considerable start on us and that night was approaching, I reluctantly returned to the Post."

The colonel reported that he could not "hold the commanding officer at the Post blameless that he did not have a stronger Guard and an officer in command of it." Carson was "satisfied," however, that the soldiers on duty at the time of the attack had "done their duty."[19] Carleton was not so tolerant of the fiasco, and he chided Carson, remarking that "if they [the Indians] prowl around your herds in this manner, some stratagem might be used so as to decoy them to the neighborhood of a force strong enough to destroy them."[20]

Carson tried to make amends by sending troops after the raiders and the stock. On the crisp, cold morning of December 14, Carson "detached two parties—one under command of Major José D. Sena, with directions to take the trail of the Indians, and to keep it until he overtook them, or if that was not possible, to bring me positive information of their whereabouts." With two officers and seventy-two men Sena saddled up and left Fort Canby, heading south and west. Near the Ciénega Amarilla, Sena sighted a trail left by the Indians who had stolen the stock. He followed it in a southwesterly direction toward Pueblo Colorado and camped on the top of Fort Defiance Mesa.

On the second day out the troops continued their march toward Pueblo Colorado, but were forced to call a halt "on account of a

An elderly Navajo woman. Such women were respectfully called shimasani *("grandmother"). Courtesy Navajo Community College.*

heavy snow storm." Three inches of snow blanketed the ground and made it "impossible to find the trail." After a short rest Sena's soldiers continued their march and soon "discovered a smoke to our left in the direction of Pueblo Colorado." The command headed toward the smoke, which smelled of sweet cedar; traveled "through a long strip of heavy timber;" and finally arrived at an Indian village.

The Navajos must have known that the troops were approaching, for the only person that the command found in the ranchería was an old woman who was unable to make her escape. It should have been obvious to Sena that this *shimasani* ("old grandmother") had nothing to do with the raid. It should have been just as apparent that the woman was too old to travel, or she would have effected her escape. Nevertheless, Sena set her on a mule and took her along. Tracks of two men and a woman were spotted, but these Navajos could not be found. Sena journeyed on to Pueblo Colorado before turning northeast into a sandy, hilly desert but failed to find any fresh signs of the Diné. The old woman became a "burden" to Sena, and, after "it was reported . . . that the Indian woman was dying," the major "ordered her to be left in some deep arroyo." The woman was abandoned there to die of cold and hunger.[21]

On the evening of December 16, Sena made camp at sundown in Beautiful Valley, or Chinle Valley, approximately six miles south of the Cañon de Chelly. The next morning his troops discovered smoke on the northwest, and Sena headed his command in that direction. The smoke that had lured Sena northward came from the fires of another detachment of troops that Carson had dispatched. It was commanded by Lieutenant Donaciano Montoya, who was pleased to see his comrades. Sena left Montoya that afternoon and headed south to track Navajos along a mule trail, which turned out not to be a mule trail at all. Nonetheless, the major continued south and finally "came to a trail of about 13 Indians on foot," which he followed for about four miles. As might be expected, Sena became confused about the direction he should take, but when his spies spotted "fresh tracks of mules and Indians," he decided to follow this new lead. Just as he was about to turn his men and start on the new trail, however, one of his men sighted

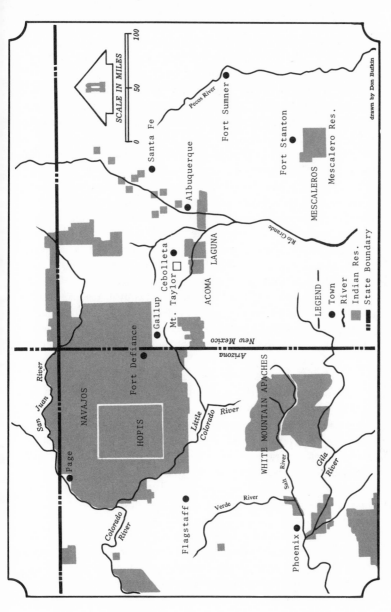

New Mexico and Arizona. Overview of the Southwest from the reservations to the Bosque Redondo "two Indians and commenced to cry out as loud as he could Los Indians! Los Indians!" Sena ordered his men to charge the Indians, because "at the time" he mistakenly thought that "there was plenty of them." He started after the Indians "double quick," but when he came to a ravine, he found only their tracks. Sena sent his men off to find the Indians, but even with the snow to help him he was unable to find his quarry.[22]

On the west, toward the Hopi mesas, Sena happened upon an Indian village "consisting of six houses." The Indians had learned of the army's approach and had fled their hogans because of the threat of a superior force. The Navajos had not been gone long when Sena arrived, for their fires were still burning. Again Sena could not ascertain the direction the Indians had fled, so he decided to head back to Pueblo Colorado. He and his men discovered a few cornfields and plenty of fresh signs of Indians and animals, which indicated to Sena that the Indians were moving toward the Cañon de Chelly. He did not follow them, however, but instead returned to Fort Canby. Carson met Sena at the fort and was upset to learn that the major had not recovered the horses. Kit's disappointment did not match Carleton's, however, for the general was thoroughly disgusted with his troops.[23]

In the closing months of 1863 it appeared to Carson and Carleton that the Navajo campaign was failing miserably, mainly because the troops had yet to find, confront, or frighten any large numbers of Navajos. Carson was frustrated and confused about his inability to engage the Diné, with their skill in evading the soldiers and vanishing into the ravines, forests, and mountains of Dinetah. Kit was upset that his horses and mules were broken down and hardly able to travel, and he was amazed that his soldiers were unable to stop the Navajos from raiding the herds that grazed so close to the fort. He was distressed because he could not send wagon trains to Fort Wingate without fear of attack, and, besides, he was running dangerously low on ammunition. No doubt the great scout and Indian fighter was embarrassed about his performance as a field commander and thoroughly disgusted with himself for his failure to execute the campaign in the manner prescribed by General Carleton.

After several months in the Navajo country Kit was ready for a rest. He was nearly fifty-four years old, and the pressures of the campaign, as well as the many hours he spent in the saddle, had doubtless taxed both his body and his mind. Customarily the frontier army did not continue a war into the winter because of lack of forage. Carson wanted to call a halt to his campaign during the winter of 1863 and 1864, and he hoped to spend these months with his wife and children in Taos. Carleton would hear none of this, however, and ordered Carson to continue the Navajo campaign by invading the Cañon de Chelly. Carson again displayed his loyalty to Carleton by immediately beginning preparations for the march into the magnificent cañon, though he was "of the opinion that but few, if any, Navajoes are in the canon." Unknown to him at the time, Carson was about to begin that portion of his campaign that would bring about the surrender of thousands of Navajos.[24]

CHAPTER 5

"You Have Killed Us. . . . We Are Suffering"

Natural beauties abound in northern Arizona, particularly in the eastern portion of the Navajo country. Sand, wind, and water have swept the land for aeons and have formed a magnificent wonderland of deserts, buttes, and mountains. All the monuments are glorious in their own right, but none of these works of nature matches the elegance, grace, and beauty of the Cañon de Chelly. Three major branches compose the cañon: Monument Cañon, Cañon del Muerto, and Cañon de Chelly itself. The main branch, the Cañon de Chelly, lies east to west and is skirted on the south by Monument Cañon and on the north by Cañon del Muerto. The ancient Pueblos, or Anasazi, the first inhabitants of the cañon, abandoned their well-constructed rock, adobe, and plaster homes along the sheer ledges and in the caves of the cañon. The Navajo people then made the cañons their home, for the land was fertile and the trees bountiful along the edges of the cañon's sandy floor. A gently flowing stream snaked its way through Cañon del Muerto and provided precious water for the Indians residing there.[1]

Spaniards, or Nakai, knew of the Cañon de Chelly and its branches, but no American is reported to have traversed the cañon until 1859, when Captain John G. Walker (not the Walker of the 1847 expedition) made his trek through it.[2] Colonels John M. Washing-

Cañon de Chelly, through which Carson's troops marched during the last major engagement of the Navajo campaign. Courtesy Southwest Museum.

ton and Edwin V. Sumner explored portions of the cañon in the mid-nineteenth century, and Colonel Dixon S. Miles once warned about the perils of ambush that awaited troops who attempted to enter the cañon. Carson and Carleton knew little about the dimensions of the Cañon de Chelly and less about its topography. Nevertheless, Carleton told Carson on December 5, 1863, that it was "desirable that you go through the Cañon de Chelly."[3]

The previous August, Kit had entered the cañon from the west entrance and had destroyed some crops. Carson was convinced that "there are very few Indians in the Cañon, and these of the very poorest." He believed that his summer scout had ruined the Indians who resided in the gorge, for they had no stock "and they were depending entirely for subsistence on the corn destroyed by my command." The Indians in the cañon had few choices: they could starve, migrate to the Bosque Redondo, or flee south. Even after Carleton ordered him to invade the cañon, Carson was reluctant. He was confident that he would find few Navajos there, and he was satisfied that the army would reap no benefit from the invasion. "Were I not of the opinion that but few, if any, Navajoes are in the Cañon de Chelly," Carson wrote Carleton, "I should have paid it a visit long since." However, the colonel obediently added that "as soon as the animals are sufficiently rested I shall send a command to examine the Cañon de Chelly, and the smaller Cañons which intersect it."[4]

On December 11, Colonel Carson began preparations for the campaign. His first move was to order Captain Francisco Abreu and approximately 150 men to explore the western end of the great cañon. This reconnoitering force was told to collect any information that would "be of use to the Colonel Commanding in an Expedition which he will lead against the Indians in the Cañon." Kit told Abreu to examine the depths of the cañon "as far as practicable" and with tongue in cheek commented that the chasm was "supposed to be the stronghold of the Navajoes—and which has heretofore been a *terra incognita* to all the Commands operating against the Navajoes." Carson insisted that no terms should be made with Navajos operating within the region surrounding the cañon, except for "the one mentioned by the Department Commander, namely: Immigration to the Bosque Redondo." If the Indians agreed to comply with this policy, they were to "be permitted to take with them their families and all they possess, and be assured all possible protection." At about that time Major Abreu received word that he had been transferred and promoted. Carson congratulated the new lieutenant colonel and expressed his sorrow that he was departing the Navajo country. Abreu's reconnaissance of the cañon was canceled.[5]

Exploration of the cañon was further delayed after the Navajos attacked the herd at Fort Canby and made off with several mules, which Major Sena was again unable to recapture. "Owing to the loss of Mules," Kit commented to Carleton, "these operations will be necessarily delayed until some Mules arrive here, which I trust will be soon." Although the campaign was delayed, Carson continued to pursue the Navajos. The colonel determined that while the troops at Fort Canby were waiting for mules and other mounts they would be "kept in the field so as to allow the Indians no rest for the circumference of one hundred and fifty miles of this post." During this time Kit obtained a very significant piece of information from a Navajo woman who claimed that she had been inclined toward peace since 1860 but had been forced by the Bilagáana to follow the path of war. This woman, Carson reported, pointed out that Herrera Grande desired peace and that "many of the Indians would be glad to come in and comply with our terms." However, they hesitated to so because of the fate of one emissary that the chief had sent to Fort Canby to talk peace. This Indian had gone to the fort on August 31 desiring to talk peace with "his white brethren." The ruthless Major Blakeney had seized him, thrown him into the guardhouse, and killed him during an alleged escape attempt. This was Blakeney's story, but the Indians looked upon the killing of the emissary as cold-blooded murder, and they were very reluctant even to consider surrendering after this incident. It was more honorable to face death from starvation than to surrender and be murdered like animals.

Even Colonel Carson could not "blame these people for distrust-

Kit Carson in formal attire, ca. 1864. Courtesy Navajo Community College.

ing the good faith of the Troops at this Post, from the manner in which their Messengers have been received at it on more than one occasion." Kit "deplored" the campaign at this point and lamented, "I have one way of communicating with them—through the barrels of my Rifles." Carson had initially helped bring on this situation by killing or attempting to kill every warrior he encountered without thought of peace councils. By the winter of 1863, Kit was slowly changing his policy, giving some thought to the possibility of talking with Navajos about their surrender and their removal.[6]

After Abreu was transferred, Carson ordered Lieutenant Montoya to make a reconnaissance of the area surrounding the Cañon de Chelly. On December 14 the lieutenant left Fort Canby with orders from Carson "to visit the Country South and West of Cañon de Chelly and to Surprise and punish any bands of Savages that might be found in that vicinity." Over one hundred enlisted men and another officer accompanied Montoya "with ten days rations and forty rounds of ammunition to each man besides One Box of extra ammunition which was taken along to meet any emergency." The troops were prepared to engage the Navajos as they headed south from Fort Canby and turned west in the region of the Ciénega Amarilla. On the first day out, Montoya's men discovered "a trail bearing the prints of two Mules and two Oxen that had been driven by perhaps Nine Indians." The lieutenant reasoned that the tracks had been made by the Indians who had raided the government herd and that the animals they were driving were stolen. Montoya had no proof of this and did not really care whether his assumptions were true or not. His sole objective was to fight the Indians whenever and wherever he found them. He followed this trail in "double-quick" fashion until nightfall, when he was obliged to camp. He awoke the next morning to find that a heavy snow had fallen. Although the soldiers could not follow the now snow-covered trail, they headed in the direction they thought "the Indians had taken expecting to see the Smoke of their Village or encampment."[7]

Piñon and sage were white with the new-fallen snow, but the

beautiful sight had no appeal to Montoya's men or to the Indians, who were starving and freezing. "The Snow fell heavily all day to the great discomfort of the Command," Montoya reported. Progress was slow through the snow, and the command camped "on a high Mesa building the Camp fires in a deep Arroya and establishing pickets on the Most elevated points with instructions to report the appearance of Smoke Signals or fires as well as other indications of the presence of Indians." Nothing of significance occurred during the night, and the next morning the command continued its journey in a northerly direction toward the mouth of the Cañon de Chelly. About an hour out, Montoya encountered rough, broken country, which he feared was a perfect place for Navajos to "elude" his command "by hiding in numerous furrows and ravines in my vicinity." As a precaution he detailed Sergeant Antonio Nava and eight men to scout approximately a mile in front of the column. These men were told to report to Montoya immediately if they discovered any sign of the Indians.

For four miles Montoya's men labored over reddish rocks, hardened sand dunes that were covered with snow and ice. Then, with a burst of jubilation, Sergeant Nava rushed back to the column with the news "that he had observed Several Smokes about two miles ahead and South of My line of March." Montoya told one of his sergeants to remain with forty-five men and protect the pack mules. He ordered Lieutenant Charles M. Hubbell to gather the remainder of the men, sixty-five in number, and follow him. Although the adrenalin was pumping through his veins, Montoya attempted to calm himself and "proceeded cautiously towards the Smokes." Two hundred yards from where the smoke was lazily drifting into the turquoise sky, Montoya hesitated and listened in the still air. He then deployed his men in "open order."

The crack of Montoya's voice broke the silence of this wilderness, as he shouted a charge. With the command "each man rushed forward with a cheer charging the Indians who fled in Confusion." The bellowing of orders and the screeching yelps alerted the Navajos. They scrambled in many directions, each one attempting to escape on his own. "A rapid and accurate fire was kept up by My

Navajo man and woman. Studio portrait probably by A. Frank Randall.
Courtesy Smithsonian Institution.

Men for about five Minutes on the Indians who numbered about thirty Warriors." The Indians fought back as best they could, but the soldiers managed to capture thirteen women and children. They were herded together as prisoners of war. Several warriors were spotted nearby "in the thick Cedar brake," no doubt hoping to save some of their loved ones. Realizing, however, that their efforts would only lead to additional pain and death, they decided not to attack. According to the soldiers, the Indians suffered during the charge: "I saw one Indian killed dead, his body remaining in the Captured Camp, and another Indian was shot through the right Side but Succeeded in escaping through the tangled underwood." The son of the wounded warrior "reported that his father died amongst the rocks" in a heavy arroyo. This grieving young man of ten must have been filled with sorrow at the death of his father and was no doubt frightened greatly when he was captured by the soldiers. Montoya maintained, with great arrogance, that the boy was "very intelligent for an Indian."[8]

The soldiers found several items of interest in and about the six hogans they had charged. Several Navajo rugs, woolen yarn, baskets, pottery, and moccasins were discovered, along with a supply of fresh meat that Montoya assumed had been procured by the recent raid at the fort. Some of these "trophies" were taken by the soldiers, while others were gathered together in a large pile and burned. The hogans were likewise put to the torch so that the Indians of the ranchería would have no shelter from the winter. After resting and eating, the troops left the encampment and headed west toward Black Mesa, or Mesa de la Vaca, as the soldiers then called the great mountain.

Leaving Lieutenant Hubbell behind with the pack mules, Montoya marched out of camp with forty men on a three-day scout in which he "expected to Surprise Indians." Six miles from camp one of Montoya's "spies," Juan Marcos, sighted two Indians just ahead of the column. Again Montoya ordered a charge. Corporal Marcos was quick to respond to the order as he galloped his mount in the direction of the Indians and discharged his revolver. Marcos "shot the leading Indian through the back," and the Navajo fell

Zedeke, Navajo medicine man. Portrait by Christian Barthelmess. Courtesy Smithsonian Institution.

off his horse. Just as the corporal approached the Indian to assure himself of a kill, "the Indian arose at the same moment and drawing a revolver shot the Corporal through the wrist." The soldier, despite his wound, managed to reload his weapon. The wounded warrior tried to make his escape, seizing a woman who had hidden in the brush during the attack and fleeing with her into the woods. Sergeant Nava charged the warrior, fired a shot at him, and captured the woman. Nava was to pay dearly for this, for the Indian wheeled in his tracks and fired a few arrows at him, two of which found their mark, striking Nava's head and side. Although wounded, the sergeant charged the Navajo again and knocked him down with the butt of his rifle. Nava also collapsed on the ground, weakened by loss of blood. The Indian was up in a flash and reloaded his revolver.

Just then Montoya arrived on the scene and fired at the Navajo. His fire was returned, but neither bullet hit its mark. The warrior managed his escape in "the thick brushwood," but the young woman was not so fortunate. She was captured, and when the soldiers returned at Fort Canby, she was placed with the other captives, who were destined to be sent to the Bosque Redondo. By and large, Montoya's expedition through Navajo land provided no new information to Carson about the region surrounding the west entrance to the Cañon de Chelly, and he did not recover any of the stock previously stolen from the fort. His journey, however, probably prompted several Navajos living in the region to either move into the Cañon de Chelly for protection or flee to the west across Black Mesa.[9]

Carson believed that many Navajos had fled to Black Mesa, just north of the Hopi villages. Therefore, on December 21, 1863, he ordered Captain John Thompson and one hundred soldiers to scout that region. Thompson was told to march southwest to Pueblo Colorado before heading northwest to the "Mesa la Baca." Carson gave explicit orders that when the troops reached the Pueblo Colorado they were to have no fires after dark, and they were to preserve "the utmost silence . . . and permit no smoking whatever." Kit commanded Thompson and his men to "allow no noise or fires" and to employ "every exertion and precaution to enable you to overtake and chastise them."

Captain Thompson followed orders, departing Fort Canby on schedule and moving first to Ciénega Amarilla and then west to Pueblo Colorado. When the captain arrived at the high, table-top mountain base of Black Mesa, he found that "it would be utterly impossible for the pack mules to ascend the mountain as the snow was some five or six inches in depth and it is still snowing." Thompson had been assigned a difficult task, for the ridge of Black Mesa was very steep and difficult to climb, even without the hindrance of snow and ice. Nevertheless, after establishing a camp at the base of the precipice, Thompson "sent a party consisting of fifteen men of Capt. Berneys company and fifteen men of my own company under command of Sergt. Romero of company 'D' to reconoitre [sic] the mountain."

With extreme difficulty and exertion the soldiers climbed to the top of the mesa. Romero marched across it and surprised a party of Navajos. A skirmish ensued, and one Indian was killed and twelve were captured. No details were reported, but it can be assumed that the fight was a fierce one, for Romero chose not to pursue the Navajos and returned instead to the base camp. When he reached camp, Thompson decided to detach Sergeant John W. Dorsett and twenty men "to ascertain whether any more Indians were in the vicinity of the mountain." While Dorsett and his men were again scouting the top of the mesa, they captured one Indian and wounded another, who "succeeded in making his escape." The sergeant remained on the mesa until nightfall without sighting another Navajo, and he decided that there was no reason for him to stay any longer. Deciding that the two skirmishes had scattered the Navajos, he returned to Fort Canby by the same route, taking with him fourteen "prisoners," all women and children.[10]

When Captain Thompson returned to the fort, he immediately reported to Carson. After talking with Thompson about his scout, Kit went to see the captives. He was shocked by their condition, for the women and children were freezing and starving. "Judging from the appearance of these captives," Kit observed, "the generality of the Navajos are completely destitute." Carson was correct, for most of the Indians were "almost entirely naked," and were starving to death. Most Navajos were living off piñon nuts collected in the fall of 1863, and any other food they found in the forests and mountains of Dinetah. The women and children brought in by Thompson "must have been without any description of food" for some time. Their bodies were thin, except for their bellies, which were pitifully swollen from malnutrition. Their eyes were far back in their heads and were as dark and empty as those of the dead. It was a gruesome sight that foretold the grave condition of the rest of the tribe. Carson attributed their destitute condition largely "to the destruction of their grain amounting to about two Millions of Pounds by my command on its first arrival in this country."

Utter starvation gripped the Navajo Nation during the long, cold winter of 1863-64. Their condition was rendered worse because of their fear of building fires for warmth, for fires might lead soldiers to their hideouts. "The dread of being discovered by my Scouting parties which are continually in the field," Kit commented, "kept the Indians from harvesting crops, building shelters, and, in general, preparing for winter." Carson realized that all these things combined to add "greatly to the horrors of their Situation, when all the severity of the winter in the Mountains must be borne by them without protection." The colonel knew that his campaign was having disastrous effects on the tribe, and he may have felt some sorrow about the death and destruction that he had caused the Navajo people.

He did not want to end the campaign, but he did ask Carleton to furnish him with blankets to help clothe the Indians who had surrendered at Fort Canby and Fort Wingate. Carleton soon realized that Carson's campaign was taking its toll and that there was, indeed, a need for blankets, but, as often happened, the bureaucracy was slow in providing them, as well as clothing and food. In early December the general wrote to the War Department requesting blankets for the naked Navajos, stating that "many of the Navajoe women and children which we capture are quite naked;

Navajos in front of shelters like those constructed at the Bosque Redondo. Courtesy Navajo Community College.

and the children, especially, suffer from the extreme cold." All too often the Navajos would suffer severely because of such inefficiency by the federal government.

Neither Carson's nor Carleton's concern for the Navajos at this stage could affect the over-all condition of the Navajos, for they were in a desperate state. Not only had they been unable to harvest their crops or build their hogans in preparation for winter, but also they had been unable to raid the New Mexicans who ranched and farmed along the Río Grande. In essence, their traditional lifeway was shattered and their means of subsistence was gone. The Navajos were starving and freezing. Both old and young were suffering, and death made no distinction between the two.[11]

No doubt the army realized that the Navajos were suffering from the winter campaign, but not even Carson knew or understood the gravity of the Navajos' situation. He looked to the future and anticipated a continuation of the war. "There can be no doubt whatever," he wrote, "but that by prosecuting the campaign with the vigor which has heretofore characterized it, during next spring and summer—so as to prevent them from planting their grain, that actual Starvation will compel any who may hold out that long to come in and avail themselves of the means offered them of sharing in the plenty." Carson reasoned that many of the Indians who remained hostile after the winter would sooner or later capitulate so that they too could enjoy the benefits already possessed "by those of their people now on Reservations."

He feared that a portion of the tribe might continue to fight, however, and offer the army and citizens of New Mexico a great threat. Carson argued that "the desperate condition of these people may drive them to bolder attempts than heretofore to supply food for their families from the Herds of the People of the Territory." Gallant attempts by Navajo warriors to feed their families had occurred before, and just as Kit was writing his report of January 3, 1864, word reached him that 150 Indians had attacked Russell's supply train, killing Wagonmaster Russell and wounding four other men. One Navajo was killed, but his starving band managed to drive off twenty head of mules. The attack occurred near present-day Gallup, New Mexico, and not far from there the Indians halted to slaughter and cook a mule, demonstrating, as Carson put it, "that they are desperate from want."[12]

By the late months of 1863, Carson was completing his plans for the invasion of the Cañon de Chelly. On December 26, he told Carleton, "I have made all necessary arrangements to visit the Cañon de Chelly, and will leave this post for that purpose with my Command on the third or fourth of next month." His plan was to establish a supply depot at the west end of the cañon near present-day Chinle, which he would personally command, and to send another column to operate from the east entrance of the cañon. The command that was to enter the east entrance was to march through the cañon and rejoin Carson at the west end. Kit was totally unaware that there were three branches to De Chelly and more than one entrance.

Carson was pleased about the weather, which seemed to be in his favor. "In the last few days," Kit commented, "we have had a Considerable fall of snow which will greatly facilitate my operations against the Cañon de Chelly." With great confidence, and even a tone of pomp, Carson told Carleton, "Of one thing the General may rest assured that before my return all that is Connected with this Cañon will Cease to be a mystery." Kit promised that the cañon would "be thoroughly explored, if perseverance and zeal, with the numbers at my Command can accomplish it."

For the first step of the invasion, on January 3, 1864, Carson dispatched two companies with the "supply train under the command of the incompetent Major Sena to Pueblo Colorado, there to await the balance of my command." He planned to leave Fort Canby for the Cañon de Chelly by way of Pueblo, Colorado, three days later.[13] On the morning of January 6, he and 389 soldiers made their departure from Fort Canby en route to the Cañon de Chelly. Carson must have gazed about and watched his men busily making their last-minute arrangements before heading out. The mountains north and west of the fort were a sight of magnificence and beauty. The piñons, cedar, and juniper in Cañon Bonito and Cañon Azul were covered with new snow, which clung to the green branches, bending them toward the ground. The air was clean but filled with a wintry chill. From this serene setting Carson set out on his mission of death and destruction.

Carson led his men southwest toward Pueblo Colorado, while Captain Albert Pfeiffer and thirty-three men were dispatched in a northerly direction to find and penetrate the great cañon of Dinetah. Carson's command marched south to the Ciénega Amarilla that morning, and for three days his soldiers trudged toward Pueblo Colorado, their travel being hampered "owing to the depth of snow on the Mountain which divides the valley of this section with those of the Pueblo Colorado." One Indian was unfortunate enough to be caught in the line of march, and one of Carson's

141

men sent a bullet through his body, breaking the silence of the forest and killing him.

The colonel was much "disappointed" when he arrived at the Pueblo Colorado, because he arrived there about the same time as Major Sena, who had been "sent forward on the 3rd with the expectation that he would have had time to recuperate his animals before the arrival of my command." It had taken Sena five days to march twenty-five miles on a route that usually took only one day. If Carson was upset about the time Sena spent crossing the mountain, he was livid after learning that the major had lost twenty-seven oxen on the trip. Kit was naturally "upset" with the bungling major, who made it necessary for the colonel "to lighten the loads and leave one wagon" at the Pueblo Colorado. Carson was also forced to leave behind ten days' rations and twenty-five soldiers to guard them.[14]

Slowly the command made its way north through Beautiful Valley and Chinle Valley, both of which were snow-covered. On January 12, Kit's command neared the west end of the low, sandy mouth of the Cañon de Chelly, but just before arriving at the opening of the chasm, Kit took an escort and rode cross-country toward the southern branch. Riding pell-mell across the hard sandhills southeast of present-day Chinle, Carson arrived at the cañon about six miles above its mouth. The sides of the cañon dropped radically into the depths and appeared as if they had been sliced clean with a sharp knife. A multitude of warm colors radiated from the cañon walls, but the scene seemed stark because it was winter. In the middle of the day the sun's glowing rays produced a yellow tint, though a rusty red dominated the cañon walls. The outline of a small stream could barely be seen, almost hidden by a layer of snow that covered the cañon floor.

Carson wanted "to reconnoiter a little previous to commencing operations," and for this reason he decided to ride "up the Cañon on the South side some four or five miles further." As the colonel rode carefully along the sheer cliffs, his eyes were fixed to his left in search of a passage which would take his men down into the depths of the cañon. Soon, however, Carson realized that he

Carnero Mucho, ca. 1879, who was a young warrior at the time of Carson's campaign. Courtesy Smithsonian Institution.

"could find no possible means of descending the bottom of the Cañon." He and his men were awed by the height of the cañon walls, which rose "about one thousand feet and nearly perpendicular."

Carson's small column continued its march along the south rim of the Cañon de Chelly and reportedly "saw several Indians on the opposite or north side of the Cañon, but out of range of our small arms." There is little doubt that the Navajos rapidly spread the word that Carson was operating along the cañon and would soon invade their natural stronghold. The cañon campaign had begun.[15]

After traveling up the cañon ten miles above its mouth, Kit decided to turn around and head west to rejoin his main command. His short reconnaissance made him a little more familiar with the cañon and alerted some Navajos to his presence. Certainly not all the Indians living in the Cañon de Chelly were aware of his march into the cañon country. When the colonel reached camp, he was surprised to learn that his men had already engaged the Navajos. Sergeant Andrés Herrera and fifty men had been ordered to explore the area around the cañon's mouth before the main column established a camp there. Carson learned that "at daylight [Herrera] discovered a fresh trail, and following it up rapidly overtook the Indians as they were about to enter the Cañon." Families of Navajos—men, women, and children—were trying to make their escape from the troops, for they had no quarrel with the Bilagáana and did not care to fight. Nonetheless, they were overtaken by the soldiers, who "immediately attacked them." Eleven Navajos were killed, but the records are not clear whether they were men, women, or children. Two women and two children were captured in the foray, and the soldiers rounded up 130 sheep and goats. Colonel Carson was pleased to hear of the attack and was much impressed by "the energy and ability displayed by the Sergeant." Once again Carson's soldiers had spoken to the Indians through the "barrels of their rifles" rather than through a peace council. That was indeed unfortunate, for Kit could have prevented bloodshed if he had instructed his soldiers to capture and hold council with the Indians instead of killing them.

144

The next day Kit viewed the site of the skirmish. Strewn about the sandy floor of the cañon lay "eleven dead bodies and five wounded (two mortally)." Three of the Indians Carson found were still alive, "though badly wounded." They were taken back to camp and cared for by Dr. John H. Shout. This was Kit's first contact with the Navajos at the Cañon de Chelly, and it proved to be a violent one.[16]

Carson's second phase of the campaign was to order "two commands to operate on each side of the Cañon, with three days Rations in Haversacks." Captain Carey was to lead one party along the south rim, while Captain Joseph Berney was to take another party to survey the north rim, which Carson later learned was actually the rim of the Cañon del Muerto, not of the Cañon de Chelly. The colonel himself chose to accompany Captain Carey, "wishing to gain a knowledge of the topography of the Cañon with the view to operations within it." Carson was also particularly interested in traveling with Carey because he was "very anxious about the safety of Capt. Pfeiffer's command, whom I had sent from Fort Canby to operate from the East opening."

Carey and Carson moved along the rim of the southern branch of the Cañon de Chelly until they reached "a point whence the view of the Cañon was unobstructed to near its Eastern outlet." Their route took them along the rim, which skirted many natural and man-made wonders. Not far from the mouth of the cañon Kit saw one of many adobe ruins built by the Anasazi, the Ancient Pueblos. The first was White House Ruins, the main portion of which was nestled in a long, horizontal cave. The stone and adobe used in its construction had been taken from the cañon walls, thus creating a natural blend of materials and colors in walls, cave, and buildings. This was a sacred place to Navajos, who believed that a *yei,* or spirit, once lived there. No less sacred were two natural pinnacles that stand eight hundred feet high and are collectively known as Spider Rock. The important figure in Navajo religion known as Spider Woman once lived on top of the rock.

Foremost among Carson's concerns was the fate of Captain Pfeiffer's command, which had been ordered to traverse the Cañon de Chelly from east to west. Carson rode the southern rim to Spider

Rock and continued his scout along Monument Cañon, not knowing that the main branch split and continued inland along a more easterly route. He had searched the entire length of the rim without finding Pfeiffer or any trace of his command. Carson calculated that Captain Pfeiffer should have begun his march through the cañon by that time, and he reported that he was "unable to discover any signs of Captain Pfeiffer's command, or any fresh signs of Indians." He feared that the captain and his men had been ambushed and annihilated. Although his mind was filled with concern for his troops, he decided to return to his main camp at the mouth of the cañon.[17]

"I found to my great surprise and gratification," Carson wrote, "Captain Pfeiffer and his party in camp—having accomplished an undertaking never before successful in Wartime—that of passing through the Cañon de Chelly from East to West" (Carson was not aware that Captain Walker had earlier made an east-to-west trek through the cañon). Carson was both relieved and excited to see that his comrade and friend was alive.[18] It would soon become apparent to Kit that Pfeiffer's march was a crucial part of the campaign.

Like Carson, Captain Pfeiffer had left Fort Canby on the morning of January 6 "*en route* for the East opening of Cañon de Chelly." Although snow had recently fallen in the region, Pfeiffer and his men made good time on their march north, making their first camp nine miles from Fort Canby at a wheat field. The second day out, the column discovered "a few Indian tracks," and Pfeiffer ordered Lieutenant Clemente P. Ortiz with a party of men to scout the area for additional Indian signs. When no Indians were found, however, Pfeiffer's small command continued north, though with great difficulty. Six inches of snow hampered their progress, and the closer they came to the Chuska Mountains near White Cone and Tsaile Butte, the deeper the snow became, in some places two feet deep.[19]

Just past Laguna Colorado, or Red Lake, as it is called today, the soldiers passed a large rock formation with a green tint. The

146

Navajos believe that at one time this green monument was a large snake and that the spirit of that snake still resides in the mountain. As the soldiers proceeded northward, the land became even more mountainous. In front of them was a glorious sight: large, pine-covered mountains and sheer, bald-faced cliffs. As the soldiers wound their way around these wondrous mountains, they came to Whiskey and Wheatfields creeks, and it was in this region that the bluecoats smelled the sweet aroma of a juniper fire and "observed smoke in the distance." Upon this sighting, Pfeiffer dispatched Sergeant Luciano Trujillo and fifteen soldiers "to discover if possible that locality from which the smoke arose." The sergeant made his way toward the smoke and found eight Navajo women and children huddled together "in an almost famishing condition." Fortunately Trujillo did not attack them but showed them great consideration and compassion. He took them back to Pfeiffer, where they were given food and blankets. At this time the weather was unbearably cold, and Pfeiffer reported that two of the soldiers suffered severely when their feet froze. Their wretched condition, however, could not approach what the Navajos were enduring.[20]

A piñon forest dotted the landscape as Pfeiffer approached the eastern entrance to Cañon del Muerto. Behind the soldiers, on the east, rose stupendous mountains: Tsaile Butte, White Cone, and Black Pinnacle. Stretching out north of them lay the red cliffs of the Lukachukai Mountains, whose bare, red faces were pocked with caves.

Snowstorms can come with unexpected speed and severity in this region of Dinetah, quickly isolating those who would brave the region in that season. Pfeiffer's soldiers faced such storms as they moved north, and with much hardship they trudged through the heavy snows. If the fate of the troops was miserable, the plight of the Navajo people was worse still. The weather brought misery and suffering to the Diné, who were dying from the blizzards because they had little shelter and few blankets. Although the weather was punishing to the soldiers and their animals, perhaps they drew some comfort from the beauty of the mountains that

147

paralleled them to their right. The barren cliffs of sandstone looked redder than ever before because of their contrast with the white snow.

Pfeiffer followed Tsaile Creek in an easterly direction until it entered an innocent-appearing little cañon, which was peaceful and quiet, except for the crow's call that occasionally broke the still air. A few large, gray boulders lay on the cañon floor, which stretched about twenty yards from side to side. The walls of the cañon were gentle at first and covered with a few large pines. The frozen creek meandered through the middle of the valley, and the soldiers had to pick their steps carefully to avoid slipping and falling on the slick surface of ice. After entering the cañon less than one hundred yards, Pfeiffer realized that the walls of the cañon were growing steadily upward and that the passage through the valley was becoming narrower. This gentle valley was deceptive, for it would soon open into the staggering dimensions of the famous red chasm of Cañon de Chelly. To protect the main body of the command from attack, the captain sent out an advance party of scouts to clear the way. Bringing up the rear was another small detachment, which was to protect the flank. All three groups, however, were told to be cautious and "to keep as closely connected as possible, and to move as one body." Pfeiffer placed himself in front of the column, "at the most dangerous points," where he could "move free and observe the strategems of the concealed foe."[21]

Enchanting vistas awaited the soldiers as they continued their trek through the Cañon del Muerto, which was a sight of awe, beauty—and danger. As Pfeiffer moved, deeper into the cañon, he reported that his travel

> for the first twelve (12) miles was accomplished on the ice of the bed of the stream which courses through it. During the passage of the Cañon I observed plenty of Oak, Cottonwood and Scrub Oak, which grew on both sides of the Mountainous declivity. The sides at the entrance for the first twelve (12) miles "jutting down" almost perpendicularly to the level of the Cañon, which was very narrow and confined to the channel of the creek.

148

Travel was made most difficult by the snow and ice, which were worse for the animals than for the men, owing to their weight. Pfeiffer later reported to Carson:

> Lieut. C. M. Hubbell, who was in charge of the rear, had a great deal of trouble in proceeding with the Pack Train, as the Mules frequently broke through the ice and tumbled down with their loads. All the Indian Prisoners taken thus far were half-starved and naked. The Cañon has no road except the bottom of the creek. We traveled mostly on the ice, and our animals breaking through every few minutes, and one mule split completely open under the exhausting fatigue of the march.[22]

Travel through the cañon was incredibly rough, especially for the Indians, who were sick and cold. Progress was slow as the party cautiously crept on the ice, fearing that around each bend of the sandstone cliffs a war party waited in silence to trap the Bilagáana in the Cañon of the Dead.

The troops' first night in the cañon brought no reprisals for their invasion of the Indian stronghold. Pfeiffer reported that the next day brought more action, for very early on the morning of January 12 the Navajos began "whooping and yelling and cursing, firing shots and throwing rocks down upon my command." The day was filled with skirmishes as the Navajos used every means at their disposal to discourage the troops from continuing their march through the cañon. According to Pfeiffer, his men killed three Navajos that day, including two "Buck Indians in the encounter, and one Squaw who obstinately persisted in hurling rocks and pieces of wood at the Soldiers." One party of soldiers under Lieutenant Hubbell chased "some Indians in a tributary Cañon, but could not overtake them on account of the steepness of the hill sides."

The Indians were able to outmaneuver the soldiers in the cañon because they were familiar with the many trails throughout the gorge. Along some walls the Indians used special routes, tiny foot- and handholes pecked into the rock. They were very difficult to see, and only the Indians knew of their existence. The sides of the cañon, ranging from 1,200 to 1,500 feet high, were so sheer that Pfeiffer reported that "nothing save an Indian or a Mountain Goat could make their way" up their sides. Six more Indians were captured that day before sundown, and the captain camped "in a secure place, where plenty of wood was to be obtained."[23]

As Pfeiffer moved through the narrow passage, he was awed by the "High Projecting Rock, and Houses built thereon, perforated with caverns and mountain fastnesses." His troops traveled over deep sand throughout the second day and camped on the bottom-lands near the Mummy Cave Ruin, which the captain called Castle Carey in honor of Captain Asa B. Carey. Pfeiffer was much impressed by the ruins in the cañon, and he correctly recorded that these "old Indian lodges" were usually "located high up among the Rocks, solidly built, and remarkable for its substantial and beautiful masonry." In a racist tone, however, the captain explained that the dwellings denoted good "taste on the part of the rude Barbarians, where most probably some of the Chiefs of the Tribe resided in Summer." These dwellings were not, of course, Navajo resort lodges but ruins left by the Anasazi who had once inhabited the cañon.

Most of the ruins were "inaccessible to the footprints of the White Man," as Pfeiffer reported, and served as excellent hiding places for the Navajos. Several ruins were held in "mountain fastnesses, three or four hundred feet above the ground." From these high, projecting precipices the Navajos hurled their curses at the Bilagáana. With great mobility and agility they were able "to jump about on the ledge of the rocks, like Mountain Cats, hallooing . . . swearing and cursing, and threatening vengeance on my command in every variety of Spanish they were capable of mastering." From time to time the troops dispersed the Indians, and according to Pfeiffer, "A couple of shots from my soldiers with their trusty Rifles caused the Red Skins to disperse instantly, and gave me a safe passage through this celebrated Gibralter of Navajodom." The oral history of the Navajos reports this event. One Navajo, Teddy Drapper, Sr., states that his grandmother remembered that "some of our people were shouting at the soldiers, calling them names, swearing, cursing and threatening them in the Navajo tongue."

The third day of the invasion found Pfeiffer and his men at a place where the cañon widened. "At some places it spreads out like a beautiful savanna, where the Corn Fields of the Savages are laid out with farmer-like taste," the captain commented. Although he was in an odd position to call Navajos "savages," he was correct about the graceful fields that lined the cañon floor, for they were works of art and skill. Many of the fields were irrigated from the stream that flowed through the cañon, while others depended upon the yearly rainfall that blessed this land.

Orchards of peach trees were huddled along the cañon wall and the streambed. They had been planted by Navajos years before from seeds procured from the Spaniards. The oral tradition of the Navajos contains hundreds of tales about how Carson's soldiers cut the trees and burned them. Pfeiffer, however, recorded that "on account of the fighting and the necessity of being on the constant lookout, I was unable to destroy them." Pfeiffer's statements are supported by the journal of John Thompson and the fact that the captain moved his troops through the cañon at such a quick pace that they did not have much time to destroy the trees. Nonetheless, the Indians still contend today that Carson's troops destroyed their peach trees.[24]

On the evening of the third night the captain camped at a place where "the curl of the Smoke from my fires ascended to where a large body of Indians were resting over my head." This may have been Fortress Rock, where the Navajos say they harassed the soldiers while they camped near a favorite watering hole at the base of the mountain. The soldiers saw the Indians from the camp, but they were so high up the cliffs "that the Indians did not look larger than crows." The Navajos and the soldiers "were too far apart to injure each other," and Pfeiffer reported that no harm "was done, except with the tongue, the articulation of which was scarcely audible." Navajos disagree and state that about twenty of their warriors were killed by the soldiers' rifle fire and were buried at the west end of Fortress Rock.[25]

In his report on the march through Cañon del Muerto Pfeiffer mistakenly stated that January 13 was his final day in the cañon. Actually it was January 14, and on that day he and his men

151

marched about ten miles, following the zigzag course of the mean-dering stream. "As I proceeded West," Pfeiffer stated, "the Cañon became more gently sloping and spreading out wider, but mostly overflowed by the River which runs in a Westerly direction, and rises and sinks every few alternate miles, until it disappears in the bosom of the earth." The cañon, indeed, began to widen as the soldiers neared the western opening, and the floor of the gorge became increasingly sandier. The rock formations changed dra-matically as they lost their sheer, smooth nakedness and gave way to sandstone, which swirled about in thick, deep-red circles.

After a four-day march through the harrowing depths of Cañon del Muerto, the soldiers were overjoyed to meet Major Sena at the mouth of the gorge. Later that winter's day Carson returned from his scout of the southern rim of the cañon and was elated to see that Pfeiffer and his men had arrived in safety. He had feared greatly for their lives, and rightfully so, for, had the Navajos not been suffering from hunger and cold, they could have prevented Pfeiffer's passage through their stronghold without great difficulty. The Cañon of the Dead offered the Indians several sites where they could have surprised the invaders and cut them to pieces. The Navajos, however, were in no condition to plan, organize, or execute such an operation. With rocks and sticks, bows and arrows they tried to discourage the Bilagáana from moving through their stronghold, but they could not prevent them. Many Navajos prob-ably would have agreed with Carson's statement that "we have shown the Indians that in no place, however formidable or inacces-sible . . . are they safe from the pursuit of the troops of this command."[26]

When Pfeiffer reached the mouth of the cañon, he made a report of his march and stated that his troops had captured nineteen half-starved women and children and had killed one woman and two men. In addition he reported seeing two Navajos who had frozen to death. Of course, Pfeiffer and Carson left written reports of these events as they saw them at the time. The Navajos also left accounts of the cañon campaign, and these are too often omitted from histories dealing with events that involved them directly.

Navajo woman. Such women provided vivid accounts of the war and the Long Walk. Courtesy Navajo Community College.

Navajo oral traditions are rich with accounts of the campaign through Tseyi', as the Navajos call Cañon de Chelly. The stories make a significant contribution to the understanding of Kit Carson's most important scout, and Navajo accounts of the cañon campaign present an added insight into the manner in which the Diné viewed the war launched against them. Sometimes these oral traditions can be verified through written accounts, but sometimes they cannot. Navajo accounts occasionally contradict the soldiers' stories, particularly those statements regarding Navajo deaths, which Navajos say numbered far more than those recorded by Carson and his men. Perhaps the numbers grew in the retelling of stories by Navajos; perhaps the Mexicans and Utes who worked with Carson failed to report their kills. The explanations could be endless, but despite the discrepancies Navajo accounts are a significant part of the story and must be presented to balance the accounts made by the army.

As Carson's troops marched through Dinetah, the Navajos usually knew of their approach because of their system of establishing sentries at key locations to observe the troops. Chahadineli Benally, a respected medicine man and historian who was eighty-five at the telling of his account, stated that as Carson's troops marched toward Cañon de Chelly "the Navajos watched them from the high mountains as they moved up the Chinle Valley." While Kit's troops scoured the region in search of Navajos, they reported finding only a few people, and these all were at the mouth of Cañon de Chelly. Benally argued, however, that his grandmother knew of a woman who had been hunted down and shot by a few soldiers in the Chinle Valley:

> The riders were approaching the woman rapidly and found her where she stood among some tall grass. They rode up close and started circling around her on horseback, and they grabbed at her clothes and soon ripped all the clothes off and left her completely nude except for the water jug which still hung from her neck. When they ripped off the waist band they saw something tied to her waist with a strip of deer hide—two small bags. She started singing one of her witchcraft songs, and the enemies understood

154

then that she was a witch and that she had her poison pollen in the two small bags. When her song ended, she told them they all would vanish at exactly noon. Then she was shot in the head, slowly fell to the ground and died. One of the raiders went to her and cut the two small bags away from her waist, taking care not to touch them, and pushed them into a fire, which was built for that purpose, and burned her poison pollen. They took her water jug and rode away.[27]

Navajos remembered that as Carson's troops moved north to the Cañon de Chelly they watched for the soldiers, who were seen traveling north in white covered wagons. Covered wagons were new to many Navajos, for they "didn't know what they were because they never had seen such things." The Navajos "tried to figure out what was coming, some thinking they were big snow balls rolling along the trail." It should be recalled that as the wagons neared the mouth of the cañon Kit left the main command to ride overland to Cañon de Chelly. While he and his small detachment rode east in search of Pfeiffer, the rest of his troops continued north and camped near the east entrance of the cañon at the present site of the Thunderbird Ranch and Trading Company. At the age of ninety, Akinabh Burbank gave this account of Sergeant Andrés Herrera's attack on the Indians near the wide, flat mouth of Cañon de Chelly:

The people did not sleep. They were observing what was going on at the enemy camp where tents were pitched and the enemies settled for the night. The next morning the intruders started moving around early. They were bringing in their horses and saddling up. Then they started moving on horseback toward the cliffs where the people were hiding. Before long, the enemies confronted the people who were hiding in the caves to which the captives had led them. Otherwise, the enemies never could have found them. The enemies opened rifle fire on the people in the caves, while the people fought back with bows and arrows. Some people were shot; some were falling off the cliff.

Then firing ceased for a while. An enemy party had moved and was coming down from above. The man named Bitl'ízhííyée (His

155

Navajos in front of Sam Day's trading post, at the mouth of the Cañon de Chelly. Courtesy Navajo Community College.

Bladder) had led the enemies down to where the people were. After more dreadful fighting, dead people were lying here and there, and many wounded were crawling around. Some fell from the cliff, including men, women, children and babies.

After the fight, the leader of the enemy party observed the tragic scene, and it frightened him. He broke down and wept, saying, "What a terrible thing we have done to these people."[28]

Although there was some fighting at the mouth of the cañon, most of the Navajos' oral histories tell of the conflict that occurred as Pfeiffer's men marched through the bottom of the Cañon del Muerto. One of the many accounts of the fighting in Tseyi' was handed down to Betty Shorthair by her grandmother. According to that account, the grandmother was a young woman during the last Navajo war, and, like most other Indians, she and her family were starving. When the family learned that there was cactus fruit in the cañon, four women of the family entered the gorge to gather some. The women spent the night in the cañon, and the next morning the young woman went outside a hogan and discovered five men on horseback riding toward her. The girl was in shock but finally managed to run inside and announce that "something in blue has come up from where we came up, my mother."

The Navajo women and other Indians in the area made their way into some caves in the side of the cañon. From there the Navajos heard a lot of gunfire as "the White Men came with *biináji̇ihí* (gunpowder) meant for the Navajos." Moreover, they saw some of the fighting. Betty Shorthair's grandmother recalled:

Two girls who went into a cave in the cliff were shot down, and they were hanging from the cliff. As my mother's group was running along, there was a woman walking toward them with blood flowing from her hip. She had been shot by the soldiers. It was late afternoon. Another lady was walking along, and they caught up with her. There were many footprints, and still the noise of the guns continued. Then they found a ladder going up the cliff, like the White Man's ladder, made out of spruce with poles going horizontally on top of each other and with chopped ropes made out of yucca that were hanging down beside the ladder. They used those to help climb up the ladder to the top of the cliff. When they reached the top a few Navajo survivors were sitting around. The number is unknown. All of the others had been killed. My mother's mother wasn't there, and my mother kept crying, "I think they killed my mother." She and her sister were sitting among the groups. A little way off a lady kept coming out of a shelter and telling everybody, "Don't be walking around over here, stay over there." The two girls spent the night there.

At midnight they heard someone talking. It sounded like their mother. Then the voice said, "I wonder if all of my children are killed or if one survived." Then she came near them. Something called chi'di (tanned buffalo hide) was wrapped around her shoulders, and she was carrying a small bag of rye, also a small grinding stone inside her bag. The story that my mother used to tell me was very scary and unbelievable. While the woman was standing there with the bag on her back, the soldiers were still shooting at the

157

men as they were gathering the empty bullet shells. Still she was standing there, with some of the other Navajos trying to push her aside. The soldiers were shooting at her and the two men beside her. The men were called Késhiini'biye' (Cane Son) and Choo'yiní (Hunchback). They were the only three who had survived in the cave on the cliff.

At dusk, someone spoke. It was a White Man who was with the Enemy Navajos. Then one of the Enemy Navajo said, "Tomorrow all of you will gather at Chinle—all that have survived; and from there you will go to Tséhootsooí (Fort Defiance)." The White Man said, "I wonder if one of the Diné survived." Not one of the Diné spoke. After the White Man and the Enemy Navajos left for Chinle, darkness appeared, and the Navajos came out and started following them.[29]

A medicine man from Nazlini provided another account of fighting in Cañon del Muerto. Eli Gorman was seventy-two at the time he gave the oral account about the cañon campaign that his father had told to him as a small boy. Gorman's father explained to his son that Bi'éé' Lichíí'í (or Red Clothes, as the Navajos called Kit Carson because of the color of his long underwear) kept the Diné on the run for many months. Gorman recalled: "Peaceful Diné were picked up peacefully, but many women were killed. Men were slaughtered. Children usually were not killed. They were taken as captives and often sold as slaves." When the family learned that Carson's troops were moving north from Pueblo Colorado, they decided to flee into the cañon and hide out at a place known as the Rock Struck by Lightning. The family knew of a cave in the side of this rock that was hard to find and get into. They left Nazlini with some sheep for food and made their way to the Rock Struck by Lightning.[30]

Pfeiffer reported that on January 12 he attacked a band of Navajos who were impeding his march through the Cañon del Muerto. Eli Gorman's father remembered this fight and recalled that it began "when the snow got to be knee high." One cold morning while his family was hiding at the Rock Struck by Lightning, Gorman's people were attacked by the Bilagáana. Down the cañon the family heard rifle fire, and soon the fighting came closer and closer to their hideout. Gorman recalled these events:

> Then another shot was heard, and another and another. The firing gradually picked up, and soon it sounded like frying, with bullets hitting all over the cave. This went on nearly all afternoon. Then the firing ceased, but, by that time, nearly all of the Navajos were killed. Men, women, children, young men and girls were all killed on the cliffs. Some just slid off the cliffs down into Tsébo'osni'í. At the bottom were piles of dead Diné; only a few survived. Blood could be seen from the top of the cliffs all the way down to the bottom. This was about 108 years ago. Our people never had a chance to kill any of the enemies, even though they had bows and arrows. However, one man was sitting by a rock near the cliff bottom when he saw a portion of an enemy's leg; so he shot an arrow at it, but all he did was wound the heel of an enemy's foot. With the few who were living when the enemies' firing ceased, my grandfather, grandmother and my father waited and listened. While my grandfather, grandmother and my father were in the cave, waiting and listening, they could hear people talking. The waiting went on through the night, with the survivors staying in the cave.
>
> At dawn the next morning, a man was heard yelling from the edge of Canyon de Chelly, from a place called Aláhdeesáh (Last Point). The man said, "Nearly all of us are killed, my fellow men. Is anybody still alive? Our men disappeared just before noon yesterday. They were all killed, and that was the last of us Diné. There are piles of dead at the bottom of the canyon. What shall we do? Our men are all gone. They are all killed. We must figure out a way to contact our enemies. They have moved out to Ch'íníli (Chinle)."[31]

After Pfeiffer left the Rock Struck by Lightning, many Navajos decided that their situation was unbearably desperate, and most of them would have agreed with Carson's contention that they were "in a complete state of starvation, and that many of their women and children have already died from this cause."[32] For these reasons many Indians decided that surrender was the best policy, but most of them feared that they would be shot if they gave themselves up to Red Clothes' soldiers. The Diné had good reason to question the idea of surrender, for they knew the fate of Navajos who had surrendered at Fort Canby. Had not those Navajos been killed? And what of Carson's policy up to this time? Had he not attacked, killed, or captured every Navajo he could find? With good reason the Navajos questioned Carson's intentions, and yet they were starving and freezing and dying. Could anything be worse than to see the children and the old people, the women and the warriors, suffer and die? Three brave Navajos decided that they would rather die trying to bring peace to their people than watch them perish in such a pitiful manner. Eli Gorman's father recalled:

> Among the survivors there was a man named Hastiin Biighaanii (Mr. Backbone), a woman and another man. These three left the cave and walked through the Canyon de Chelly [del Muerto] wash. They had decided to give themselves up, no matter what happened. They thought it would be all right if they were killed.[33]

Carson also recorded this incident, which has survived through Navajo oral tradition. Kit reported that he parleyed with three Navajos who came to him "with a flag of truce, requesting permission to come in with their people and submit." Through a Navajo interpreter, Enemy Navajo, the colonel stated that "they and their people might come unmolested to my camp up to ten o'clock A.M. next day." If they failed to comply with his command, he threatened, he would hunt them down like animals and destroy them unmercifully. The Navajos remember the meeting of the three Indians with Red Clothes:

> As the three approached the camp, the soldiers just stood and stared. As the Diné got closer, they spread out. One soldier gave the Diné a hand signal to go right into a tent; so they went in. When they got to the center the three sat down. Surrounding them was a crowd of soldiers, staring at them. Then one of the Diné spoke to the commander and his officers. When the Navajo spoke, one of the officers asked, "What?" Then the Enemy Navajos began to interpret. Hastiin Biighaanii said, "You have killed most of us. There are no more Diné now. They are gone. Maybe a few are alive in other areas. You have killed us, and there is nobody left for you to kill. Besides, we have nothing; we are suffering very much from hardship. We want to stop here; we want peace."[34]

Navajo elder. Courtesy Navajo Community College.

According to this Navajo account, Carson told the Indians that "there will be peace." He instructed them to bring all their people to him because he truly wished for him "to be saved." The three Navajos returned to the cañon to tell their people what Carson had said, particularly his promise that "we will have food and everything for you people here."[35]

Word spread throughout the cañons as well as other areas of Dinetah that "an agreement had been made between the White Men and the Navajos not to fight any more." The Indians were told "to move to Fort Defiance [Canby] for supplies of food." Since the starving and freezing Navajos were to be "cared for" and would be given "plenty to eat," some decided to surrender.[36] Other Navajos were not convinced, however, believing that "he is just going to kill us, for no reason."[37] Despite the Navajos' fear that they might be lined up and shot by Carson's troops, they decided to give up the fight. Their families and friends were dying from the elements, and there was a flicker of hope that, by surrendering and throwing themselves on the mercy of the troops, at least some of them would survive.

Carson's policy was intended to weaken the Navajos' resistance to the point that submission seemed the only alternative, and it was beginning to succeed. The next day, before the time designated, sixty Navajos arrived in Carson's camp and "expressed their willingness to emigrate to the Bosque Redondo." Several of the Indians told Carson that "they would have come in long since, but that they believed it was a War of Extermination." Carson correctly recorded the sentiments of the Diné, whose feelings were clearly justified.[38]

Carson soon became convinced that his show of force at the Cañon de Chelly had thoroughly "convinced a large portion of them that the struggle on their part is a hopeless one." He noted that, when the Navajos entered his camp to surrender, they "were agreeably surprised and delighted" when they learned that they would not be lined up against the walls of the cañon and shot down. Carson treated the Navajos fairly when they surrendered, and he hoped that by doing so he "demonstrated that the intentions of the Government toward them are eminently humane." He gave them meat and blankets and permitted them "to return to their haunts and collect the remainder of their people."

On one occasion four Navajo warriors cautiously came into Carson's camp to talk peace terms. The colonel reported that "they had great fears of being killed on approaching our camp, but that their necessities overcame their fears." They told him that "many rich Indians would come in but were afraid." Carson furnished them with supplies and asked them to "go to those Indians and assure them of the protection of the troops, providing they came in with the *bona fide* intention of immigrating." Each time Carson met with a band of Navajos, he reportedly told them the same thing — they had to emigrate to the Bosque Redondo, for there was no other policy. Some Navajos disagree, however, stating that they were trapped into surrender by the offer of food. Chahadineli Benally maintained that "it was a trap because the Navajos had no knowledge of the White Man's plans."[39]

Carson was not convinced that this was the end of the campaign. Quite the contrary, he felt "certain that now is the time to prosecute the Campaign with vigor, and effect the speedy removal of all the Indians." While Carson was still camped at the mouth of the Cañon de Chelly, Captain Berney returned from his scout along the north rim. He told the colonel that his "party surprised and killed two Indians and captured four." Once Berney's command returned, there were no other troops in the field operating against the Indians. Thus Colonel Carson "determined to return to Fort Canby for the purpose of being present to receive the Indians as they arrived, and to take measures to send out 'Expeditions' in other directions." Kit headed south with most of the command to Pueblo Colorado, and there he left his Navajo "prisoners," three companies of soldiers, and the ox train in the care of Major Sena. The colonel and two companies, along with the mule train, pushed across the Fort Defiance Mesa and on to the Ciénega Amarilla. Carson's thoughts probably ran in two veins. He reflected on the destitute condition of the Navajo prisoners, but he also thought of the pleasure of being able to return home to his wife and children.

163

Kit arrived at Fort Canby on January 21 "after an absence of sixteen days."[40]

A portion of Carson's command did not return to the fort by way of Pueblo Colorado. These soldiers marched through the Cañon de Chelly and returned to the post across Fort Defiance Mesa about thirty miles north of where Carson crossed the mountain. Kit sent seventy-five men under the command of Captain Carey to traverse the cañon from west to east. This party was ordered to destroy "all the Peach Orchards" in the gorge as well as the hogans of the Navajos. In a constructive vein the colonel assigned an artist to accompany Carey's command to make some sketches of the cañon. Unfortunately these sketches have not come to light. What a prize they would be if they could someday be found.[41]

Captain Pfeiffer accompanied Carey's command on a "Scout against the Navajoe Indians," which left the mouth of the cañon on January 16. Four miles into the cañon Carey came to the open, majestic junction of the Cañon del Muerto and the Cañon de Chelly. The captain decided to take the southern branch, which Captain Pfeiffer had not traveled, because "knowledge of this almost unknown stronghold of the Navajoes [would be] a valuable acquisition for future operations." He proceeded up the trail for a few miles before halting. "Indians were discovered on the north side," Carey recalled, "on the cliffs almost immediately above us and beyond rifle shot." Immediately upon sighting the Navajos, the captain called his column to a halt "for the purpose of ascertaining if the side of the Cañon could be ascended but found it impossible."[42]

The Indians increased in number but looked as small as crows from their cañon-floor vantage point. They made "signs and gestures" to Captain Carey, indicating that they desired to come down from the sandstone cliffs and parley with him. Through a Navajo interpreter Carey conversed with the warriors: "I communicated to them that if they desired to come to me they could do so when I would make known to them the intentions of the Department Commander." The Indians told Carey that they would meet with him farther up the cañon. After Carey had made camp on the wide, sandy bottom of the cañon, he noticed that the Navajos "had followed my line of march and soon came into camp in large numbers." Carey "disposed of" the Indians "in such a manner as to prevent injury in my command should they prove treacherous." He was unnerved by the large gathering of Navajos, which by nightfall numbered "one hundred and fifty full grown Indians . . . besides many children."

Carey "informed them of the humane intentions of the Department Commander concerning them and that a full and complete submission to his wishes was required and that under no other circumstances would they be treated with except as Enemies to be fought." These Navajos "surrendered themselves" to the captain but asked permission "to return to their homes in the mountains to collect and bring in their families." Without hesitation Carey gave the Indians leave, "stating to them that within ten days they must report themselves with their families at Fort Canby." The Indians agreed to comply, and they fulfilled their promise.[43]

On the cold, blustery morning of January 17, Carey continued his journey through the cañon. After a march of only two miles he began his ascent out of the cañon. He was probably following Bat Trail, at the entrance to Monument Cañon. Carey was unaware that he had not traversed the entire length of Cañon de Chelly, which continued for fifteen more miles. The captain ordered his command "to gain the table land on the south side of the Cañon by the *only* practicable trail leading out of this branch." Carey wrote that "the trail was very difficult" and he soon "found it necessary to unpack my mules in order to Enable them to go up the trail with the men carrying the loads." Carey left the cañon and marched across Fort Defiance Mesa, which he described as "a broken country covered with pine and piñon." He found very little grass or water as he plodded through snow one to two feet deep. The captain moved as quickly as possible, marching in a "direct line" for Fort Canby. By the time Carey reached the post on January 18, 105 Navajo adults and a number of small children were following his column. Carey arrived at the fort before Carson, and he reported that several Indians were "coming in, in parties of from three to ten." This trend continued and greatly increased after Carson arrived back at the post.[44]

Four days after Carey's arrival Carson returned to the fort. He rested for a few days and then began to write his report of the cañon campaign. Most of his comments were short and to the point, though the colonel displayed an unusual flair for verbiage toward the end of his report. In summing up the results of the campaign, Carson stated that he wanted to record that twenty-three Navajos had been reported killed, while thirty-four had been forcefully taken prisoner. Another two hundred "souls" had voluntarily surrendered, and the troops seized two hundred head of livestock. "In addition we have thoroughly explored their heretofore unknown stronghold," Kit asserted, "and Cañon de Chelly has ceased to be a mystery." This statement was inaccurate on two counts. Other expeditions had entered the cañon before 1864, and the Cañon de Chelly and its many branches would hold many mysteries for years to come.

Colonel Carson's statements in his report to Canby are very important because they illuminate Kit's thoughts and ideas, his character and personality. Carson looked on his "accomplishments" with a great deal of pride, but he argued that "it is to the ulterior effects of the 'Expedition' that I look for the greatest results." He thought first of all that the Indians had learned a lesson, because henceforth they would not be safe anywhere "from the pursuit of the troops of this command." Kit was secure in his conviction that for "a large portion of them . . . the struggle on their part is a hopeless one." He felt that the campaign had demonstrated to the Navajos "that the intentions of the Government toward them are eminently humane; and dictated by an earnest desire to promote their welfare." Carson would have been hard pressed to find an Indian who was willing to agree with such a view without coercion or who believed "that the principle is not to destroy but to save them, if they are disposed to be saved." As soon as the Navajos "understood" this, Carson commented, and as soon as they became "convinced" that he would destroy all those who resisted, "then they will gladly avail themselves of the opportunities afforded them of peace and plenty under the fostering care of the Government." Carson concluded his report with several compliments to General Carleton's "wise policy" toward the Navajos, which could "not be too highly estimated." Carleton's concept of removing the Navajos from their traditional lands and placing them on a reservation at the Bosque Redondo would, in Carson's opinion, help the Navajos tremendously, for "their wants will be supplied, until such time as by their industry they are able to supply themselves."[45]

Carson's command had invaded the land of the Navajos many times, and now the soldiers had even penetrated the Navajo stronghold, the Cañon de Chelly. Carson's campaign at Tseyi' was not a great military victory, for no large battles had been fought. The colonel did not crush the Indians with his superior army, and the Indians did not suffer a severe defeat at the hands of the Bilagáana. Yet Kit Carson's cañon campaign was heralded as a great victory throughout the Territory of New Mexico because it had the effect of a great military victory. After Kit's return to Fort Canby large numbers of Navajos arrived at the post to surrender. Thus the significance of the cañon campaign was not to be found in military action but in Carson's success in reaching a large number of Navajos. The Indians had eluded him many, many times, and whenever he found them, he had spoken through the barrels of his guns rather than through a council of peace. This was very unfortunate, because it had caused needless bloodshed, prolonged the war, and convinced the Navajos that Red Clothes' campaign was a "war of extermination." Thus the Indians felt that they had no choice but to remain fast in their mountains and to avoid the onslaught of the troops, who they feared would murder them if they surrendered.

The significance of the Cañon campaign came from Carson's success in talking to the Diné and demonstrating that his policy was not to murder them in cold blood. After Carson conversed with a few warriors, the Indians returned to their families to gather their belongings and then surrender. Carson told them that he was under orders from Carleton to tell all Navajos that the government had but one policy—removal. The Indians had a choice of either migrating to the Bosque Redondo or holding fast to their homes, where they might starve and freeze. Death seemed ever present to the Navajos at this time, for untold numbers of them had died from lack of food and warmth. The Indians were sick, and their children were crying from hunger. Everyone was freezing from the cold winds and the blowing snow. Carson's proposal of removal was not an attractive alternative, but to the Navajos it was the only chance for survival.

CHAPTER 6

Long Walk to Hwééldi

In his report to Washington on February 7, 1864, General
Carleton reported his joy at the success of Carson's cañon
expedition, calling it the "crowning act" of the colonel's long
life "in fighting the savages among the fastness of the Rocky Mountains." The general was optimistic about the future course of the
campaign, for he believed that "this will be the *last* Navajoe War."
Carleton did not realize the magnitude of his statement, and he
did not comprehend the long-lasting effects of Carson's campaign
at Tseyi'. Thousands of Indians would surrender at Fort Canby and
Fort Wingate in the coming months, and the army would be totally
unprepared for the situation. Severe confusion would result, and
the Indians would suffer greatly as a result of Carleton's blunders.

Besides Carleton's unpreparedness, one of the chief causes of
Navajo starvation, sickness, and deaths was his miscalculation of
the number of Navajos. Indians by the score began arriving at the
forts after Kit returned from the cañon campaign.[1] In mid-January,
Carson reported that Major Sena had returned to the fort with the
ox train and 344 Navajos. "I have now over five hundred Navajos
at this post," Carson told Carleton, and the colonel learned from
Cabara Blanco, a Navajo chief, "that Navajos from various points
to the number of over one thousand are *en route* to this post to
immigrate." The surrender of the Navajos and their subsequent

"Long Walk" to Hwééldi, as the Navajos call the Bosque Redondo, is remembered by the Diné as the most significant time in their past. In Navajo history the Long Walk period includes the years from 1863, when the first Diné were removed to the Pecos, to 1868, when they were permitted to return to their homelands. It is the period from which Navajo time is measured, and it is most clearly remembered for the severe suffering associated with defeat and the forced walk of over three hundred miles. Kit expressed few feelings toward the Indians as they surrendered, for he was eager to leave Navajo country and return home to his family.[2]

In November, 1863, Carson had written Carleton asking him for a leave of absence, which the general denied him. Carleton told him, however, that as soon as he had secured one hundred captives and had gone through the Cañon de Chelly he could have a leave. As soon as Carson returned to Fort Canby, he hurried to put his affairs in order so that he could make his trip to Santa Fe and Taos. On January 26 he left the fort with 240 Navajos to begin their Long Walk. When he reaches Los Pinos, he left the Indians, who were transported to the Bosque Redondo at a later date. Carson would take a lengthy leave of absence, for he would not return from his visit with his wife and children until March 19. While he was gone, Captain Carey was left in charge of the fort and the field operation of the Navajo campaign.[3]

Carson's route from Fort Canby took him south and east toward Fort Wingate. The landscape was very similar to what the colonel had seen in the Navajo country. It varied from high desert spotted with occasional trees to sloping mountains covered with an assortment of piñon, juniper, and cedar. As the colonel hurried toward Wingate, he passed along the southern end of the flat red cliffs that paralleled his march for the next several miles. Colonel Carson and his Navajo prisoners marched onward toward the Río Grande.

While he was at Fort Wingate, he learned of the actions of Delgadito, an important chief from the Wingate region. This headman and 187 of his followers had surrendered in late November, 1863, and had been transferred to the Bosque Redondo. After only a short stay at the Bosque, Delgadito and three other Navajos

Kit Carson's home in Taos, New Mexico. From Peters, Kit Carson's Life and Adventures.

returned to their homeland with a special mission. Carleton ordered them "to induce" other Navajos to surrender and move to the Bosque Redondo. The chief visited many Navajos and found the same situation everywhere—his people were dying from cold and hunger. He urged them to surrender and move, for he had seen the "fertile" valley along the Pecos River and "knew" that his people would thrive in their new home. More important, however, Delgadito told them that he had spoken to Carleton personally and that the general had threatened to pursue the Diné without mercy until they surrendered. The leaders of the various clans listened, and many agreed to lay down their arms. On the last day of January, 1864, Delgadito arrived at Fort Wingate with 680 Navajos, and within a few days the number swelled to more than 1,200. Once they learned that they would not be killed and that the government had given a solemn promise to provide for them, they agreed to surrender. Unfortunately, it would soon become apparent that Carleton would not live up to his promises.[4]

Navajos continued to surrender at Fort Canby as well as at Wingate, and Captain Carey had his hands full throughout the month of February. On the fourth of that month he sent 189 Indians, under the command of Captain Joseph Berney, to the Bosque Redondo by way of Fort Wingate. "There are still a number here for Immigration," Carey stated, "whom I could not send for want of transportation." Many Navajos were coming into the fort to parley with the captain, who told them to go to their families, gather their belongings, and return to await removal. Carey's primary problem at this point was transportation, for the Indians were arriving faster than he could find transport for them. By the middle of the month there were approximately "one thousand Navajo Indians at the post, and they are daily and hourly arriving." Their general condition was very poor, "resulting from hunger and destitution." Still they came in, and by the end of the month more than 1,500 Navajos had surrendered at Fort Canby alone. Surrender was difficult for the Navajos, a proud people who had exhibited great ability as warriors. The situation was complicated by the food rationed to them by Captain Carey. One Navajo recalled the circumstances at Fort Canby:

> Food was distributed among the people, and more food was promised if they would cooperate. Because the Navajo did not know how to fix the strange foods in the proper ways, and perhaps because of the change in diet and climate, many deaths occurred. There were medicine men, but they did not have herbs to cure the nutrition sickness. Different types of diseases also caused a lot of deaths. There was much suffering among the people.[5]

Some of the most distinguished of all Navajos arrived at the post during this time, including headmen Soldado Surdo and Herrera Grande. Surdo was the son of the famed chief Zarcillos Largos, whose role during the Navajo Wars dated back to 1846, when the first Bilagáana came to Dinetah under the command of Colonel Alexander W. Doniphan. Herrera Grande was another famous headman; Carey observed that he "has a great deal of influence and control over his people." These and other Navajo chiefs brought in their people to surrender, and because of this Carey did not deem it "expedient to send out 'Scouting Parties' for fear that they might intercept and come in collision with the Indians now winding their way to this Post." Carey feared that this would "injure or obstruct their peaceable inclinations in complying with the requisitions of the Department Commander."[6]

Captain Joseph Berney, who left Fort Canby on February 4 with 165 Navajos and 50 soldiers, was given charge of the second group of Indians to make the Long Walk into captivity. His route took him eastward toward Fort Wingate along the same trail that Carson had followed. The first night out, Berney "had the Indians disarmed, with a promise that their arms would be returned to them when they arrived at the place of their destination." Before leaving Fort Canby, each of the Indians had been given rations consisting of one pound of beef, one pound of flour, and a small quantity of coffee per day. When the party arrived at Fort Wingate, the Indians were given the same amount of flour, but instead of beef they were given

Fort Wingate, New Mexico, where hundreds of Navajos surrendered in 1864. Courtesy Navajo Community College.

bacon, which they did not like and many would not eat. The food provided to the Navajos was new to many of them and different from anything they had ever eaten. Some Navajos boiled the coffee beans without roasting them. Many Navajos thought that the Bila-gáana were trying to poison them and were warned by their leaders "about eating the strange food that was not good for them." To help alleviate the problem, the army permitted Navajos to form hunting parties to kill wild game. The march from Canby to Wingate was a difficult one owing to the wintry weather, which showed no mercy for the sick, starving people. Four Navajos froze to death during their march, and all "suffered intensely from the want of clothing," which the army had failed to provide. Carleton's promises to feed and clothe them sufficiently had proved shallow indeed.[7]

The Navajos who took this Long Walk arrived at Los Pinos on February 14. Berney reported that when he arrived at the post he "turned over one hundred and seventy five Indians to the Commander of that post, fourteen having joined me on the road." The captain received orders at Los Pinos "to send back one half of my detachment, and with the other half to await the arrival of a large number of Indians en route from Fort Wingate." Two separate escorts were required to get the Navajos to Los Pinos, where Berney herded them up like cattle into lines so that they could be counted. "There proved to be in all fourteen hundred and forty five (1445) Indians, having in their possession about two hundred horses and between three and four hundred sheep and goats." According to the soldiers, the Navajos were given "a tolerable good supply" of cotton cloth and blankets to warm their freezing bodies. The party had provisions for fifteen days, including "one pound of flour and one pound of fresh meat per day, for each Indian, and a small portion of coffee and sugar for the Chiefs."

With great difficulty Berney tried to manage the large group. During the first camp out from Los Pinos, he divided the Indians into small groups under a "chief" and issued them their first rations. The captain had the cattle slaughtered, and he instructed each chief "to divide it equally among their people: the flour was divided in the same manner." By the second day Berney had "trained" the Indians in his system of rationing, for "they would sit down in their proper places and would remain so until all had received a supply for a day." To flatter the headmen and make them "proud to be distinguished from the others," Berney "issued rations to the chiefs separately, giving each one a proportion of flour, a sheep and a small portion of coffee and sugar, for himself and his family."[8]

The destitution of the Navajos was incredible during the Long Walk; they made use of anything and everything at their disposal to survive the arduous journey. Taking the meager food provided them, they "would go to their fires, and cook and eat their entire ration of beef at once." Once they learned how to work with flour, they made a dough, "cooked it in hot ashes, or on flat stones, picked up for this purpose." The Navajos made use of the cow hides and the sheepskins that were taken from the butchered animals: "The

175

hides were worked into moccasins, and the sheepskins were dried and used to sleep on, and in some cases made into garments for protection against the cold."

In an attempt to keep up the morale of their people, the headmen would deliver long speeches each evening. According to Captain Berney, he "learned through the Interpreter that they would invariably say, that, they had been fools long enough for fighting against the white man, but now they would fight no more." The captain confidently commented that "they would do as directed by their white father, plant corn and become rich, and good people." Berney was convinced that the Indians believed themselves to be much better off now that they had surrendered and were being exiled. He stated that, according to his interpreter, the Indians would say that "heretofore they were starving with hunger, but now they had plenty to eat." If, in fact, the Indians made or believed such statements, which is doubtful, they would soon learn the truth of their plight once they arrived at the Bosque Redondo.[9]

Berney arrived at Fort Sumner with the large party of Navajos on March 12, 1864. He turned over 1,430 Navajos to Major Henry D. Wallen, the post commander, with a report that he had "lost fifteen Indians on the road, principally boys, three of which were stolen"; 10 Navajos "died from the effects of the cold &c," and two others strayed away from a camp on the Río Pecos. "The meeting between the party which I escorted and those already at the Bosque," Berney commented, "was very affectionate, and very touching." Many of the Navajos "shed tears of joy at meeting their parents and brothers and sisters," while others "wept over the loss of a deceased father or brother."

Immediately upon their arrival at the Bosque the Navajos were put to work on irrigation systems so that they could farm and be like their "white brethren." Like the Indians of old who had worked under the mission system of the Spaniards, the Navajos came "forth every morning at the sound of the bugle, with their farming implements, and proceed at once to their work." All day the Navajos toiled in the fields in an attempt to eke out a living from the barren valley along the Pecos River. Each evening the tired Indians re-

176

A gathering of Navajo exiles at the Bosque Redondo. Courtesy National Archives.

turned from the fields with a few mesquite roots that they had grubbed out of the ground to use as fuel. After a small meal of beef and flour, the Navajos retired, only to awake in the morning with hungry bellies and cold bodies to face the same monotonous routine as that of the day before.[10]

By the time the next large body of Navajos was ready to take the Long Walk, there were over 2,500 of them at Fort Canby. Of that number 126 Navajos died at the post before removal to the Bosque Redondo. Many died of hunger; some perished from the cold and still others died from diseases like dysentery caused by eating bacon and "half-cooked bread made of . . . flour to which they were not accustomed."[11] Regardless of their condition, if they could move, they were sent on the Long Walk. On the morning of March 4 the Indians were herded together and forced on their march into captivity. A total of 2,103 left Fort Canby that cold March morning and proceeded to old Fort Fauntleroy (in the present-day

177

Gallup area), where 35 more "prisoners" were added to the number. For transportation the government had provided twenty-eight wagons pulled by mules, but, owing to the lack of space, most of the Navajos were forced to walk, not ride, to the Bosque Redondo. Those Navajos who owned livestock were permitted to take them, and altogether they took 473 head of horses and 3,000 head of sheep. As Thompson moved along the trail toward the Bosque Redondo, 245 Navajos from Bear Springs, Los Pinos, and other points joined in the Long Walk. The journey was a nightmare for these Indians too, and 197 men, women, and children died on the trail. The accounts of the soldiers do not detail the deaths of these Navajos, but the Navajos say that, besides dying of the elements, lack of food, and drownings at river crossings, some Navajos were shot when they could not keep up with the main body. They lost stock on the journey, including "50 head of horses and mules which were stolen by Mexican thieves." Thompson arrived at Fort Sumner, completing this Long Walk on April 13 after a march of forty-one days.[12]

Other army officers took Navajos on their Long Walks into captivity, but most of them failed to write reports of their journeys, or, if they did, the reports have not survived. By far the most detailed of the few army reports filed on the Long Walk was that of Captain Francis McCabe, who left Fort Canby on march 20 "with eight hundred Navajo prisoners." Only twenty-three wagons had been supplied to McCabe for transportation, which meant that about thirty-five Indians were assigned to each wagon. Of course, as on the previous journeys, the army failed to provide sufficient transportation, and most Navajos were forced to walk. The army supplied each Indian eight days' rations, "consisting of one pound of meat or flour, and half a pound of bacon." To prevent raids from hustlers and thieves, and to prevent the Navajos from escaping, McCabe stationed a fifteen-man guard at the front of the wagons and another at the rear. "I placed as many of the women, children and old people as possible in wagons," the captain wrote, "and had one empty wagon placed every morning under control of the Officer of the day for the purpose of traveling with the Guard to receive such sick and aged Indians as might have given out on the march." In this fashion the party began its journey eastward to Fort Wingate.[13]

The second day out from Fort Canby, "a very severe snow storm set in which lasted for four days with unusual severity, and occassioned [sic] great suffering amongst the Indians, many· of whom were nearly naked and of course unable to withstand such a storm." McCabe refused to camp while the storm waged its ugly war on the party, and the trip was made with a great loss of life and spirit. The weather finally cleared on March 25, and after a short rest the party moved on, arriving at Fort Wingate four days later.

Disappointment and despair greeted the group upon arrival at the post, for there was a severe shortage of provisions. McCabe was given a supply of rations, but only half of what he expected to receive. He was given only a "half pound of flour and half a pound of beef" for each Navajo, and he was uneasy about his failure to receive the clothing and transportation promised to them. Their condition was made even worse by the weather, and there was a danger that insufficient food might bring on a revolt and further bloodshed. McCabe became very concerned "that this unexpected diminution of their rations would have the effect of shaking their faith in the government, and of creating mistrust and suspicion which if not promptly removed might lead to serious consequences." For this reason, the captain "called the principal chiefs and warriors together, and told them that I believed they would receive their full amount of rations at Los Pinos." He added that "the present diminution was but a temporary arrangement occassioned [sic] by the scarcity of provisions." McCabe reported that the headmen "seemed" satisfied with his remarks and "that they had every confidence in the word of the Genl. Comdg." It is questionable whether the Navajos still had faith in the promises of Carson, Carleton, or any other white man, but they were in no position or condition to protest. Therefore, according to the officer, the Navajos "cheerfully" agreed to move on to their reservation.[14]

Between March 30 and April 14 the Navajos proceeded on their Long Walk from Fort Wingate to Los Pinos. "In passing the Pueblos

Navajos at the Bosque Redondo, after the three-hundred-mile Long Walk across New Mexico. Courtesy National Archives.

of Acoma and Laguna I noticed a disposition amongst the Indians of these villages to induce the Navajoes to remain amongst them." McCabe had to send out guards to ride the perimeter of the column so as to prevent the Indians from having "improper communication." The party continued eastward from Laguna Pueblo, but many Navajos slipped from the main column, as they had done since the march had begun at Fort Canby. Many of these "cheerful" Navajos fled and made their way back to Laguna before returning to their homelands.

When McCabe's main party arrived at Los Pinos on the fourth of the month, the wagons were taken away from McCabe, who had to remain at that post for twenty days with the Navajo captives. This stay at Fort Pinos afforded the soldiers and the Indians the opportunity to rest and recuperate from their arduous march. "During my stay here," McCabe later reported, "the Navajo women were generally employed in weaving blankets—the men if called on to police camp, or perform any fatigue duty whatever very willingly complied." With an air of superiority McCabe remarked that he "noticed a spirit of activity and industry amongst them, which promises well for their rapid and complete civilization."[15]

With adequate rations and a good quantity of blankets and utensils, the party continued the Long Walk to the Bosque Redondo on
April 24. McCabe also had "received 130 Captive Navajoes from
Capt. C. Deus," who had warned McCabe that among this group
of Indians "was a notorious character named Pino Baca." Deus did
not care for Baca, who was considered a degenerate in "the frontier
village of Cebolleta where his habits (naturally bad) had been still
more depraved by the class of associates he lived amongst." According to McCabe, Baca was despised by the other Navajos, who considered him Diné Ana'aii, or an Enemy Navajo, who had sold other
Navajos into slavery. Three days out from Los Pinos, Baca escaped
with "about twenty five women and children who were doubtless
pursuaded by him to escape." Many of the women and children were
recaptured and sent on to the Bosque Redondo, but Baca cleverly
made his escape.

"During the remainder of the march," the captain wrote, "nothing unusual occurred, and I arrived at Fort Sumner, N.M. on the
11th day of May 1864." McCabe marched the Navajos smartly into
the fort and had them sit in lines so that they could be counted.
A total of 788 Navajos arrived at the Bosque with McCabe, who
had left Fort Canby with 800 people and had "received" 146 more
while en route. The captain accounted for the discrepancy by stating
that 110 Indians had died, while 25 had fled with Pino Baca, and
"the remainder I think returned to Canby or Ft. Wingate on account
of inclement weather." Although the Indians had suffered severely
from the Long Walk, McCabe had the utmost faith in the experiment along the Pecos, for he remarked that the "Navajos were
greatly delighted and expressed great satisfaction with what they
saw." This was McCabe's personal view, and it is doubtful that he
truly represented the feelings of the Indians.[16]

Before General Carleton took command of the Military Department of New Mexico in October, 1862, various agents of the
United States government had asked for a reservation to be established for the "wild Indians" of the territory. "One of two things
will have to be done with them," wrote James F. Collins, superintendent of Indian Affairs of New Mexico in 1861, "a total breaking

up of the nation, verging upon extermination, or placing them upon a reserve."[17] The Indian Bureau felt that the best Indian policy was to set aside reservations for them; to do so was in the best "interest to the whites and Indians." In 1862, Collins again argued that "the reservation system is the one which should now be adopted and effectually carried out" in the Territory of New Mexico. "If we consider it in the light of humanitarians," he argued, "then our desire to promote the welfare, increase the happiness, and prolong the existance [sic] of these portions of the race, call aloud for reformation."

The superintendent believed that it was "easier and much more economical to manage the Indian tribes when they are subjected to the regulations and confined to the limits of reservations than it is to control them whilst they roam at large."[18] Superintendent Collins felt that the Navajos should be removed from their traditional lands to a reservation, where they could be concentrated, confined, and contained. He did not agree with Territorial Secretary, William F. M. Arny, a former Indian agent, who maintained that the Indians should be permitted to remain in their own lands, where they could raise stock and till the soil. The controversy over the proper location of a Navajo Reservation was not a new one when Carleton began directing Indian policy in New Mexico, and his decision to remove the Navajos to the Río Pecos did not end the controversy.[19]

Several ranking officials in New Mexico had wanted the Navajos removed in 1864, believing that Navajo land was "as rich if not richer in mineral wealth than California."[20] Henry Connelly, governor of the territory, as well as the New Mexican legislature, reported to Congress that "vast deposits of gold, silver, and other valuable minerals" could be found in the mountains of Navajo country. The reason that these mineral deposits had not been exploited by whites was because they were "in possession of the savages, who are living on the flocks and herds of our people."[21] The Indians were not "developing" these natural resources, and many leaders and inhabitants of New Mexico favored their removal from the mountains and deserts as a means of stealing Navajo lands and establishing "legal" claims for the mineral wealth they fully expected to find.

Carleton shared this economic view. He asserted that Navajo land was "a magnificent pastoral and mineral country . . . a country whose value can hardly be estimated."[22]

There was little opposition to such views, for in the eyes of the whites the Indians were not making proper use of this "God-given" wealth. New Mexicans and Anglos knew the value of the minerals, and they did not mind demanding removal of the Indians so that they could rape the land for the wealth they expected to find. Fortunately for the Navajos the mineral-mongers found little to attract them to Navajo land once the Indians were removed. Of course, they knew little or nothing about coal, oil, natural gas, or uranium.

Carson and Carleton believed that mineral and other natural resources could be exploited in Navajo land, but that was not the primary reason for removal. General Carleton, the "humanitarian," was the architect of the Long Walk and of the concentration of Navajos on a reservation far removed from their homeland. He was convinced that such was the best policy for the Navajos. He considered his policy "righteous" and "humane," right not only for the government but for the Indians as well. When Carleton took over the military department, he began his plan of sending Carson after the Mescaleros and the Navajos, though at that time he did not have an exact location for the reservations. At the end of October, 1862, however, Carleton ordered a military post constructed in east-central New Mexico, at a place along the banks of the Pecos River known as the Bosque Redondo. It was his purpose to use this post as a focal point for a reservation for the Mescaleros, and he later decided to use the same spot as a reservation for Navajos. The first Navajos to arrive at the Bosque Redondo were from Sandoval's band of Diné Ana'aii, who had resided near Cebolleta and who had oftentimes been an ally of the Spaniards and Anglos.

Carleton envisioned the Bosque Redondo as an ideal place for the Navajos, assuming that they could change their lifeway and learn to live like whites. Like so many others of his era, Carleton had little regard for the unique history and culture of Native Americans—in fact, he would not have thought the Navajos capable of possessing anything that could be considered a culture. Most impor-

Fort Sumner, New Mexico. Navajos constructed most of the post buildings. Courtesy Fort Sumner, New Mexico State Monument.

tant, he would not have acknowledged the fact that Navajos had a religion of their own, for to him these "barbarous and savage" people were "heathens." Carleton's Calvinist background prevented him from seeing and appreciating the beliefs and mores of the Navajos. He was steadfast in his Christian belief that no religion save his own was worthy of existence. Few of the so-called humanitarians of the nineteenth century were interested in preserving Navajo culture and religion, and Carleton was no exception. They were interested in destroying the native religion and making their "red brothers" Christians. Carleton's missionary spirit encouraged a zealous belief that the Navajos should be removed, civilized, and Christianized for their own good in this world and for salvation in the next. One of the primary reasons for removal was to place the Navajo on a reserve where Carleton could "teach them the truths of Christianity."[23]

"To collect them together, little by little, on to a reservation," was Carleton's foremost desire. He wanted to take them "away from the haunts, and hills, and hiding places of their country" and resettle them where he could "be kind to them; there teach their children how to read and write." The general saw the reservation as a place to "teach them the arts of peace" so that they would eventually "acquire new habits, new ideas, and new models of life." He yearned for the day when "the old Indians will die off, and carry with them all latent longings for murdering and robbing." The general had faith that the younger Navajos would "take their places without these longings, and thus, little by little, they will become a happy and contented people."[24]

Carleton believed in the righteousness of Indian removal, for to him the war and the subsequent exile of the Navajos was a holy experiment. Like the Puritans of old, Carleton hoped to establish a "City Upon the Hill," which would serve as an example and a beacon to all national leaders who had to deal with the fate of the Native Americans. He was convinced of the absolute necessity of removal and of his "mission" and "duty" to his God and his country. His dogmatic position was based on a sense of "obligation" to whites and Indians alike. Carleton conceived that he had a duty to discharge—to educate, to Christianize, and to "civilize" the red man in New Mexico.

Few whites in New Mexico disagreed with Carleton's demand for removal, except those who favored outright extermination. Most people supported the reservation system, because in this way the Indians would be subdued and confined. Some citizens would profit from the sale of produce and beef to the authorities at the new reservation. There were, however, those individuals who openly opposed Carleton's removal of the Navajos from their traditional lands. The most vocal of all his opponents was Dr. Michael Steck, who had replaced James Collins as the superintendent of Indian Affairs. When the first Navajos were sent to the Bosque Redondo, Steck ordered Indian Agent Lorenzo Labadie not to take charge of them, because they were "prisoners of war" and thus the responsibility of the War Department, not the Interior Department. The Indian Department, Steck maintained, did not have sufficient funds to feed the Navajos in addition to the Mescaleros. Indeed, the department was having difficulty feeding the Apaches, and the

185

situation became so critical that the superintendent decided to arm the Apaches and let them hunt for food to supplement the meager government rations. Steck opposed placing the Navajos on a reservation away from their homeland, because the Bosque Redondo was not large enough to support both the Apaches and the Navajos. Moreover, he knew that the two tribes were traditional enemies and that the settlement of both on the same reservation would only lead to difficulties. Only a fool would place both the Apaches and the Navajos at the Bosque Redondo, Steck stated—and that fool was Carleton.[25]

Steck was sincere in his belief that there was "no place so well calculated to make a permanent home for those Indians as on the Colorado Chiquito in the western part of the country now occupied by the tribe." He based his feelings primarily upon the advice of the former commander of New Mexico, General Canby, who once argued that the Little Colorado River afforded the Navajos "the proper place" for their reservation. The superintendent stated that in 1862 Canby had "agreed with several of the principal chiefs to send a party to select a proper location upon that river." Many of the Navajo chiefs had agreed to settle on the Little Colorado, and Canby had agreed to permit the Indians to remain on their traditional lands, but only along the river. The general had planned to construct a fort on the location to prevent renegades from "jumping" the reservation and to protect the Indians from the illegal incursions of New Mexican citizens. Circumstances beyond Canby's control "prevented the consumation of his plans," however. Those "circumstances" were the invasion of the Confederates into the territory. Canby had to turn his full attention to fighting Confederate Major Henry H. Sibley and his men. Steck maintained that the reservation should have been established on the Little Colorado. Furthermore, he opposed Carleton's experiment, as well as his attempt to have the Indian Department assume responsibility for the Navajos. The doctor took his view to Washington in hopes of thwarting Carleton's efforts. The Navajos froze and starved while the bureaucrats fought among themselves.[26]

Both Carleton and Carson were outraged by Steck's opposition

Bosque Redondo, Fort Sumner, 1863. Carleton's dream was to turn these arid lands into productive fields of grain and vegetables. Courtesy National Archives.

to the reservation at the Bosque Redondo. A feud between Steck and Carleton erupted in Washington and New Mexico over the general's grand experiment with the Indians and quickly grew into a political controversy between the territorial and national levels of government. Officials in the War Department and the Interior Department took sides on the matter, as did the politicians. Carson, of course, threw his support to Carleton. Kit stated, "The wisdom of removing the Navajoes from this country cannot be too highly appreciated, nor do I think that any other or better location could be found for them than their present Reservation." According to Carson, it was folly for anyone, especially Steck, to believe it prudent to establish a reservation on the Navajos' own lands. The colonel commented that "permitting them to remain in their own country would have the same effect as a Treaty of Peace." History had shown, Carson stated, that such treaties with the Navajos had proved to be worthless because "little attention has been paid to

187

them by these savages." The idea of establishing a reservation in Navajo country was "ridiculous" according to Carson, who added, "It astonishes me not a little that Dr. Steck . . . should display such ignorance of this country and of the Indians who inhabit it."[27] The battle between the general and the superintendent raged for two years, until the spring of 1865, when Steck decided to resign.

While the politicians fought, the Navajos were removed, and they continued to suffer because of government inefficiency. The major problem was that the army could not feed the large number of captives who came in, and Carleton was "embarrassed" by the fact. While the general was proud to report that Carson's troops had ended "every shade of atrocity, brutality and ferocity," he was extremely upset to report that the Indians were starving and freezing to death. *"These six thousand people must be fed"* he emphasized, and clothing was needed for "these poor women and these little children." The number of Navajos surrendering at Fort Canby and Fort Wingate caught Carson, Carey, and Carleton by surprise, though Carey kept insisting that only half of the tribe had surrendered. Carleton continually underestimated the number of Navajos, and he refused to acknowledge that the tribe was much, much larger than he had expected.[28]

In March, 1864, Carleton exclaimed that "we can feed 6000 Navajoes, but not . . . more." The general was convinced, or perhaps he convinced himself, that "they will not overrun 6000." Things were so critical that he demanded that "The *greatest* care must be had of food. Every ounce must be made to tell." Captain Carey responded that the Indians had informed him that only half of the "Navajoe Nation" had surrendered and that there were an additional six thousand at large.[29] When Carson returned to active duty on March 19, he agreed with Carey on the number of Navajos remaining in their homeland, but he eased Carleton's mind somewhat by stating that some Indians had told him "that all who are likely to come in and emigrate are already in, and that no more need be expected at this Post."

Carson recommended that Fort Canby be abandoned and that the garrison at Fort Wingate be reduced. He also asserted that

Navajos awaiting government rations at Fort Sumner. Courtesy Arizona Historical Society.

the Indians should receive sufficient food to "convince them by our treatment of them of the kind intentions of the Government towards them." Carson, however, did not have any suggestion about where the general might get more food, for the army could not adequately feed the Navajos who had already surrendered. Carleton and Carson had too many Navajos, and they were not interested in transferring any more to the Bosque Redondo.[30] "They are starving and must be fed," wrote one government official. Although the government had been repeatedly advised of the Navajos' wretched condition, it was slow in reacting to their needs. Again and again the Navajos would suffer as a result of the inefficiency and political constipation of the government, and no one understood this suffering better than the Navajos themselves.[31]

189

The Navajo accounts of the campaign and the Long Walk record the miseries experienced by the Diné during this era. "These Navajos had done nothing wrong," one Navajo stated, for injuries committed against the Nakai or Bilagáana in the past were inflicted by a few undesirables in the tribe who "killed white people . . . and took their belongings." For the actions of a few the entire tribe had been pursued by soldiers of Red Clothes, or "Rope Thrower," as some of the Navajos called Kit Carson. Several stories have survived telling the Navajo view of their surrender and exile. These Long Walk stories are important contributions to the understanding of Kit Carson's campaign and of the removal of thousands of Navajos from their traditional homelands. Florence Charley, an elderly Navajo whose family lived near the mouth of the Cañon de Chelly during the fighting, said that her family and friends were

> evacuated out of the Canyon by the Army and were informed that they were to be driven way off somewhere to a place called Hwééldi. They had hardly any clothing, not like jeans and shoes like today; and, in that way, they were driven out. Also, the few who survived didn't have anything on hand to cook with, like pots or kettles. (Pots were made of mud-clay, and I don't know what was boiled in them—probably juniper blueberries or prickly pear fruit. Rabbits would be caught at times and rabbit stew would be prepared.)[32]

When the Navajos surrendered at Fort Canby and Wingate, they were promised food and clothing. The military accounts of the surrender tell of the grave problems the soldiers had in securing sufficient supplies for their prisoners. In their oral tradition the Diné also have many stories about the plight of their people after they surrendered to Carson and Carey. Rita Wheeler was an elderly Navajo woman from Round Rock whose grandfather had told her that, when the Indians arrived at the fort, "the people started eating the strange food, they had diarrhea which caused a lot of deaths among babies, children, and old people."[33] Florence Charley recalled one of the stories she was told about the Navajo Long Walk:

> According to my great-grandmother, when the journey to Fort Sumner began the Diné had hardly anything to comfort them or to

190

Navajo woman. Courtesy Navajo Community College.

keep warm, like blankets. Women carried their babies on their backs and walked all the way hundreds of miles. They didn't know where they were headed. Finally, the Diné reached their destination, but they were to shed many tears during their stay at Hwééldi. The rations that were given out were unfamiliar to them and made them sick, and many died of the food. It took some time for them to get used to it.[34]

One of the most detailed of the Navajo accounts dealing with the Long Walk was presented by a prominent member of the Bitter Water Clan. His name is Howard Gorman, and he has been a member of the Navajo Tribal Council since 1937. Today Gorman resides in Ganado, Arizona, on the site of what Carson called Pueblo Colorado. The seventy-nine-year-old Gorman heard the following stories from many forebears who made the Long Walk in 1864. Gorman's account provides a detailed presentation of Navajo view of removal:

> From Fort Defiance the Navajos started on their journey. That was in 1864. They headed for Shash Bitoo' (Fort Wingate) first, and from there they started on their Long Walk. Women and children traveled on foot. That's why we call it the Long Walk. It was inhuman because the Navajos, if they got tired and couldn't continue to walk further, were just shot down. Some wagons went along, but they were carrying army supplies, like clothes and food. Jaanééz (mules) pulled the wagons. So the Navajos were not cared for. They had to keep walking all the time, day after day. They kept that up for about 18 or 19 days from Fort Wingate to Fort Sumner, or Hwééldi.
>
> On the journey the Navajos went through all kinds of hardships, like tiredness and having injuries. And, when those things happened, the people would hear gun shots in the rear. But they couldn't do anything about it. They just felt sorry for the ones being shot. Sometimes they would plead with the soldiers to let them go back and do something, but they were refused. This is how the story was told by my ancestors. It was said that those ancestors were on the Long Walk with their daughter, who was pregnant and about to give birth. Somewhere beyond K'aalógii Dzil (Butterfly Mountain) on this side of Bilín (Belen), as it is called, south of Albu-

192

querque, the daughter got tired and weak because of her condition. So my ancestors asked the Army to hold up for a while and to let the woman give birth. But the soldiers wouldn't do it. They forced my people to move on, saying that they were getting behind the others. The soldiers told the parents that they had to leave their daughter behind. "Your daughter is not going to survive, anyway; sooner or later she is going to die," they said in their own language.

"Go ahead," the daughter said to her parents, "things might come out all right with me." But the poor thing was mistaken, my grandparents used to say. Not long after they had moved on, they heard a gunshot from where they had been a short time ago.

"Maybe we should go back and do something, or at least cover the body with dirt," one of them said.

By that time one of the soldiers came riding up from the direction of the sound. He must have shot her to death. That's the way the story goes.

These Navajos had done nothing wrong. For no reason they had been taken captive and driven to Hwééldi (Fort Sumner). While that was going on, they were told nothing—not even what it was all about and for what reasons. The Army just rounded them up and herded them to the prison camp. Large numbers of Navajos made the journey. Some of them tried to escape. Those who did, and were caught, were shot and killed.[35]

The last is one of the most common themes running through the Navajo oral tradition: if Navajos became too tired or too sick to travel, they were either left behind or killed. No American officer who guided the Navajos on the Long Walk recorded the cold-blooded killing of a single Indian, but almost every historical record made by the people who took the Long Walk tells of such murders. It is difficult to assess the discrepancies; if an officer or a soldier killed an Indian because of the individual's inability to keep up, there would probably be no record of such an atrocity. There is little doubt that the Navajo stories have a basis in fact and that Navajos were left behind and sometimes "put out of their misery."[36]

The Navajos tell of the long hours of travel and the weeks of hunger and cold. By any standard the Long Walk was a grueling

Irrigation canal dug by Navajos at the Bosque Redondo. Courtesy National Archives.

and exhausting experience. Things were little better when they arrived at the Bosque Redondo. A prison atmosphere met the Indians when they arrived, and their every activity was watched and guarded. The Navajos had little to eat other than army rations, which they continued to have trouble eating and digesting. Those who survived starvation, disease, and the freezing weather were expected to work, digging canals, building hogans, tilling fields, and building a fort. The stick-and-mud hogans failed to protect the Diné from the fierce winter and later the spring rains. Other problems arose. Whiskey peddlers and gamblers cheated and robbed the Indians and caused conflict and ill feelings. Venereal disease spread, as did smallpox. All these conditions were recorded by Navajos in their oral tradition, and many of them were reported by the officers and soldiers who commanded Fort Sumner.[37]

Mose Denejolie, of Piñon, Arizona, provided one of many Navajo stories about conditions at the Bosque Redondo. His discussion of

Navajo starvation is graphic testimony to the severity of the food problem. He reports that the Navajos were so weak that rabbits could defeat these former warriors and that the shortage of food was so critical that Navajos had to dig through fecal matter in order to survive:

> At the time of the Navajo roundup, some Diné got pretty weak, especially while on the Long Walk. When they chased a rabbit into its hole they would start digging after it. When a Navajo got hold of a rabbit's hind leg, the rabbit would just run off his hands; or, when a rabbit ran out of a hole and bumped into a man, the man would fall down, and the rabbit would run over him. The U.S. Army fed corn to its horses. Then, when the horses discharged undigested corn in their manure, the Diné would dig and poke in the manure to pick out the corn that had come back out. They could be seen poking around in every corral. They made the undigested corn into meal. Plenty of hot water was used with a very small amount of corn; and it was said that hot water was the strongest of all foods. The Diné spent four years at Fort Sumner living in a most miserable way.[38]

Other Navajo accounts show how starvation diminished the tribal population. Even when there was food, the Navajos could not trust it to be edible. Sometimes the flour was filled with bugs, and at times meat was of the poorest quality or even spoiled. Howard Gorman provided this account of the starving time of his people:

> As I said, a large number of our people went on the Long Walk, and, when they started back several years later, more than 7,500 made the return trip. Since many of them had died, this means that there must have been a great number who walked to Fort Sumner. I don't know exactly in what formation they walked. Maybe they marched in two lines or went in single file. That is one thing I never have heard. "We were just being driven," they said afterward. And when they reached Hwéeldi, which was located across a river, they saw that, on the other side of the river, some adobe or mud shelters were being started. The Diné helped build those shelters.
>
> The Army selected some of the Navajos to be in charge of their people. The captives were divided into groups. The selected men

were put in charge—one for each group. If these leaders wanted to go somewhere for a short while, they had to get permission, or a pass, from the Army officers. They were not allowed to leave confinement without permission, and they had to have good causes and special reasons. The Navajos had hardly anything at that time; and they ate the rations but couldn't get used to them. Most of them got sick and had stomach trouble. The children also had stomach ache, and some of them died of it. Others died of starvation. The prisoners begged the Army for some corn, and the leaders also pleaded for it for their people. Finally, they were given some—one ear of corn for each member of the Diné. Some boys would wander off to where the mules and horses were corraled. There they would poke around in the manure to take undigested corn out of it. Then they would roast the corn in hot ashes to be eaten. They had nothing to grind corn with at that time, like the stone corn grinders that the Navajos have now.

Also, the water was bad and salty, which gave them dysentery. They were given medical treatment, but extreme hardships stayed with them for about a year after they arrived at Fort Sumner, and they had a bad time throughout the imprisonment. Large numbers of the Diné lost their lives. A few would ask permission to hunt small game like gah (rabbits), and permission sometimes was granted. The Diné also hunted na'azísi (gophers) along the river bank and used them for food.

Gorman said that the Navajos suffered from lack of food, wood, and housing. He stressed that the people had to endure all this because the government forced them to move to a foreign land where they were supposed to be farmers. Gorman continued his discussion of the Navajo confinement at Hwééldi:

After several years at Fort Sumner, life became very hard for the Navajos. There was no wood for fires; there weren't enough seeds to grow their crops, which hardly could grow in the poor ground, anyway; and insects ate what did come up. The White Man used to kill cattle for them, but there was not enough meat to go around, just a small piece for each person. In this way, some cow meat, as well as some from pigs, kept the people from starvation. After another year at Fort Sumner, things became even worse. As they

Navajo stick-and-cloth shelters at the Bosque Redondo. Courtesy National Archives.

had done before, the Navajos pleaded, "Release us back to our lands, back to our patches that we used to eat upon. There must be still some of our native foods that were left, such as sumac berries, prickly cactus fruits, and yucca from which we made yucca fruit cake, as well as wild potatoes that used to grow along the Dzil Lijiin (Black Mountain). Such plants used to be our food; let us return there."[39]

These and a multitude of other problems plagued the Navajos throughout their captivity at Hwééldi. The Diné have never forgotten the four years their people were imprisoned at the Bosque Redondo, and this era has become a pivotal point from which Navajo time is measured. It was a most traumatic and significant period in the Navajos' history, even though an estimated five thousand of them did not make the Long Walk. Some fled with their families to the western end of Navajo country. Others remained in the eastern portion of Dinetah, which was their home, and refused to surrender even in the face of hunger, cold, and aggressive enemies. Such was the case of many Navajos whom the Bilagáana labeled "hostiles."

197

CHAPTER 7

"I Will Never Go Voluntarily"

When Colonel Carson left Navajo land in January, 1864, the campaign was winding down. Hundreds of Indians were surrendering at Fort Canby. Captain Carey was left in command, and it was he, not Carson, who dealt with the first transfer of Navajos to the Bosque Redondo. Because of the large number of Indians surrendering, Carey decided to cease military operations against the Navajos so as not to "injure or obstruct" any peaceful intentions of the Diné. Carey and the army did not authorize a scout against the Navajos during most of the month of February, but the New Mexicans and Utes continued operations against them.

On February 26, for example, "a party of Mexican Citizens [New Mexicans] arrived at this Post from an unsuccessful pursuit of a party of Navajo Ladrones [thieves] who had robbed them of some stock." These adventurers, from northern New Mexico, had crossed the Chuska Mountains to search the eastern edge of the Cañon de Chelly for Navajos. The New Mexicans were discouraged because they had seen only "one Indian, whom they killed." The captain informed them that "active operations would not be redeemed" as long as the Navajos continued to surrender. Furthermore, he told them that if they had any claims against the Indians they could file them with the government. Carey asked these citizen militiamen to end their foray against the Navajos, for, if they continued, it "would in all probability injure those who were coming in in good faith."[1]

The Hispanos agreed to return to their homeland and complied with Carey's wishes. Carey was impressed with the efforts of this group. Like so many officers before him, in his support and loyalty he rested with the New Mexican marauders, not with the Indians. Captain Carey maintained that "citizens cannot be blamed, but must on the contrary be praised for their energy in pursuing so far the robbers of their flocks—their hereditary foe—the Navajo." The captain was concerned, however, about the presence of the New Mexicans in Navajo country, not because they might murder innocent Indians but because he feared that they might "place a barrier in the way of carrying out the wise measures now in successful progress of freeing this Territory from the lawless acts of these people." Neither Carey nor most of the other commanders who operated in Navajo land ever stopped to consider that the New Mexicans were raiding the Indians not just in retaliation but to profit from their venture. Some New Mexicans had genuine grievances against the Navajos, but many were simply out to steal sheep, horses, cattle, and slaves for profit.[2]

Hispano raids against the Navajos did not end, continuing to be a problem throughout the spring of 1864. Not only were these civilians attacking Navajos in Dinetah, but they were stealing children along the route to the Bosque Redondo. According to the accounts of the whites and the Indians, the New Mexicans captured women and children on the Long Walk and sold them into slavery. The age-old practice continued even as large numbers of Indians were surrendering.

Carleton was disturbed about these reports of New Mexican forays, for he had promised Delgadito that he would free Navajos held as slaves in the villages of the territory. At the end of February the general dispatched Lieutenant George W. Campbell to Cebolleta, Cubero, and other villages to collect Navajo slaves confined in them. The lieutenant was able to persuade a few of the inhabitants to give up their slaves, and most of these people handed

Manuelito Segundo, son of Chief Manuelito and Juanita, 1874. Courtesy Smithsonian Institution.

them over "with a very bad grace." Campbell was convinced that he had only secured about half of the number of Navajos held by the Hispanos, because the residents had hidden their slaves and refused to cooperate with the government. This was probably true, because slaves were viewed as personal property and were expensive to purchase. Few people were quick to hand over slaves that had cost them so much to acquire.[3]

Carleton was well pleased with the release of the slaves, but he was concerned about New Mexican raids into Navajo country. After Carson returned from his leave on March 19, he too was upset over the "various parties of citizens" who had ventured "into this country for the purpose of robbing from the Navajoes." He was particularly irritated that some of the Hispanos had "carried their audacity so far as to steal from those under my protection at this Post." Carson was afraid that if the New Mexicans were permitted to continue their raids against the Navajos "the Chiefs and others of their tribe" would stop "coming in with their stock, and complying with the instructions of the Department Commander." For this reason Colonel Carson suggested that a detachment of soldiers be assigned "to pursue and capture whatever band of citizen marauders" might then be operating "for the purpose of thwarting the laudable action of the Government in removing the Navajo Indians to the Reservation assigned them at Fort Sumner."[4] Kit's actions would soon become a source of agitation to the Hispanic citizens of the territory, who made large profits from the sale of slaves and property that they stole from the Navajos.

Like his friend Carleton, Henry Connelly, the territorial governor of New Mexico, was worried about the groups of citizens raiding the Navajos. He issued a proclamation to the effect that all "hostilities on the part of the citizens with the remainder of the Navajo tribe . . . shall cease." The governor told his constituents that "the more hostile part of that tribe is now reduced to and located upon the reservation at the Bosque Redondo" and that other members of the tribe continued to surrender. He warned that "any hostile demonstration upon the part of our citizens towards the said In-

Cayatanita, a brother of Chief Manuelito, 1874. He fought with his brother in the 1860s. Courtesy Smithsonian Institution.

dians . . . would frustrate the intentions and efforts of the government in the peaceable removal of the remainder of the tribe." For these reasons, Connelly not only ordered the New Mexicans to halt their raids against the Indians but also "positively prohibited under the severest penalties" any incursions by them into Navajo country. The governor threatened that all "parties of armed men,

202

with hostile intentions, hereafter found in this Navajo country, will be immediately arrested by the United States troops." Connelly ended his proclamation by warning "the people against further traffic in captive Indians." All of this must have come as a surprise to the citizens of New Mexico, because their governor and his predecessors had consistently sanctioned such forays against the Navajos. Unfortunately the proclamation did not end Hispano raids against the Indians or the illegal "traffic in Indian captives." Some Hispanos were indignant over the proclamation. They had raided the Navajos for decades, and they could not understand the propriety of halting their attacks in 1864 when the Navajos were so vulnerable.[5]

As if this were not enough, the Navajos were pursued by Utes and Pueblos, who caused havoc by killing and stealing. Most of the reports of these raids are preserved in the oral tradition of the Navajos and other tribes, but a few reports were recorded by agents and officers. On one foray against the Diné the Pueblos reported having killed twenty-two Navajos and captured 1,200 head of sheep and 40 head of horses and mules.[6] The people of Jémez Pueblo were reported "at war with the Navajoes." Indeed, there were "in the Pueblo over Fifty scalps of Navajos, many of which have been taken recently." According to these Pueblos, several Navajos who were "tired of the war" came into their village to "throw down their arms and beg for peace."[7] Other reports suggest that the Pueblos of Pojoaque were operating against the Navajos, to say nothing of the Utes. In one account Steck stated that "a party of Utahs passed the Abiquiu agency on their return from the Navajo Country." The Utes reported to the doctor that they had killed nine Navajos and captured an additional forty, who would be sold into slavery. The Navajos were receiving fire from many sources that were not checked by the army. A formerly powerful adversary had now been weakened, and many parties were quick to take advantage of the Navajos' vulnerable condition. Not all Navajos, however, were willing to surrender; many of them stood firm against the army, the Hispanos, and the other tribes of the territory.[8]

While Kit was moving against the Navajos in 1863 and 1864, some warriors continued their raids and fights in New Mexico. Navajos attacked the herds in east-central New Mexico and captured stock right "under the nose" of officials of the Bosque Redondo. As early as November, 1863, "some 300 Navajo warriors passed near this fort with a robbery of near 20,000 sheep, 12 Mexican captives, oxen, asses, &c." This was the report of Lorenzo Labadie, Indian agent at Fort Sumner. When the warriors were spotted, a column of Apaches led by Captain John Cremony was sent in pursuit. The Apaches followed the Navajos for "sixty miles in one day over a sandy country" but their animals grew too tired to continue, and "the Navajos got off with their booty." The Indian agent stated that "other depredations, murders, and robberies have been committed by the Navajoes upon the citizens of the county of San Miguel; and Rio Abajo, Cadette, and Ojo Blancos."[9]

The Navajos struck again in early December, when a band attacked Agent Labadie's supply train, which was en route from Albuquerque to the Bosque Redondo. Thirty miles southeast of Albuquerque near the village of Chilili, Navajo warriors charged the wagon train. The fight was sharp and quick, and the Indians were briefly pushed back for a time owing to the spirited fire of the teamsters. While the Indian agent and his men reloaded, however, the Navajos charged the wagons in hopes of capturing two Mexican boys who were accompanying the train. The Indians would have succeeded had it not been for some fierce fighting by José Carrillo. A fierce, quick fight took place, and in the heated action one Navajo and one wagoner were killed and several people were wounded. The Indians were successful in driving the soldiers from the wagons, and they pressed the teamsters so much that they were able to score a victory. The Indians destroyed all the wagons and their contents before heading east with the oxen taken from the wagons.[10]

Other hostile warriors attacked the inhabitants in northeastern New Mexico above Carson's home in Taos. While the scout was invading their homes, the Navajos rode through Kit's homeland, bringing fear to the hearts of New Mexico's citizens. The scale and intensity of Navajo raids, however, did not match the scorched-earth warfare of Kit Carson. Some Navajos concentrated their efforts in the mountainous region of the Red River near where it flows through the little town of Questa. The Navajos raided some of the flocks that grazed in the forests, cañons, and broken country of the region, killing a few citizens and capturing a few others. As the warriors were about to cross the Red River, however, they were surprised by a detachment of troops. The Indians and the soldiers fought along the pine-covered banks of the river. Rifles boomed and arrows flew in a rapid exchange of fire. Two of the captive Mexicans were freed, and a few Indians were killed or wounded. Nonetheless the Navajos regrouped, gathered their stolen animals, and rode safely away from the Red River country.

The Navajos' operations against the whites were not planned and organized by the tribe as a whole. Rather, individual leaders of various bands planned and carried out their strikes independently, as they saw fit. Thus, while one band attacked northern New Mexico, another struck central New Mexico, probably unaware of the other band's activities. In mid-December, for example, Navajo warriors struck Fort Sumner, driving off over five thousand head of sheep, as well as some horses and burros. The warriors also succeeded in raiding the agency storeroom, taking rifles, blankets, and moccasins. The cavalry and the infantry and a band of Apache volunteers were called out to chase the Navajos. The Mescaleros had no love for the Navajos, and they were interested in pursuing the Diné for several reasons. First, it gave them an opportunity to break the monotony of reservation life, which was very dull for the former warriors. Moreover, they too suffered in the Navajo raid, losing blankets and moccasins. For these reasons the Apaches took off after the Navajos, and their role in the upcoming fight by far overshadowed that of the soldiers.

It was the Apaches who first found the fleeing Navajos. Labadie and the Mescaleros waited for the cavalry to catch up, but when it became apparent that they were moving too slowly the Apaches attacked without the army's support. For four hours the battle

Ganado Mucho, or Much Cattle, a famous Navajo leader of the region near present-day Ganado, Arizona, 1874. Courtesy Smithsonian Institution.

raged, with lead and arrows flying in about equal proportions. The Navajos, however, proved no match for the angry Apaches that day. Labadie reported "leaving twelve dead Navajos on the field of battle, our loss being one Apache mortally wounded." The Diné decided to abandon the stock and flee. The Apaches recovered most of the herd and the provisions, but Labadie and his warriors had not seen the last of the Navajo raiders.[11]

The year 1864 brought renewed raids by the renegade Navajos, who refused to surrender. On the cold, stormy morning of January 4, Navajos slipped to within a mile of Fort Sumner under the cover of darkness. As quietly as possible they attacked the horse herd, driving off sixty animals. Again the Apaches and the soldiers joined forces to recover the stock. With sixty Apaches and a detachment of soldiers Labadie was off again in hot pursuit of the Diné. They had followed the trail for nine miles when they overtook the Navajos, who were lying in wait for the party. Despite the cold weather, the fighting was very hot. From eleven in the morning until sundown the fight raged across the plains as the Apaches and soldiers fought a running battle with the Navajos. The smell of gunpowder was heavy, and the odor of death hung over the field of battle. Motionless and groaning bodies were strewn all along the banks of the Pecos. The Navajos were approximately 120 strong, but they were no match for the Apaches and the soldiers. As before, the Navajos received the worst of it; between forty and sixty of them were killed in the battle. Agent Labadie reported that fifty-two Navajos "were left dead on the field, and others escaped wounded under the cover of the darkness." This was a terrible loss for the Navajos operating against the army in central New Mexico. Nevertheless, they did not end their forays.[12]

Wagon trains, express riders, and New Mexican citizens continued to be harassed during the spring and summer of 1864. In early August of that year, a band of Navajos swept down upon the Río Grande settlement Santa Clara and made off with twenty-three head of stock belonging to Ramon Virgil. Several days later the Indians struck again in northern New Mexico near the picturesque town of Abiquiu, stealing several head of horses, sheep, and cattle. Hostile Comanches, Apaches, and Navajos continued to steal cattle from the herds at the Bosque Redondo. The headmen confined at the reservation tried unsuccessfully to end these depredations, which hurt them much more than they did the government officials. The combined forces of the army and the reservation Indians failed, however, to halt the raids on the herds at the Bosque Redondo. The Mescaleros and Navajos confined there suffered accordingly.[13]

The raids continued, and the citizens of New Mexico demanded that the army take action to prevent the forays of the hostiles. In an attempt to halt these raids, Captain Carey ordered scouting parties to begin operating from Fort Canby against the Navajos. The captain was interested not only in ending the raids but also in encouraging more Navajos to surrender. His intentions were to survey the regions north and south of Fort Canby, and to this end he ordered Captain Francis McCabe to take fifty men and head south for old Fort Fauntleroy.[14]

On February 24, 1864, McCabe and his men moved out from Canby in search of hostile Navajos. When the captain arrived at Fort Fauntleroy, which had become a small station for the army and express riders, he inquired about the Navajos in the vicinity. McCabe learned that the soldiers who were stationed there were new and that "none of the men then on duty at the Station knew anything about the locality of the hostile camp." A Navajo captive was found at the mail station. He agreed to act as guide and interpreter for McCabe's column. On March 1 the troops marched south toward Zuñi Pueblo until nightfall, when they encamped for a short while. At moonrise the captain put his party in motion on the trail leading to the Indian camp. Although the night air was cold, the stars were bright, and the troops were able to march easily by moonlight. The shadows cast an erie scene as the soldiers moved west along the valley of the Río Puerco before turning north onto "an elevated ridge with a growth of evergreens."

At sunrise "the smoke of the enemy camp fires" was sighted, and, after regrouping, McCabe planned his attack. The soldiers charged across a plain toward the camp and had advanced two-thirds of the distance to the encampment when the alarm was

*Navajos under guard at the Bosque Redondo. After they surrendered,
they were treated as prisoners of war. Courtesy National Archives.*

given by three Indians who had left the camp in search of water.
Word of the advancing soldiers had "spread so rapidly that by the
time the head of my command reached one side of the camp the
last savage was retreating under cover of the forest timber." With
lightning speed the Navajos fled their camp without a single injury.

"In their flight the indians [*sic*] abandoned all their camp equip-
age," McCabe reported, including their "cooking utensils, and even
portions of their clothing." The soldiers found a large quantity of
wild potatoes that the Indians had been eating, and much to the
delight of McCabe's men they found a number that had been
roasted. The soldiers ate these with great gusto, for they had been
without food since the previous day. The Indians who had abandoned their homes so quickly were not far away, and, no doubt,
they observed the activities of the Bilagáana. Their hearts must
have sunk to new lows as they watched Carson's men devour their
only food and pondered the fact that the soldiers were pursuing
them again.

As soon as the bluecoats had taken the camp, Captain McCabe

sent his interpreter "forward to the crest of a knoll in the vicinity with instructions to hail the dispersed Navajoes, and tell them that unless they came in, and surrendered themselves, I would divide my command and pursue them immediately." No quarter was to be given the Navajos, McCabe said. The Indians had but one choice: They were to surrender and take the Long Walk in to the Bosque Redondo. Otherwise they would be killed. Realizing that there was no other choice, the Navajos sent their headmen to parley with the interpreter. For months they had held out and refused to go to Hwééldi. They had suffered starvation and bitter weather. Their time was up, and they were forced to surrender to the troops. According to the captain, many of the warriors who surrendered said that they were "very willing to remove to the reservation." The Indians asked and were permitted to gather up their families. True to their promise, the Navajos gave themselves up and, the captain returned to Fort Canby with 112 Navajos who were later marched off to the Bosque Redondo.[15]

The Indians brought in by McCabe only added to the problems at Fort Canby. Captain Carey was preoccupied with the large number of Indians who were surrendering daily at the post, and he had little interest in trailing hostile Indians who still roamed the regions south and west of Fort Canby. His orders, however, were to put men in the field to capture them, and on March 8 he ordered Sergeant José M. Chávez to take twenty-five men to scout the mountains north of the fort. For four days the soldiers surveyed the mountains west and east of the Chuska Valley but saw no sign of Indians. On the west side of the valley, however, about twenty miles from the fort, Chávez found three dead Navajo warriors who had been murdered by Hispanos. According to a Navajo informant a party of New Mexicans had killed the Indians, "who were on their way to this post to go to the Bosque Redondo." Carey ordered another detachment to scout south and west of Fort Canby, but this scout failed to find a single Navajo.

Although forbidden by the army, a group of civilians operated independently of the United States government against the Navajos in the spring of 1864. These "volunteers," from southern Colorado, had ridden west to the San Juan River before heading south to Black Mesa. They encountered no Navajos until they reached the mouth of the Cañon de Chelly. There they surprised a band of Navajos and immediately "raised the rifle" against the Diné. The Indians must have been shocked by this sudden encounter, and they probably scattered in a frenzy of confusion. The Colorado volunteers murdered three Navajos and captured four others. It is not known whether they killed women and children or warriors, because Captain Carey failed to report such details. In his report of the affair the captain condoned the actions of this force and even supplied them with government rations. With full stomachs and spirits stimulated by adventure, the "Indian fighters" returned to Colorado.[16]

Throughout the spring and summer of 1864 small patrols scouted the Navajo country in search of hostile Indians. The patrols were of little consequence, for as early as mid-April of that year, Carson was claiming that "the Navajo War, so far as active operations are concerned, is ended." Kit admitted that there were "a good many Indians still to come in, but there will be no trouble in connection with their removal." The colonel had returned to Fort Canby only a short while before asserting that his "services here are no longer required." He wanted to be transferred to Santa Fe, where he could be close to his wife and children, and he also sought to tender his resignation. In late April the old scout relinquished his command of the Navajo Expedition and departed for Santa Fe, leaving Captain Carey in charge of Fort Canby. Kit's days of fighting Navajos were over, but, after a brief visit with his family in Taos, Carson was asked by Carleton to serve his country once again, by supervising Fort Sumner.

From the beginning "Fair Carletonia" had been plagued by problems ranging from disease, shortage of supplies, and insects to fraud. Carleton hoped that Kit could save the ill-conceived experiment in civilization, but the problems were too grave and the frustrations too great for Carson. After struggling with administrative bureaucracy for nearly three months, Kit refused to remain at the Bosque Redondo, despite his loyalty to Carleton and his

211

sense of duty to his country. He resigned his post as "supervisor" and returned to Taos.[17]

While Carson was at the Bosque Redondo, warfare continued in the Navajo country. United States soldiers and civilians continued their operations against the hostile Navajos, but the fighting was limited. By the summer of 1864, Carleton had far too many Navajos to feed, clothe, and house. Nevertheless, he was eager to secure a few important Navajo chiefs, particularly Barboncito and Manuelito. Orders went out from Santa Fe to Fort Canby to secure the principal headmen of the tribe, and in compliance Carey sent troops into the field. In early August, 1864, Captain John Thompson and a small column of men were scouting the Cañon de Chelly when they surprised a small band of Navajos —six men, a woman, and a child. That in itself would not have been a great discovery except that one of the warriors was the famed chief Barboncito. The chief and his tiny band were taken completely by surprise, and they had no choice but to surrender. Fortunately for Barboncito, the soldiers were not as trigger-happy as the "volunteer" forces had been, and instead of being shot down between the red walls of their cañon he and his band were taken prisoner. They were captured with a herd of fifteen hundred sheep, whose bodies were visibly weak, torn by wind, snow, and sleet. Thompson's troops took their prisoners to Fort Canby and from there forced them on the Long Walk to Hwééldi.

The spirit of the warrior burned bright in Barboncito, and he hated captivity. He waited for his opportunity and sprang for freedom less than a year after his capture. On July 15, 1865, Barboncito bolted from the reservation with Ganado Blanco and a large band of Navajos. The Indians fled west to Coyotero country, living in the mountains of the Apaches. There they stayed for more than a year, until November, 1866, when the sick, impoverished band of Barboncito again surrendered at Fort Sumner. Ganado Blanco met a similar fate; he too was forced to return to the reservation.[18]

Of all the hostile Navajos who remained at large, none was as well known and revered by his own people as Manuelito. In some

Barboncito, Navajo warrior and leader of the region surrounding Cañon de Chelly. Courtesy Smithsonian Institution.

respects his life and personality were similar to those of the famed Apache Geronimo. Both were great warriors who fought Mexicans and Anglos, both were respected by their people, both possessed strong medicine, and both remained hostile at a time when most of their tribesmen had surrendered to the whites. Like all other Navajos, Manuelito and his band had suffered from Carson's campaign, but unlike many members of his tribe, the great war chief refused to surrender. In late April, 1864, Captain Carey reported to Carleton that Manuelito and his band were coming in to Fort Canby to surrender, but the captain was disappointed when Manuelito appeared at the post but refused to go to the Bosque Redondo.[19] On May 9, Carey personally parleyed with Manuelito, who told the captain that he and his people wanted to remain in the lands of their fathers and live in peace. Manuelito suggested that his band could live near the fort, where they would remain at peace and plant their crops. Carey, however, "told them there was but one peace for them, and that was to go to the Bosque."

Manuelito was not moved by Carey's words. He would not go to the Bosque Redondo. He sincerely feared that the Navajos "were to be collected at the Bosque and massacred as they were at Fort Fauntleroy in 1861." The war chief refused to consider migrating to the Bosque Redondo without first consulting some of the Navajos already living at the reservation to learn of their fate at the hands of the Bilagáana. He specifically asked to see Herrera Grande, who was then the principal "chief" at the Bosque Redondo. Manuelito and his band were very "suspicious" of the army's intent, Carey wrote, "but if they consult with and obtain a knowledge of the Bosque from some Indian of influence who has been there all will go well." The captain knew that if he attempted to force Manuelito and his band to migrate they would disappear into the cañons and mountains, where they could not be tracked. For this reason Carey decided not to press the matter with the chief and his people. The captain was keenly aware that not only was Manuelito afraid of being rounded up and shot down, but he and his band were weary because they had been attacked recently by a party of New Mexicans. The army had failed to protect the Navajos and prevent

214

Manuelito, the most famous of the Navajo war chiefs, 1874. Courtesy Smithsonian Institution.

incursions into Dinetah by Hispanos. Even Carey could not blame Manuelito for distrusting the army.[20]

Throughout 1864, Manuelito remained at large in Navajo land, where he faced the adversities of famine, thirst, disease, and death. His condition was made much worse by the raids continually launched against him by Hispanos and Utes, who preyed upon the sick, weak bands of Navajos. Still Manuelito refused to surrender. As time went by, however, Carleton became even more eager to corral the hostile Navajos, especially Manuelito, who represented the defiant spirit of his people. The general was under great fire from the superintendent of Indian affairs, who maintained that over half the tribe still remained at large. Although this information had been confirmed by both Carson and Carey, Carleton called Superintendent Steck a liar. In February, 1864, Major Ethan W. Eaton made a scout of Navajo land and reported on the number of hostiles. He insisted that the only Indians still at large were Manuelito's band. This was a false claim, because Eaton had scouted only along the eastern edge of Navajo country. Nevertheless, Carleton used Eaton's report to bolster his position that few Navajos remained in Dinetah and that they were of Manuelito's group. For that reason Manuelito became the object of Carleton's wrath. The general wanted the last war chief corralled and wanted him taken immediately.[21]

Late in January, 1865, two Navajo runners were dispatched to find Manuelito and inform him and his band "that they must come in at once, that they may be sent to their reservation in time to plant the coming season." With firmness and purpose "Manuelito answered that he would not leave his country; that he was doing no harm to anyone, and he intended to die there." The chief insisted that "he was not stealing, neither would he allow thieves with his party," and he felt it unjust to ask his people to surrender for having committed no wrongs. Manuelito "had no fears and did not intend to run away." Instead he informed the Navajo runners that he was going to plant his own crops in the Cañon Bonito and that the army could find him there. The Navajos told him that the army would destroy his crops and force him to move.

216

The war would commence again, they told him, but the chief stood firm. Manuelito refused to leave his land, and he told the runners that "he wanted to die where he was."[22]

Manuelito remained at Cañon Bonito and stood firm in his determination not to go to the reservation voluntarily. The chief venerated the land of his father and his mother and remained willing to die in the defense of his land and his beliefs. To Manuelito the land was not property to be bought and sold or carved up into individual lots. The land was part of what Navajos call the "Navajo Way"; it was an important part of their religious beliefs. Dinetah was sacred ground, a gift of the spirit world, or Holy People. The Navajos believe that they traveled through three worlds before arriving in the fourth, or present, world. When they emerged into the Glittering World, they found themselves in the lands they call Dinetah. Four mountains border Navajo land on the north, south, east, and west, and all the lands within the boundaries of these mountains are sacred to the Diné. Thus the land is not only part of the physical being of the Navajos but also part of their spiritual being. Manuelito loved this land and vowed to fight to the death to remain in it.[23]

While Manuelito stood steadfast in his country, the Navajo messengers returned to Santa Fe, where they met with Carleton. They told the general what Manuelito had said and reported that the chief agreed to meet with Chief Armijo. Carleton gave serious thought to Manuelito's message and then decided that, instead of sending troops after him, he would send a small delegation of Navajos to confer with the chief. The general selected Herrera Grande to lead a group of Indians in search of Manuelito, mainly because Herrera supported Carleton's efforts at the reservation. Carleton told Herrera "to tell Manuelito and other Indians still in that country that they must go to the Bosque." As Herrera Grande and his delegation headed west, a feeling of excitement must have stirred in their hearts, for they were returning for a brief visit to their homelands. They rode their mustangs across the hills and plains until they entered the broken forest country leading to Zuñi Pueblo. When the Navajos rode into the dusty adobe village, they were greeted by Manuelito himself. "They embraced when Herrera told Manuelito he had come to see him."

Herrera and Manuelito did not remain in Zuñi very long, for, shortly after greeting one another, they rode southwest ten miles to a camp at Deer Springs. Manuelito, probably fearing that he might be trapped at Zuñi, led Herrera to an encampment well protected by Navajo warriors. The two chiefs sat and talked, and it took but a short while for Manuelito to discern that Herrera supported Carleton's removal policy. Herrera told Manuelito that he and his people should surrender and go to the reservation, and Manuelito reportedly replied that "he would be willing to go to the Bosque, but his animals were poor." There is no doubt that Manuelito's mounts and his sheep were in a wretched state and would have had great difficulty traveling to the reservation. It is questionable, however, that he was sincere in stating that he would go to the reservation despite the condition of his stock.

Because of a recent raid on Manuelito's band by the Utes, he told Herrera, it would take time for him to round up his people so that they could consider their course of action. Herrera reported that Manuelito's band and their animals were in a very poor state indeed, and that the Navajos were starving. The people were eating wild roots, cactus, and berries. Herrera talked to these people and tried to persuade them that life would be better on the reservation. If Manuelito had in fact originally considered Herrera's proposal of surrender and removal, he then changed his mind and decided that he would not go to Hwééldi. He told Herrera that the earth was his mother and that he would not abandon the lands given to him by the Holy People. Herrera tried again to convince Manuelito that he should give up, but his words fell on deaf ears. When it became obvious that Manuelito would not surrender, Herrera became angry and frustrated, saying that "it was no use to discuss the matter." He told Manuelito's band that "if they did not go to the Bosque worse would come to them," for they would lose not only their livestock but their lives as well. With grave warning Herrera told Manuelito's people to remember that "the dead could not be called back and they had better think of this."[24]

Juanita, wife of Chief Manuelito, who surrendered with her husband and was imprisoned at the Bosque Redondo. Courtesy Smithsonian Institution.

When the women and children heard Herrera's words, they reportedly "commenced to cry—as they seemed to foresee the consequences of remaining behind." They well knew that their leader would not surrender but would rather die in his "native hills." Sensing correctly that his efforts were in vain, Herrera stated that "it was no use to remain longer; that he had delivered his message and would now go back to the Bosque." Manuelito could not go to the reservation, he told Herrera, because "his god and his mother lived in the West and he would not leave them." Besides, according to Navajo tradition, he and his people could not cross the rivers that encircled Dinetah—the Colorado, the San Juan, and the Río Grande. The headman named three sacred mountains that his people would have to pass if they surrendered and moved to the Bosque, and this too they would not do. Most important, Manuelito would not leave his home in the Chuska Mountains, for they were a part of him and thus were sacred. He told Herrera that he would rather "suffer all the consequences of war or famine" than surrender. Manuelito had no more to lose, he said, but his life. Herrera looked at Manuelito with great disappointment in his face and told him that he had done all he could and had given his best advice. "I now leave you," he said to Manuelito, "as if your grave were already made." Manuelito later summed up his position when he told an interpreter, "I will not go, and it is no use killing up horses in coming for me: I will never go voluntarily."[25]

When Carleton learned the details of the parley with Manuelito, hate and anger welled up in him. His mind began churning with ideas and methods of deception by which he could catch the elusive Navajo. Carleton hoped to "make certain arrangements with the Indians at the Zuñi village, where [Manuelito] frequently comes on a visit and to trade." The general was convinced that the Zuñis would cooperate in the capture of Manuelito. Of course, Carleton wanted these "arrangements" to be "honorable," and he eased his conscience by claiming that Manuelito's "capture would doubtless save his people from being robbed and perhaps exterminated." Carleton felt certain that many Navajos would again surrender once winter blew its breath of freezing wind, rain, sleet, and snow, but

220

he had little hope that Manuelito would surrender peacefully. "Try hard to get Manuelito. Have him securely ironed and carefully guarded," he ordered. He preferred to take Manuelito alive, but he wanted him alive or dead. "It will be a mercy to others whom he controls to capture or kill him at once." If Manuelito tried to escape once he was caught, he was to be "shot down." These were the words of General James H. Carleton, humanitarian and Christian.[26]

Manuelito was a hard, proud man, and he had spent his life fighting Utes, Pueblos, Hispanos, and Anglos. His worst enemy, however, was nature, which did not favor the chief and his band during the cold winters of 1864 and 1865. The warrior fought on throughout the early months of 1866, but he was able to elude the Bilagáana better than he was the traditional enemies of his people. Manuelito was surprised by Utes near Black Mesa, and his people had to scatter in every direction. Then the Hopis attacked his band, now physically and spiritually weakened. When the Hopis attacked, Manuelito's people were taken by surprise. A confused fight erupted as men, women, and children ran for their lives. They sought protection behind rocks and trees, trying to make their escape through the ravines that scarred the land. They fought as best they could, but many of them were wounded or killed. Manuelito himself was wounded in the skirmish, and he entirely lost the use of his left arm. Rumors spread that Manuelito was dead or dying in the mountains of Dinetah. The rumors must have pleased Carleton, who had become obsessed with capturing or killing the clever chief. On September 1, however, it was learned that Manuelito was still alive, for on that day the gallant leader and his bedraggled band surrendered to the troops.

Manuelito arrived at Fort Wingate with only twenty-three followers. The chief was tired and sick at heart, for he had seen the death and destruction brought on by the last Navajo war. Many of his warriors were dead, and those who were still alive were unable to fight. The women and children were suffering the most. Manuelito's people had no food, no clothing, and no blankets. They had stood up against the Bilagáana, the Nakai, and their other

221

*Navajo prisoners constructing an administration building at Fort
Sumner. Courtesy Fort Sumner, New Mexico State Monument.*

enemies, but now they could stand up no longer. Their spirits and
their bodies were broken, and by the fall of 1866 they could
fight no more. As autumn came to Dinetah, the leaves on the
aspen trees changed to a deep yellow and then fell to the ground.
Manuelito's band was in the autumn of its years, and, like the aspen
leaves, it, too, had changed. Some of its members would not survive the winter and would fall to the ground like the leaves. Others,
however, would survive and bring forth new leaves in the springs
to come.

As for Manuelito, he was not permitted to remain in the land he
loved. He was removed and forced to live without the freedom,
dignity, and honor that he had known as a warrior and chief in
Dinetah. He and his band were herded off on their Long Walk
to join over eight thousand other Navajos confined at Hwééldi.
Although Manuelito would one day return to the land of the Holy
People, many other Navajos would not. Many would die on the
walk or at the reservation because the government of the United

222

States failed to provide for the Indians as they had promised. Many Navajos would never again see the red buttes and the deep cañons of their homelands. Many would never again smell the piñon or the fragrance of the sage and sand after a thunderstorm. Many would never again touch the rough earth that held the bones of their ancestors. Gone forever for many was the laughter of little children as they played in the deserts, mountains, forests, and cañons of Dinetah. Many of Manuelito's people left the sacred mountains forever and would never see the Mother Earth that had been given to them by the Holy People. Kit Carson's campaign had ended, and the last Navajo war had come to a close.[27]

CHAPTER 8

"Gather Them Together Little by Little onto a Reservation"

Che reasons for the Kit Carson campaign did not emerge in the 1860s; they had developed long before Carson, Carleton, or Manuelito were born. The last Navajo war had its roots deep in the past, when the first white men arrived bearing the cross and the sword of Spain. At first the Nakai had very little direct influence on the Navajos, but as contact gradually increased, the Indians took bits and pieces of Hispanic culture and meshed them with their own. From the Spaniards the Navajos procured livestock that became the basis of their economy and lifeway. They obtained horses and, like their Apache kinsmen, adopted the horse culture. Raiding became part of the Diné economy, and in this way they acquired sheep, cattle, mules, and more horses from the Hispanos. Although the Navajos were primarily hunters and gatherers, they also practiced some farming. Their economy was closely linked to that of other tribes. Livestock and food in other villages invited Navajo attacks, and, again through raiding, Navajos easily acquired animals, grain, and metal. Once the raiding cycle was established, it was nearly impossible to break. This was not a new practice; the raiding economy was worldwide. The Navajos raided because the opportunity was there, and it was advantageous to do so.

Cultural elements acquired from the Spaniards, such as livestock herding and crop cultivation, became so much a part of the Navajo lifeway that by the time of Carson's campaign the Indians had become dependent upon them. When horses, sheep, and fields of wheat and corn were destroyed in Kit's scorched-earth campaign, the Navajo economy collapsed, for these items had become the basis of the Navajo lifeway. While Navajo raids helped perpetuate the war in the Southwest, New Mexican raids on the Navajos also inflamed the conflict between the two peoples. Thus raiding was not a one-way practice; the residents of the Río Grande stole large numbers of Navajo women and children, whom they sold into slavery. True, the Indians took captives as well, but they did not practice slavery as a business enterprise on the scale of the Hispanos. Raids and retaliation were the order of the day during the era of Spanish and Mexican settlement. Little changed when the Bilagáana arrived in the arid Southwest in 1846.

By the time the Anglo-Americans arrived, the Navajos were recognized as one of the most powerful tribes in the region. The Diné had held their superiority for over two hundred years, and neither the Spanish nor the Mexican government had been able to defeat them. The Anglos felt that the Nakai had failed because of incompetence, yet the soldiers of the United States spent nearly twenty years trying to subdue the Diné. Even with the aid of the Navajos' traditional enemies, the Pueblos, Utes, and Comanches, the United States was unable to defeat the Diné. Other Navajos, the Diné Ana'aii, scouted and fought for the Anglo soldiers, but even they could not overcome their stubborn foe. Just before the outbreak of the Civil War, however, the Navajos met their match militarily when a white warrior named Canby launched his campaign against them.

Colonel Edward Canby inaugurated a kind of warfare that Kit Carson would later adopt, and its effectiveness proved too great for the Diné. Canby pursued the Navajos relentlessly, burning their crops, destroying their homes, and killing their sheep. He pressed the first scorched-earth campaign against the Navajos, and it brought about the surrender of many Navajos, including several prominent war chiefs. Many leaders laid down their arms and signed Canby's treaty, which called for a permanent peace. Their lands were to be limited under Canby's agreement, and they would lose approximately one-third of Dinetah. There were no provisions for removal, however, or for a reservation to be established far from their homelands. Many Navajos, including Manuelito, Cayetano, Barboncito, Old Herrero, Ganado Mucho, and Herrera Grande, agreed to the treaty. These men had faith in the treaty and in the author of the agreement, but their faith was soon betrayed. New Mexicans took advantage of the weak condition of the Navajos and began raiding and plundering. The Bilagáana were unable to control these punitive expeditions, mainly because of the pending invasion of the Texans. To the Navajos it was a severe breach of faith, and they lost all respect for the soldiers and their promises. The precarious peace of 1861 was irretrievably broken after many Navajos were gunned down in the mindless massacre at Fort Fauntleroy. In the wake of the Civil War came a new leader of the Bilagáana who would plan and direct the final campaign against the Diné.[1]

When General Carleton assumed command of the Military Department of New Mexico in 1862, he faced many "Indian problems." The Mescalero Apaches and the Navajos had increased their raids and had been very successful in their war against the New Mexicans, primarily because United States troops had been transferred from their lands to meet the Confederate invasion. Not long after he took command of New Mexico, Carleton began formulating plans to defeat the Apaches and Navajos, and to this end he ordered Colonel Kit Carson to launch his campaign against the two tribes. Although Carleton contemplated the removal of the Indians from their homeland, he did not make his plans public at that time.[2]

Before the arrival of Anglo-Americans in the Southwest, the Navajos had known of and had felt some effect of Spanish and Mexican Indian policy. They had no experience, however, in dealing with Anglos, whose policies toward Indians were somewhat different from those of the Nakai.[3] White Americans of English stock had a long history of dealings with the Indians. Over two hundred years before encountering the Navajos they began developing a course of action in dealing with the tribes that was advantageous to them—at the expense of the Indians. Thus the pattern of Anglo-Indian policy that was to influence Carleton's course of action toward the Navajos had roots in American history dating back to 1607, and even to some degree to 1492. Certainly the Europeans' preconceptions about American Indians had some of their origins in the first contacts between Columbus and the Indians of the Caribbean.[4]

New Englanders had long viewed Indians as devils who worshiped Satan through their medicine men, whom the English colonists had labeled "witch doctors." Indians were also seen as "heathens" or "pagans" and as primitive barbarians who blocked the expansion and progress of Christian civilization. Unlike the Spaniards, who tried to incorporate the Indians into their society, the English and their descendants at first had little interest in assimilating the Indians into their culture. There was no interest by the dominant Anglo-American society in including the Indians in the national destiny, and Native Americans came to be considered outsiders in "American" society. Indians were viewed as barriers, standing defiantly in the way of civilization, progress, and Christianity. By the time of Carleton's ascendancy to power in New Mexico, some Anglos were gradually changing their views about Indian policy and the treatment of the tribes. This change, however, would not come into full bloom until after the Civil War, when some of Carleton's policies would be implemented on a national scale.[5]

For generations a major element of American Indian policy was the treaty. The Navajos had had much experience negotiating treaties with the whites before Carleton's arrival in New Mexico, and members of their tribe had signed many formal agreements with the Bilagáana by 1863. Treaties were instruments used by Anglos to bring peace, protection, and stability to the territorial limit, which was called "Indian country." Whites interested in securing Indian land and resources drafted "legal" agreements or treaties with the Indians that were most advantageous to the whites. If the treaties did not provide the desired results, the whites expanded on them, taking Indian lands and resources by right of conquest.[6] Ironically, Carleton could declare in 1863 that the Navajos had "deceived us too often and robbed and murdered our people too long" and in lieu of further treaties order Carson to pursue the Navajo people until they ceased "to exist or move."[7]

Through the use of treaties the United States had also established a unique relationship with the Indian tribes. By negotiating and ratifying treaties with the Indian nations, the United States acknowledged the sovereignty of tribes as political bodies. Since Indian lands were in areas claimed by the United States, however, the original inhabitants had no "natural" rights to their lands unless the government recognized that right through treaties. Moreover, the United States continually extended its jurisdiction over Indian lands and renegotiated treaties, nullifying relationships established by earlier treaties. The United States had negotiated several treaties with the Diné, recognizing certain limits to Navajo land. Carleton's decision to ignore past treaties was not a new development, and his decision to remove the Navajos superseded all past agreements between the Diné and the Bilagáana.

After personally abrogating past treaties, Carleton's next step was to redefine his policies in terms of removal to a reservation. Removal of Indians from their ancestral lands was not a new policy in 1863. Removal had been practiced from the time the first Europeans arrived in the New World. When the English landed in Virginia and Massachusetts, their relations with the Indians were at first relatively peaceful, because the newcomers needed the Indians, who held the keys to survival. The Indians helped the white settlers by teaching them how to cultivate, harvest, and prepare foods. The Indians taught the English how to survive, but once the whites had learned these lessons, they no longer needed or wanted their native teachers. While the Indians lived in areas already cleared and farmed successfully on those lands, the English created the myth that the Indians were not making "proper" use of the land to justify the theft of Indian territories. Through treaties and war the white people removed the Indians from their traditional lands, pushing them farther and farther into the interior.

Presidents George Washington and John Adams were in no

position to launch a national policy of Indian removal after the American Revolution because their political attentions were needed elsewhere to keep the young Republic alive and healthy. In Thomas Jefferson's administration, however, Indian removal became a prominent issue, and the third president drafted a constitutional amendment calling for the exchange of Indian lands in the East for lands in the West. Although the amendment was never ratified, the idea was not forgotten. Indeed, the administrations of both James Monroe and John Quincy Adams supported the concept of voluntary removal. Forced removal became the next national Indian policy after the election of Andrew Jackson in 1828. Thousands of Indians were coerced into accepting new homes, and many were forced at gunpoint to remove to the trans-Mississippi West. Except for a few tribes who were left in the East in the backwash of conquest, the vast majority of the tribes were removed to the "Indian Country" west of the great river.[8]

New lands were opened up for resettlement by whites after the Indians were removed to the West. Yet there was never enough land, and the desire for more obsessed thousands of Anglo-Americans during the 1830s and 1840s. The desire to expand the boundaries of the United States from shore to shore became the national doctrine labeled Manifest Destiny. Like other Indians, the Navajos were directly influenced by the effects of this aggressive philosophy. No doubt General Carleton was taken by the belief that his country was destined by God to possess the lands of the American Southwest and to enlighten the "heathen red men" of that savage wilderness. Carleton was a Christian soldier who marched into New Mexico ready to solve the Indian problem by removing the "wild Indians" from their homelands and settling them on a reservation.

Although there had always been an Indian country that segregated the whites from the Indians, the idea of a reservation, or an island of Indians surrounded by whites, was new in the nineteenth century. The reservation system began as a national policy in 1853, when Edward Fitzgerald Beale, the superintendent of Indian affairs in California, inaugurated the program in the Tejon Valley. Beale's plan was to make the Indians of southern California self-sufficient

General William T. Sherman, framer of the Navajo Treaty of 1868. Courtesy of National Archives.

through the "civilized" activity of farming. Carleton set out to do the same thing in New Mexico with the Navajos and Apaches. The reservation was to be the institution through which Carleton would civilize the Navajos. By removing the Diné from their homeland and isolating them on a reservation, Carleton hoped to break down the Navajo lifeway and rebuild it with the religion, habits, and language of Anglo-Americans. He felt that, once on the reservation, the Navajos would give up raiding and the practice of their traditional religion. Their love for Dinetah and their pride in being Diné would slowly fade away. The vacuum left by their physical and cultural dislocation and their economic disintegration would be filled with the only true civilization—that of the Anglo-American. These were new concepts in Carleton's day, and the general was called a humanitarian.[9]

Up to the 1840s there was no government-sponsored program to "civilize" or Christianize the Indians; Native Americans were either forcefully removed or exterminated. Carleton hoped to change this policy by providing an alternative, believing that even the Navajos and Apaches, whom he considered wild, barbaric, and savage, could be pacified, civilized, and Christianized. Although it may seem obvious, it is extremely important to emphasize that the term "civilized" was defined by Carleton, not by the Navajos. To be civilized according to Carleton's standards, the Navajos had to live in a community or pueblo, where they could be given a formal Anglo education as well as Christian instruction. The Navajos were expected to surrender forever their lives as warriors and herders and live the life of farmers. Carleton's relationship to the Navajos was to be like that of a parent to his children. The general was convinced that he knew what was best for the Navajos, and he promised to make his dependents behave and follow his teachings. Carleton himself said it best when he wrote:

> To gather them together little by little onto a Reservation away from the haunts and hills and hiding places of their country, and there be kind to them: there teach their children how to read and write: teach them the art of peace; teach them the truths of Christianity. Soon they will acquire new habits, new ideas, new modes of life: the old Indians will die off and carry with them all latent longings for murdering and robbing: the young ones will take their places without these longings: and thus, little by little, they will become a happy and a contented people, and Navajoe Wars will be remembered only as something that belongs entirely to the Past.[10]

231

Navajo prisoner at the Bosque Redondo, photographed in military dress. Courtesy Navajo Community College.

There was an economic consideration linked to the removal of the Navajos to the Bosque Redondo. Not only was there a desire for an end to raiding and a hunger for Navajo land, but also there was the added consideration that mineral wealth might be found in Dinetah. Some New Mexicans would have agreed with Carleton that Navajo land was "as rich if not richer in mineral wealth than California." Fortunately for the Navajos, no gold or silver was found in their homelands. The mining potential of Navajo country was certainly a consideration with regard to removal, but it was only a minor consideration. The major reason for Navajo removal was Carleton's desire to establish the perfect system through which the United States could deal with Indians. "Fair Carletonia," as the reservation was called, was to serve as an experiment in American Indian policy. If it was successful, Carleton's program would shine like a beacon and provide the light by which future policies could be designed.[11]

Carleton's decision to remove the Indians and establish a reservation on the Pecos appears to have been doomed from the outset. The general had underestimated the number of Navajos, and the army was totally unprepared to deal with the more than eight thousand Navajos who surrendered. Food, clothing, blankets, shelter, and transportation were insufficient for the Long Walk and at the destination, Hwééldi. The Navajos were caught between the political feuds of General Carleton and Steck, the superintendent of Indian affairs in New Mexico. Steck was strongly opposed to Carleton's efforts to keep the Navajo reservation on the Pecos. The superintendent favored the reservation system but argued that the best site for the reservation was along the Little Colorado River in a portion of Dinetah. After Carson's campaign and the removal of the Navajos, Carleton tried to transfer the responsibility for the Navajos from the War Department to the Interior Department. Steck refused to accept responsibility for the Navajos, maintaining that the Diné were prisoners of war. In addition, Steck argued that he did not have sufficient funds to care for the Mescalero Apaches at the Bosque Redondo and had no extra funds to provide for the thousands of Navajos. Thus while the bureaucrats squabbled, the

Kit Carson (seated, center) with General Carleton (seated, right) and members of the general's staff. Courtesy Museum of New Mexico.

Navajos perished from the lack of promised provisions and the effects of weather and disease.[12]

The success of the experiment was in doubt as early as the summer of 1864. Many problems had arisen, not the least of which was political criticism. Carleton moved to avert disaster to his experiment by appointing Kit Carson as military superintendent of Indians at the Bosque Redondo. He hoped that Carson's stature would help rescue the faltering program on the Pecos. In July, Carson arrived at Fort Sumner to parley with the Indians and survey the situation on the reservation. He was convinced that all was well and that the Navajos and Apaches were living in a "most perfect harmony." In a report to Carleton the colonel congratulated the general on "the entire success which has crowned your efforts in ameliorating the condition of the Indians and in giving permanent Peace to this Territory." Despite Carson's report the reservation was in trouble, and problems grew worse as time went on.[13]

234

Carleton's popularity and influence dwindled after Carson's campaign. Steck discredited Carleton in Washington, and several New Mexicans criticized him publicly, particularly in the newspapers. The territorial legislature went so far as to address a memorial to President Andrew Johnson asking for Carleton's removal. The efforts of Steck and the citizens of New Mexico were successful, and in April, 1867, Carleton was relieved of his command.[14] The Navajos were then transferred from the War Department to the Interior Department, and Carleton's career rapidly declined. The citizens of New Mexico were elated to see the general's downfall, and the *Weekly New Mexican* reported that the only thing Carleton had earned was "the detestation and contempt of almost the entire population of the territory."[15] Carleton lived to see the destruction of Fair Carletonia and the end of his dream. After he left New Mexico, his health deteriorated, and he died of pneumonia on January 7, 1873.[16]

Carson's career did not decline as rapidly as did Carleton's. The colonel worked at the Bosque Redondo for a few months in 1864 before heading for the Great Plains late that year. Carson was at the Battle of Adobe Walls in November, 1864, and he was promoted to the rank of brevet brigadier general in March of the next year. Kit became the commander of Fort Garland in August, 1866, but failing health forced him to resign from the army in the summer of 1867. In January, 1868, Carson was appointed superintendent of Indian affairs in the Territory of Colorado, but he was suffering greatly from an aneurysm of the aorta. Carson's wife, Josefa, died at Fort Lyon, Colorado, on April 23, 1868, and a month later Carson lay on his own deathbed. In May he was confined to a pallet of buffalo robes and blankets, suffering unmercifully from chest pains. He sat up day and night, for his condition caused him difficulty in breathing. He spit and coughed blood much of the time and was in pain until the aneurysm burst and death followed on the afternoon of May 23, 1868. The old scout was buried beside his wife at Boggsville, Colorado, but in the spring of the next year their remains were removed to their hometown, Taos, for final burial.[17]

235

Taos Pueblo, near the burial place of Kit Carson. From Peters, Kit Carson's Life and Adventures.

Most narratives describing the life of Kit Carson make a hero of him. Even studies that present Kit's weaknesses tend to express a favorable bias toward the frontiersman. Most white Americans likely do so as well, whether or not they know much about the man, his life, or his times. Kit has been popularized through the written and visual arts, and he has been portrayed favorably on television and radio and in motion pictures. There are statues and paintings of Carson. Cities, forests, buildings, and streets have been named for him. That is not surprising, for it seems that all peoples create heroes, who become part of the social fabric of their culture. Kit has been remembered through the words of his contemporaries, such as Edward Fitzgerald Beale, who wrote, "Dear Old Kit, O wise

of counsel, strong of fame, brave of heart and gentle of nature."
His biographer Edwin L. Sabin said that "Kit Carson was not a
great man, not a brilliant man. He was a great character." His
friend Jessie Benton Frémont wrote that "all who knew Carson
best, when they hear him spoken of, will not think of him only
as the brave man, or the great hunter, or the cool, sagacious, ad-
mirable guide, but first and tenderly as their 'Dear Old Kit.'"[18]

While Carson is a hero to most Anglo-Americans, many Native
Americans, particularly the Navajos, view Carson as a villain. He
is remembered as the man who murdered many innocent Navajos,
people who had played no role in the hostilities before 1863. Carson
and Carleton are held responsible for Navajo removal to the Bosque
Redondo. Yet Carson was not a ruthless murderer, and he did not
condone those who were. In 1866, two years after the Sand Creek
Massacre, Carson gave his opinion of John M. Chivington, who
had murdered peaceful Cheyennes. Kit's words provide an insight
into his personal feelings about the senseless slaughter of Indian
people:

> To think of that dog Chivington, and his hounds, up thar at
> Sand Creek! Whoever heerd of sich doings among Christians! The
> pore Injuns had our flag flyin' over 'em, that same old stars and
> strips that we all love and honor, and they'd bin told down to Den-
> ver, that so long as they kept that flyin' they'd be safe. Well, then
> here come along that durned Chivington and his cusses. They'd bin
> out huntin' hostile Injuns, and couldn't find none no whar, and if
> they had, they'd run from them, you bet! So they just pitched into
> these friendlies, and massa-creed them-yes, sir, literally massa-creed
> them in cold blood, in spite of our flag thar-women and little chil-
> dren even . . . And ye call these civilized men-Christians; and the
> Injuns savages, du ye?
> I tell ye what; I don't like a hostile Red Skin any better than you
> du. And when they are hostile, I've fit 'em-fout 'em-as hard as any
> man. But I never yit drew a bead on a squaw or papoose, and I
> loathe and hate the man who would. 'Taint nateral for brave men
> to kill women and little children, and no one but a coward or a dog
> would do it.[19]

Navajos waiting for ration tickets at Fort Sumner. Courtesy National Archives.

Harvey Lewis Carter, another biographer of Carson, stated that "it could be said of Kit Carson that he never met a man who did not like him." Obviously, when Carter made this statement, he failed to consider the opinions of thousands of Navajos who had suffered so much as a result of the campaign launched against them by "Dear Old Kit." The old scout had defeated the Navajos, and both he and Carleton were held responsible for their removal to the Bosque Redondo. With a sort of callous paternalism, Carson and Carleton were certain that the days of the Indians were numbered. Kit once commented that "I've seen as much of 'em as any white man livin', and I can't help but pity 'em. They'll all soon be gone, anyhow."[20] Carleton agreed and added his own racist views to Kit's argument, stating that Indians were analogous to prehistoric animals. According to the Christian general, God was the primary agent in the destruction of the Indian, not men like himself:

In their appointed time He wills that one race of men—as in races of lower animals—shall disappear off the face of the earth and give

238

place to another race, an so on in the Great Cycle traced out by Himself, which may be seen, but has reasons too deep to be fathomed by us. The races of the Mammoths and Mastodons, and great Sloths, came and passed away: the Red Man of America is passing away![21]

Carson and Carleton may have claimed to be sympathetic about the slow demise of Indians in general and the Navajos in particular, yet they did very little to impede the process. Rather, Carleton's policy of removal, eventuated by Carson's campaign, accelerated the physical and spiritual decline of Indian peoples. Such was the sense of mission and national destiny held by these men and their government.

According to Carson, Carleton, and other observers of the Indians, America's native people were quickly vanishing from the earth. They believed that the Indians would either be exterminated or be transformed into white people through acculturation. They believed that over the years the Indians would lose their distinguishing color, languages, religions, and culture. In other words, the Indians would cease to exist, through extinction or assimilation. Such beliefs were at the heart of certain basic assumptions held by Carson and Carleton. Both men believed that the white tide was too strong to be held back and that the Indians were too weak to check their own ultimate destruction. They had no faith in the Indians' survival, but in that they were wrong. Indians have been changed and their lifeways have been altered by the white men, but they have not disappeared. There are still Indians, and there are still Navajos, despite the destructive policy and mistaken beliefs of men like Carson and Carleton.

Fortunately for the Navajos, the grand experiment at the Bosque Redondo came to an end in 1868 as a result of the many difficulties associated with operating the reservation, particularly the high cost of maintenance. In April, 1868, Manuelito, Barboncito, and other prominent Navajo headmen journeyed to Washington to confer with President Andrew Johnson. Their message was simple: they asked to return to their traditional lands. The president did not commit himself to any course of action, saying only that a national

peace commission would decide the fate of the Diné. Upon returning to New Mexico, Manuelito and Barboncito urged their people
to bolt the reservation if the peace commission refused to allow
them to return to Dinetah. By the time General William T. Sherman and Samuel Tappan, representatives of the peace commission,
arrived in the territory, they had already decided to remove the
Navajos from the Bosque Redondo if the Diné were peaceful; if
they were hostile, however, the commissioners would recommend
that they be sent to Indian Territory (present-day Oklahoma).

Sherman was shocked by the wretched condition of the reservation and the plight of the Navajos. He wrote, "I found the Bosque
a mere spot of green grass in the midst of a wild desert, and that
the Navajos had sunk into a condition of absolute poverty and
despair." Agent Theodore H. Dodd spoke to Sherman in behalf of
his charges, stating that most had remained peaceful and indus-
trious throughout their forced captivity. The agent argued that the
Navajos should be sent back to their lands. Sherman was probably
inclined to agree with Dodd, but he decided to wait and talk to the
Navajos before reaching a decision.[22]

Meanwhile, the Navajos were well aware of the developing
events surrounding the visit of the peace commission, and they
were confident that the general would recommend that they be
returned to their homeland. Days before the arrival of the commission the Diné had held a Coyote Ceremony. In this ceremony
a group of Indians encircled a coyote. Barboncito approached the
coyote and placed a white shell bead in the animal's mouth. The
coyote had powerful medicine and would walk in the direction in
which the Navajos would be asked to go. The coyote slowly moved
west and was permitted to leave the encirclement, thus indicating
that the Navajos would be allowed to go home.[23]

The Navajos held their first parley with Sherman and Tappan
on May 28, 1868. Sherman opened the session by stating that he
knew of the Navajo Wars and the removal of the Diné. He commented that, although the Navajos had worked hard, little progress
had been made at the reservation. He asked what the Navajos
thought of the reservation.

Coyote Way Ceremony at the Bosque Redondo. Sketch by Ray Johnson.
Courtesy Navajo Community College.

Barboncito was the principal spokesman for the tribe, and he addressed the commission with poise and confidence:

> The bringing of us here has caused a great decrease of our numbers, many of us have died, also a great number of our animals. Our Grandfathers had no idea of living in any other country except our own and I do not think it right for us to do so as we were never taught to. When the Navajos were first created four mountains and four rivers were pointed out to us, inside of which we should live, that was to be our country and was given to us by the first woman of the Navajo tribe. It was told to us by our forefathers, that we were never to move east of the Rio Grande or west of the San Juan rivers, and I think that our coming here has been the cause of so much death among us and our animals.[24]

Barboncito further explained how sacred Dinetah was to the Navajos and how destructive the reservation life had been to his people. "We have all declared that we do not want to remain here," Barboncito said, and as for himself, he stated, "Before I am sick or older I want to go and see the place where I was born." With utmost confidence the headman said to Sherman, "I am speaking to you now as if I was speaking to a spirit and I wish you to tell me when you are going to take us to our country."[25]

The negotiations continued. Sherman proposed that the Navajos be resettled in Indian Territory. Sherman maintained that if the Navajos wanted to go to Indian Territory they would "get a piece of land" to call their own. He continued: "Our proposition now is to send some of you at the Government expense to the Indian Territory south of Kansas or if you want to go to your own country you will be sent but not to the whole of it, only a portion which must be well defined."

Barboncito expressed the feelings of his people when he said, "I hope to God you will not ask me to go to any other country except my own." Sherman met with the Diné again on May 29 and told them that they would be returned to Dinetah. All the Navajos were filled with joy over this news, and Barboncito thanked the commissioners on behalf of his people. The chief looked forward to the

*A gathering of Navajos on the reservation after their return from the
Bosque Redondo. Courtesy Navajo Community College.*

near future, when his people would again reside in their beloved
Dinetah: "After we get back to our country it will brighten up
again and the Navajos will be as happy as the land, black clouds
will rise and there will be plenty of rain. Corn will grow in abundance and everything look happy."[26]

With joy in his voice, Barboncito spoke firmly to General Sherman, stating that "what you have said to me now I never will
forget." Barboncito never forgot, and his people never forgot. On
June 1, twenty-nine Navajo leaders signed the Treaty Between the
United States of America and the Navajo Tribe of Indians. Ratifi-
cation was advised on July 25, and the treaty was proclaimed on
August 12, 1868. On the same day the Navajos signed the agree-

243

ment, the order was given to prepare for their removal, and by the middle of June the first group of Navajos had started their Long Walk back to the lands that held the bones of their ancestors. As the Navajos approached Albuquerque, they saw Mount Taylor in the distance. Manuelito later said that "we wondered if it was our mountain, and we felt like talking to the ground, we loved it so." Onward the Navajos marched, closer and closer to their homeland, and when they reached their Mother Earth, "some of the old men and women cried with joy."[27] After years of misery and sorrow, the Diné had finally come home to their hills and cañons, their forests and mountains. They had come home to their beloved Dinetah.

Abbreviations Used in Notes

NA   National Archives
OAG   Office of Adjutant General
RG   Record Group
LR   Letters Received
LS   Letters Sent
RCA   Records of the Commands of the United States Army
NMS   New Mexico Superintendency
CIA   Commissioner of Indian Affairs
AAG   Assistant Adjutant General
OR   Official Records of Union and Confederate Armies
SED   *Senate Executive Document*
HED   *House Executive Document*
SS   Serial Set
AGO   Adjutant General's Office

Notes

Chapter 1

1. For general sources dealing with the anthropological and Navajo views of creation, see Ethelou Yazzie, *Navajo History;* Ruth Underhill, *The Navajos.*

2. Herbert Eugene Bolton, *Coronado: Knight of Pueblos and Plains,* pp. 246-47.

3. Jack D. Forbes, *Apache, Navaho, and Spaniard,* p. 91; Underhill, *The Navajos,* p. 4.

4. Donald E. Worcester, "The Navaho During the Spanish Regime in New Mexico," *New Mexico Historical Review* 26 (1951):103-104.

5. Frank McNitt, *The Navajo Wars,* pp. 12-14.

6. Ibid., pp. 18-23. According to McNitt, the quotation by Governor Francisco Cuervo y Valdez was taken from an unpublished journal dated 1705 and written by Captain Roque de Madrid. See Madrid, "Journal of a Campaign Which Maestro de Campo Roque Madrid Made Against the Navajo Indians, by Order of Governor Don Francisco Cuerbo y Valdes, Year 1705" (Peabody Museum, Cambridge, Mass.).

7. For a better understanding of Navajo warfare, see W. W. Hill, *Navaho Warfare.*

8. J. Lee Correll, *Sandoval — Traitor or Patriot?* See also McNitt, *The Navajo Wars,* pp. 48-50.

9. Thomas James, *Three Years Among the Indians and Mexicans,* pp. 184-85.

10. "Report of a Meeting Between Vizcarra and the Navajos, Camp at Paguate, February 12, 1823" (Manuscript, New Mexico State Records Center and Archives), as cited in Myra Ellen Jenkins and Ward Allen Minge, "Record of Navajo Activities Affecting the Acoma-Laguna Area, 1746-1910" (United States Indian Claims Commission, Dockets 226-27, National Archives).

11. Ibid.

12. José Antonio Vizcarra, "Vizcarra's Navajo Campaign of 1823," trans. and ed. David Brugge, *Arizona and the West* 6 (1964).

13. Ibid.; for a further study of Indian slavery see David M. Brugge, *Navajos in the Catholic Church Records of New Mexico, 1694-1875;* see also Lynn R. Bailey, *Indian Slave Trade in the Southwest.*

14. This statement was made by George C. Sibley, one of three American commissioners sent by President John Quincy Adams to mark the Santa Fe Trail. See Buford Rowland, ed., "Report of the Commissioners on the Road from Missouri to New Mexico, October, 1927," *New Mexico Historical Review* 14 (1939):220.

15. Chief Sandoval was first called Cebolla, then Cebolla Sandoval, and then Antonio Sandoval. For an excellent survey of his activities, see McNitt, *The Navajo Wars,* pp. 71-73, 83-91.

16. James D. Richard, comp., *A Compilation of the Messages of the Presidents,* 4:442.

17. George R. Gibson, *Journal of a Soldier Under Kearny and Doniphan, 1846-47,* ed. Ralph Bieber, pp. 75-76; William E. Connelley, *Doniphan's Expedition and the Conquest of New Mexico and California,* p. 138.

18. Jacob S. Robinson, *A Journal of the Santa Fe Expedition Under Colonel Doniphan,* pp. 35-40; Marcellus B. Edwards, *Marching with the Army of the West,* ed. Ralph Bieber (Glendale, Calif., 1936), pp. 183-84.

19. Robinson, *A Journal of the Santa Fe Expedition,* p. 43.

20. Ibid., pp. 49-50.

21. Ibid., pp. 46-47, 50.

22. John T. Hughes, *Doniphan's Expeditions; Containing an Account of the Conquest of Mexico* (Cincinnati, 1847), p. 185.

23. Ibid., p. 187.

24. Ibid., pp. 188-89.

25. *Santa Fe Republican,* September 10, 1847.

26. Ibid., April 2, 1848.

27. Newby to Jones, June 17, 1848, National Archives, Office of Adjutant General, Record Group 94, Letters Received; hereafter cited as NA, OAG, RG, LR.

28. James S. Calhoun was a staunch Whig who had served during the Mexican War as a captain in the Georgia Volunteers. He received the appointment as the Indian agent of New Mexico by President Zachary Taylor, and he was inaugurated governor of the territory on March 3, 1851. For the best source on Calhoun see Annie H. Abel, comp. and ed., *Official Correspondence of James S. Calhoun While Indian Agent at Santa Fe and Superintendent of Indian Affairs in New Mexico;* hereafter cited as *Calhoun Correspondence.* For particulars regarding Calhoun's first days as Indian agent, see Medill to

Ewing, March 28, 1849; Medill to Calhoun, April 7, 1849; and Calhoun to Medill, October 4, 1849, all in *Calhoun Correspondence.*

29. Details of the tragedy can be found in Frank McNitt, ed., *Navaho Expedition: Journal of a Military Reconnaissance from Santa Fe, New Mexico, to the Navaho Country Made in 1849 by Lieutenant James H. Simpson,* pp. 61-67, 87-89. See also Calhoun to Medill, September 25, October 1, and October 29, 1849, in *Calhoun Correspondence.*

30. Proclamation of Governor Calhoun, March 19, 1851, and Proposal of Manuel Chaves, March 18, 1851, in *Calhoun Correspondence.*

31. Buford to McLaws, June 10, 1850, NA, Records of the Commands of the United States Army's Department of New Mexico (RCA), RG 98, LR; Calhoun to Lea, March 31, 1851, *Calhoun Correspondence;* Lancing P. Bloom, ed., "The Reverend Hiram Read, Baptist Missionary to New Mexico," *New Mexico Historical Review* 17 (1942):153.

32. Calhoun to Brown, June 12, January 25, 1850 *Calhoun Correspondence;* Frank D. Reeve, "The Government and the Navaho, 1846-1858," *New Mexico Historical Review* 14 (1939):86.

33. Conrad to Calhoun, April 1, 1851, and Sumner to Jones, October 24, 1851, *Calhoun Correspondence.* See Also Fort Defiance Post Returns, September, 1851, NA, RCA, RG 98.

34. Calhoun to Wingfield, September 17, 1851, and Sumner to Jones, November 20, 1851, *Calhoun Correspondence.*

35. Greiner to Calhoun, January 31, 1852, ibid.

36. Greiner to Lane, n.d., New Mexico Superintendency Papers (NMS), NA.

37. Lane to Vigil, May 9, 1853, and Vigil to Lane, May 25, 1853, NA, NMS; see also Kendrick to Sturgis, NA, RCA, RG 393.

38. Excellent accounts of Dodge's career can be found in his biographical file in the Arizona Historical Society, Tucson; McNitt, *The Navajo Wars,* pp. 224-36, 243-50, 286-97; Lynn R. Bailey, *The Long Walk: A History of the Navajo Wars, 1846-1868,* pp. 15-17, 51-57, 71-78.

39. Brooks to Nichols, July 22, Garland to Brooks, July 26, Miles to Nichols, August 26, 1858, NA, RCA, LR and LS; see also Collins to Commissioner of Indian Affairs (CIA), July 31, 1858, Collins to Yost, August 13, 1858, and Yost to Collins, September 3, 1858, NA, NMS.

40. For details of the treaty, see Collins to Mix, November 29, and Collins to Yost, December 1, 1858, NA, NMS.

41. Yost's letter, dated December 21, 1858, can be found in the *Santa Fe New Mexican.* Information regarding the Utes can be found in the following letters: Pfeiffer to Collins, May 6 and May 15, and Connelly to Collins, May 13, 1859, NA, NMS, LR.

42. Kendrick to Collins, September 24, Kendrick to Greenwood, October 4,

and Kendrick to Shepherd, October 25, 1859, NA, NMS. See also Kendrick to Collins, January 6, 1860, Kendrick's Report Navajo Affairs, 1859-1860, February 25, 1860, NA, NMS.

43. Kendrick to Collins, January 23, 1860, NA, NMS and Shepherd to Wilkins, January 17, 1860, NA, RCA, RG 393, LR.

44. Shepherd to Wilkins, February 14, 1860, NA, RCA, RG 393, LR.

45. Fort Defiance Post Returns, April, 1860; see also Shepherd to Wilkins, May 7, 1860, NA, RCA, RG 98, LR.

46. Ibid.

47. Fauntleroy to Thomas, May 20, 1860, NA, RCA, RG 393, LS; Maury to Collins, September 4, 1860, and Collins to Maury, September 5, 1860, NA, NMS, LR.

48. Canby to Assistant Adjutant General (AAG), November 17, 1860, NA, RCA, RG 393, LR; Canby to AAG, November 8, 1860, NA, RCA, RG 393, LR. For excellent secondary accounts of Canby's campaign see McNitt, *The Navajo Wars,* pp. 391-409; Bailey, *The Long Walk,* pp. 127-39.

49. See Canby's correspondence to AAG, January 14, February 6, 27, March 11, 18, 1861, NA, NMS, LR.

Chapter 2

1. Edwin L. Sabin, *Kit Carson Days, 1809-1868: Adventures in the Path of Empire,* pp. 813-15; Harvey Lewis Carter, *"Dear Old Kit": The Historical Christopher Carson,* pp. 179-216.

2. For general accounts of the Confederate invasion of the Southwest, see William A. Keleher, *Turmoil in New Mexico, 1846-1868;* Robert L. Kerby, *The Confederate Invasion of New Mexico and Arizona, 1861-1862;* Ray C. Colton, *The Civil War in the Western Territories;* Hubert H. Bancroft, *History of Arizona and New Mexico* (San Francisco, 1889).

3. Report of Major Rafael Chacon, November 30, 1911, in Sabin, *Kit Carson Days,* pp. 843-46.

4. The account is that of Colonel Joseph McClellam in General Theodore F. Rodenbough, *From Everglade to Cañon with the Second United States Cavalry: An Authentic Account of Service in Florida, Mexico, Virginia, and the Indian Country, Including the Personal Recollections of Prominent Officers; with an Appendix Containing Orders, Reports and Correspondence, Military Records, etc., etc., etc., 1836-1875,* p. 239.

5. Report of Carson to Canby, February 26, 1862, in U.S. Department of War, *War of the Rebellion: A Compilation of the Official Records of Union and Confederate Armies,* ser. 1, vol. 9, pp. 489-90, 495, 514, 518-19; hereafter cited as OR.

6. Sabin, *Kit Carson Days,* pp. 693-700, 843-48.

7. For further details of Carleton's life see Aurora Hunt, *Major General James H. Carleton.*

8. Dole to Smith, November 27, 1861, in Annual Report of the Commissioner of Indian Affairs, *Senate Executive Document,* 37th Cong., 2d Sess., no. 1, vol. 1, Serial Set 1117; hereafter cited as *SED,* SS.

9. Collins to Dole, October 8, 1861, ibid.

10. Labadie to Collins, October 25, 1862, in Annual Report of the Commissioner of Indian Affairs, *House Executive Document* 37th Cong., 3d Sess., no. 1, vol. 2, SS 1157; hereafter cited as *HED.*

11. Carleton to Carson, October 12, 1862, NA, RCA, RG 393, LS.

12. The reports of the killings can be found in RCA, RG 393, LR for October 23, 24, 1862. See also Sabin, *Kit Carson Days,* p. 704.

13. J. P. Dunn, *Massacres of the Mountains: A History of the Indian Wars of the Far West, 1815-1875,* p. 383.

14. Carleton to Thomas, March 19, 1863, in Sabin, *Kit Carson Days,* p. 706.

15. Collins to Greenwood, March 3, 1861, NA, NMS; *Santa Fe Gazette,* March 2, 1861.

16. Canby to AAG, NA, RCA, RG 393, LR.

17. Proclamation to the People of New Mexico by Henry Connelly, September 14, 1862. *HED* 37th Cong., 3d Sess., no. 1, vol. 2, SS 1157.

18. Need to Collins, May 16, 1862, NA, NMS, Miscellaneous Correspondence (MC).

19. Ibid.

20. For an in-depth look at the situation at the fort see Marc Simmons, "Horse Race at Fort Fauntleroy: An Incident of the Navajo Wars," *La Gaceta* 5 (1970).

21. An over-all view of the massacre can be found in McNitt, *The Navajo Wars,* pp. 422-29. For the best primary source, see "Condition of the Indian Tribes," *SED,* 39th Cong., 2d Sess., no. 156, pp. 331-41; hereafter cited as "Condition of the Tribes."

Chapter 3

1. Carleton to Riggs, August 6, 1863, "Condition of the Tribes"; see also Robert M. Utley, *Frontiersmen in Blue: The United States Army and the Indian, 1848-1865,* p. 234.

2. General Order no. 81, September 9, 1862, NA, Records of the Adjutant General's Office (AGO), RG 94, vol. 356. The Fort Wingate described in this narrative is not the same Wingate that is today situated fifteen miles east of Gallup, New Mexico. The Fort Wingate of Carson's campaign was

forty-five miles southeast of the new Wingate, near San Rafael, New Mexico. Cubero, New Mexico, is west of Albuquerque on the road to Gallup.

3. Carson to Carleton, February 3, 1863, NA, AGO, RG 94, LR.

4. Carleton to Thomas, March 19, 1863, NA, AGO, RG 94, LR. For insight into Navajo religious concepts see Gladys A. Reichard, *Navajo Religion.*

5. General Order no. 15, June 15, 1863, NA, AGO, RG 94, vol. 922.

6. Ibid.; for Carleton's statements see Carleton to Thomas, September 6, 1863, Annual Report of the Commissioner of Indian Affairs, *HED* 38th Cong., 1st Sess., no. 1, vol. 3, SS 1182.

7. Morrison to AAG, June 23, 1863, NA, RCA, RC 393, LR. A former Ute and Apache agent, Albert H. Pfeiffer had come to the United States from Holland, where he was born in 1822. Pfeiffer was attacked by twenty Apaches on June 20, 1863, while taking a bath at a hot spring along the Journada de Muerto (Journey of Death), a north-south route between Valverde and Las Cruces. Pfeiffer received an arrow wound in his side, but his wife, Juanita Sánchez, and a servant girl were killed.

8. Carson to Acting General, July 24, 1863, NA, RCA, RG 393, LR. Carson drafted two letters to the acting general on July 24, 1863. This citation is from letter 1.

9. Ibid.

10. Carson to Carleton, July 24, 1863, NA, RCA, RG 393, LR (letter 2).

11. Carleton to Thomas, September 6, 1863, Annual Report of the Commissioner of Indian Affairs, *HED* 38th Cong., 1st Sess., no. 1, vol. 3, SS 1182.

12. Carleton to Carson, August 18, 1863, NA, RCA, RG 393, LS.

13. Carson to AAG, July 28, 1863, Carleton to Carson, August 9, 1863, NA, RCA, RG 393, LR and LS.

14. See the service records of Morrison and McAllister in National Archives Microfilm Publications, microcopy M-427, rolls 14, 15, and 25; hereafter cited as microcopy M-427.

15. Carson to Carleton, April 19, 1863, NA, RCA, RG 393, LR.

16. Information on the bounties can be found in Carleton to Carson, August 18, 1863. Details of the expedition can be found in Carson to Cutler, August 19, 1863, NA, RCA, RG 393, LR.

17. Ibid.

18. Carson to Cutler, August 31, 1863, NA, RCA, RG 393, LR.

19. Ibid.

20. Ibid.; oral interview by author with Milton Chee, Ray Winnie, Mike Mitchell, Ruth Roessel, Teddy Drapper, and Frank Harvey at Navajo Community College, Tsaile, Arizona, in sessions dating March 1 to May 1, 1977.

21. Ibid. An excellent discussion of Blakeney's background can be found in Lawrence C. Kelly, *Navajo Roundup,* pp. 44-50.

22. Details of the Blakeney affair can be found in microcopy M-427, rolls

10, 14, and 17; Service Records of Blackeney, NA, AGO, RG 94; Blakeney to Cutler, September 5, Blakeney to Cutler, September 1, 1863, NA, RCA, RG 393, LR; see also Carleton to C.O., Fort Canby, September 18, Carleton to Blakeney, August 19, 1863, NA, RCA, RG 393, LS.

23. See the Service Records of Prentiss, NA, AGO, RG 94.

24. "Memorandum of Events at Fort Canby, September 9-12, 1863," NA, RCA, RG 393, LR.

Chapter 4

1. Carleton to Carson, September 19, 1863, NA, RCA, RG 393, LS.

2. Ibid.

3. Carson to Cutler, October 5, 1863, NA, RCA, RG 393, LR.

4. Ibid.

5. Ibid.

6. Ibid.

7. Carson to AAG, October 19, 1863, NA, RCA, RG 393, LR.

8. McCabe to Murphy, October 12, 1863, NA, RCA, RG 393, LR.

9. Sena to Murphy, October 29, 1863, Carson Copybook, Library of Congress, Manuscript Division, cited from Kelly, *Navajo Roundup,* pp. 66-68; hereafter cited as CC, Kelly.

10. Ibid. Information about Fitch can be found in Fitch to Murphy, October 23, 1863, NA, RCA, RG 393, LR.

11. Abreu to Cutler, October 16, 1863, Carey to Murphy, October 13, 1863, NA, RCA, RG 393, LR.

12. Carson to Carleton, November 1, 1863, CC, Kelly, pp. 68-69; Carleton to Carson, December 5, 1863, NA, RCA, RG 393, LS.

13. Ibid.

14. Ibid.; Carson to Cutler, November 10, 1863, NA, RCA, RG 393, LR.

15. Carson to Cutler, December 6, 1863, NA, RCA, RG 393, LR. This letter contains some excellent insights into Carson's view of the Hopis.

16. Ibid.

17. Ibid.; for Carey's report see Carey to Carleton, December 6, 1863, NA, RCA, RG 393, LR.

18. AAA General to Abreu, December 11, 1863, Sena to Murphy, December 13, 1863, NA, RCA, RG 393, LR.

19. Carson to Cutler, December 20, 1863, NA, RCA, RG 393, LR.

20. Carleton to Carson, December 31, 1863, NA, RCA, RG 393, LS.

21. Ibid.; Sena to Murphy, December 23, 1863, NA, RCA, RG 393, LR.

22. Ibid.

23. Ibid.

24. Carleton to Carson, December 31, 1863, Carson to Cutler, December 6, 1863.

Chapter 5

1. For studies of the Cañon de Chelly see David DeHarport, "An Archaeological Survey of Cañon de Chelly, Northeastern Arizona"; Earl H. Morris, "Exploring in the Canyon of Death," *National Geographic Magazine* 48 (1925): 263-300; Sam Day, Sr., "Canyon de Chelly," printed manuscript, Day Collection, Library of Northern Arizona University, Flagstaff; David Brugge and Raymond Wilson, *Administrative History, Canyon de Chelly National Monument.*

2. John G. Walker, *The Navajo Reconnaissance.*

3. Carleton to Carson, December 5, 1863, NA, RCA, RG 393, LS.

4. Carson to Cutler, August 31, 1863, Carson to Cutler, December 6, 1863, NA, RCA, RG 393, LR.

5. AAA General to Abreu, December 11, 1863, NA, RCA, RG 393, LR.

6. Carson to Cutler, December 20, 1863, NA, RCA, RG 393, LR.

7. Montoya to Sir (Murphy), December 20, 1863, NA, RCA, RG 393, LR.

8. Ibid.

9. Ibid. Officials at Navajo National Monument state that Navajos did not arrive in the cañons surrounding Keet Seel and Betatakin until Carson's campaign.

10. AAA General to Thompson, December 21, 1863, CC, Kelly, p. 91; Thompson to Carson, January n.d., 1864, NA, RCA, RG 393, LR.

11. Carson to Cutler, January 3, 1864, Carleton to Thomas, December 12, 1863, NA, RCA, RG 393, LR and LS.

12. Carson to Cutler, January 3, 1864.

13. Carson to Cutler, December 26, 1863, January 3, 1864, NA, RCA, RG 393, LR.

14. Kit's detailed account of the cañon campaign is found in Carson to Cutler, January 24, 1864, NA, RCA, RG 393, LR.

15. Ibid.

16. Ibid.

17. Ibid.

18. Ibid.

19. Pfeiffer to Murphy, January 20, 1864, NA, RCA, RG 393, LR.

20. Ibid.

21. Ibid.

22. Ibid.

23. Ibid.

24. Ibid.; Ruth Roessel, ed., *Navajo Stories of the Long Walk Period,* p. 46; Stephen C. Jett, "The Destruction of the Navajo Orchards in 1864: John Thompson's Report," *Arizona and the West* 14 (Winter, 1974): 365-78.

25. Ibid.; oral interview, author with Willard Draper, April 17, 1977.

26. Ibid.; Carson to Cutler, January 24, 1864.

27. Roessel, *Navajo Stories of the Long Walk Period,* pp. 257-58.
28. Ibid., p. 128.
29. Ibid., p. 112.
30. Ibid., p. 201.
31. Ibid., pp. 201-202.
32. Carson to Cutler, January 24, 1864, NA, RCA, RG 393, LR.
33. Roessel, *Navajo Stories of the Long Walk Period,* p. 202.
34. Ibid.
35. Ibid.
36. Ibid., pp. 130-31.
37. Ibid., p. 190.
38. Carson to Cutler, January 24, 1864, NA, RCA, RG 393, LR.
39. Roessel, *Navajo Stories of the Long Walk Period,* p. 260.
40. Carson to Cutler, January 24, 1864, NA, RCA, RG 393, LR.
41. Ibid.
42. Carey to Murphy, January 21, 1864, NA, RCA, RG 393, LR.
43. Ibid.
44. Ibid.
45. Carson to Cutler, January 24, 1864, NA, RCA, RG 393, LR.

Chapter 6

1. Carleton to Thomas, February 7, 1864, NA, AGO, RG 94, LR.
2. Carson to AAG, January, 1864, NA, RG 393, LR.
3. Kelly, *Navajo Roundup,* pp. 110-11.
4. Ibid.; Carleton to C.O., Fort Wingate, December 23, 1863, De Forrest to C.O., Fort Wingate, January 15, 1864, NA, RCA, RG 393, LS; Eaton to Cutler, February 2, 14, 1864, NA, RCA, RG 393, LR.
5. Ibid.; *Santa Fe Weekly New Mexican,* November 7, 1863; Campbell to Carleton, February 2, 1864, NA, AGO, RG 94. For a general discussion of Degadito's influence see Gerald Thompson, *The Army and the Navajo,* pp. 22, 27-29. The Navajo account was provided by Chahadineli Benally; the full text of his statements can be found in Roessel, *Navajo Stories of the Long Walk Period,* p. 260.
6. Carey to Cutler, February 4, 14, 21, 1864, NA, RCA, RG 393, LR. Zarcillos Largos was killed by Hispanos at the mouth of the Cañon de Chelly while operating in concert with Canby in 1860.
7. Berney to AAG, April 7, 1864, NA, RCA, RG 393, LR. For the Navajo accounts see Roessel, *Navajo Stories of the Long Walk Period,* pp. 82, 113.
8. Berney to AAG, April 7, 1864.
9. Ibid.
10. Ibid.
11. Kelly, *Navajo Roundup,* p. 121-122.

12. Thompson to Cutler, April 5, 1864, NA, RCA, RG 393, LR. Additional information on Navajo views can be found in Roessel, *Navajo Stories of the Long Walk Period,* p. 30.

13. McCabe to AAG, May 12, 1864, NA, RCA, RG 393, LR.

14. Ibid.

15. Ibid.

16. Ibid.

17. Collins to Dole, October 8, 1861, Annual Report of the Commissioner of Indian Affairs, *SED* 37th Cong., 2d Sess., no. 1, vol. 1, SS 1117.

18. Collins to Dole, October 10, 1862, Annual Report of the Commissioner of Indian Affairs, *HED* 37th Cong., 3d Sess., no. 1, vol. 2, SS 1157. For information regarding the significance of the Hispano-Navajo slave trade see Need to Collins, May 16, 1862, Miscellaneous Correspondence, NMS.

19. Arny to Dole, January 17, 1863, Collins to Dole, February 18, 1863, NA, NMS, LR.

20. Carleton to Halleck, May 10, 1863, June 14, 1863, "Condition of the Tribes," pp. 110, 113-114.

21. "Memorial of the Legislature of New Mexico," January 23, 1864, *House Miscellaneous Document* 38th Cong., 1st Sess., no. 1, vol. 3, SS 1200.

22. Carleton to Thomas, March 12, 1864, microcopy M-619, roll 284.

23. For Carleton's background see Hunt, *Major General James H. Carleton;* Thompson, *The Army and the Navajo.*

24. Carleton to Thomas, September 6, 1863, Annual Report of the Commissioner of Indian Affairs, *HED* 38th Cong., 1st Sess., no. 1, vol. 3, SS 1182.

25. A great deal of correspondence exists regarding the Steck-Carleton feud. See Steck to Dole, January 23, December 10, 14, 1863, NA, NMS, LR; see also Thompson, *The Army and the Navajo,* pp. 22-24, 68-99.

26. Ibid.; Steck to Dole, February 16, 1864, Annual Report of the Commissioner of Indian Affairs, *HED* 38th Cong., 1st Sess., no. 1, vol. 3, SS 1182; Cutler to Wallen, February 14, 1864, "Condition of the Tribes," p. 158; *Santa Fe Weekly New Mexican,* January 31, 1864.

27. Carson to Carleton, (two letters of the same date) April 10, 1864, NA, RCA, RG 393, LR; Carleton to Thomas, April 24, 1864, microcopy M-619, roll 284.

28. Steck to Dole, April 30, 1865, NA, NMS, LR: Frank D. Reeve, "The Federal Indian Policy in New Mexico, 1858-1880," *New Mexico Historical Review* 12 (1937): 256-60.

29. Carleton to C.O., Fort Wingate, February 26, Carleton to Carey, March 16, Carey to AAG, March 27, 1864, NA, RCA, RG 393, LS, LR; Carleton to Thomas, March 12, 1864, microcopy M-619, roll 284.

30. Carson to AAG, March 20, 1864, Carson to Carleton, April 10, 1864, NA, RCA, RG 393, LR.

31. McFerran to General-in-Chief, March 27, 1864, NA, RCA, RG 393, LS.

32. Roessel, *Navajo Stories of the Long Walk Period,* p. 148.

33. Ibid., p. 82.

34. Ibid., p. 149.

35. Ibid., pp. 30-32.

36. Ibid., pp. 23, 30.

37. The best accounts of the administrative mismanagement of the reservation are found in Thompson, *The Army and the Navajo,* pp. 28-67.

38. Roessel, *Navajo Stories of the Long Walk Period,* p. 242.

39. Ibid., p. 191.

Chapter 7

1. Carey to Cutler, February 28, 1864, NA, RCA, RG 393, LR.

2. Ibid.

3. Campbell to Carleton, March 3, 1864, NA, RCA, RG 393, LR.

4. Carson to AAG, April 13, 1864, NA, RCA, RG 393, LR.

5. "Proclamation," May 4, 1864, "Condition of the Tribes," p. 333.

6. Luna to Steck, October 5, 1863, NA, NMS, LR.

7. Steck to Carleton, September 25, 1863, NA, NMS, Miscellaneous Correspondence and Accounting Papers; Steck to Ward, September 19, 1863, NA, NMS, LR. For many accounts of Ute attacks on Navajos from 1863 to 1866, see Roessel, *Navajo Stories of the Long Walk Period.*

8. Steck to Carleton, September 5, 1863, NA, NMS, Miscellaneous Correspondence and Accounting Papers.

9. Labadie to Steck, November 25, 1863, Annual Report of the Commissioner of Indian Affairs, *HED* 38th Cong., 2d Sess., no. 1, vol. 5, SS 1220.

10. *Santa Fe Weekly Gazette,* January 2, 1864.

11. Carleton to Thomas, December 23, 1863, "Condition of the Tribes," p. 254; Steck to Dole, October 10, 1864, and Labadie to Steck, October 22, 1864, Annual Report of the Commissioner of Indian Affairs, *HED* 38th Cong., 2d Sess., no. 1, vol. 5, SS 1220.

12. Labadie to Steck, October 25, 1864, Annual Report of the Commissioner of Indian Affairs, *HED* 38th Cong., 2d Sess., no. 1, vol. 5, SS 1220.

13. McCabe to AAG, May 12, 1864, NA, RCA, RG 393, LR; Thompson, *The Army and the Navajo,* p. 65.

14. Carey to Cutler, March 6, 1864, NA, RCA, RG 393, LR.

15. McCabe to AAG, March 4, 1864.

16. Carey to Cutler, March 13, 15, 1864, NA, RCA, RG 393, LR.

17. Carson to Carleton, April 10, 1864, NA, RCA, RG 393, LR; Kelly, *Navajo Roundup,* pp. 140-69; Thompson, *The Army and the Navajo,* pp. 33-34, 42-43.

18. For Thompson's report of his expedition into the Cañon de Chelly and Barboncito's capture see Kelly, *Navajo Roundup*, pp. 161-62, 167; Thompson, *The Army and the Navajo*, pp. 88-89, 126-27, 145-46.

19. Carey to Carleton, April 24, 1864, NA, RCA, RG 393, LR.

20. Carey to Wood, May 10, 1864, with Carleton to Thomas, May 29, 1864, in microcopy M-619, roll 284.

21. See Carleton's Report, March 21, 1865, NA, RCA, RG 393, LS.

22. Eaton to Cutler, February 8, 1865, OR, vol. 48, pp. 783-84.

23. Kelly, *Navjao Roundup*, p. 164. For Navajo views of creation and emergence in Dinetah see Ethelou Yazzie, *Navajo History.*

24. Carleton's Report, March 21, 1865.

25. Ibid.

26. Carleton to Shaw, March 23, 1865, OR, vol. 48, pp. 1246-1247.

27. Graves to Cooley, September 28, 1866, NA, NMS, LR; see also the many letters written by Butler in NA, RCA, RG 393, LR. In July, 1864, the commander at Fort Sumner estimated that there were 5,916 Navajos then at the Bosque Redondo. By January, 1865, the number of Navajos had increased to 8,577: 2,361 men, 2,742 women, 3,180 children, and 1 infant.

Chapter 8

1. The best description of Canby's negotiations with the Navajos in 1861 is found in McNitt, *The Navajo Wars*, pp. 410-329.

2. Sabin, *Kit Carson Days*, pp. 700-704; Thompson, *The Army and the Navajos*, pp. 11-12.

3. An excellent discussion of Spanish, Mexican, and Anglo Indian policies in the Southwest can be found in Edward H. Spicer, *Cycles of Conquest: The Impact of Spain, Mexico, and the United States on the Indians of the Southwest, 1533-1960.*

4. Ibid.; see also Francis Jennings, *The Invasion of America: Indians, Colonialism, and the Cant of Conquest.*

5. Ibid.

6. For discussion of the relationship of treaties to American Indian policy see Felix S. Cohen, *Handbook of Federal Indian Law* (Washington, D.C., 1941); Charles J. Kappler, *Indian Affairs: Laws and Treaties* (Washington, D.C., 1903-40); and S. Lyman Tyler, *A History of Indian Policy*, pp. 32-53.

7. Carleton to Carson, September 19, 1863.

8. A general discussion of removal is found in Tyler, *A History of Indian Policy*, pp. 54-69.

9. Ibid., pp. 70-94; Thompson, *The Army and the Navajo*, pp. 12-14.

10. Carleton to Thomas, September 6, 1863. For an in-depth study of Carleton's beliefs see Thompson, *The Army and the Navajo*, pp. 10-27.

11. Ibid.; Carleton to Halleck, May 10, June 14, 1863, "The Condition of the Tribes."

12. Thompson, *The Army and the Navajos,* pp. 24-27, 31-38, 44.

13. Carson to Carleton, July 14, 1864, NA, RCA, RG 393, LR.

14. Arny to Bogy, November 24, 1866, NA, NMS, LR. The territorial newspapers were filled with criticism of Carleton. See *Santa Fe Weekly New Mexican:* November 3, 1865; January 5, 12, 26; February 16; April 6, 27; May 25; June 8, 16; July 7, 28, 29; October 13, 27; November 24, 1866; January 12, 1926; February 23; and all papers from March through July, 1866. See also *Santa Fe Weekly Gazette:* January 20; April 2; May 10; July 7, 28; September 22; October 20; December 8, 1866; January 12, 19, 26, 1867.

15. *Santa Fe Weekly New Mexican,* October 27, 1866.

16. In late April, 1867, Carleton relinquished his command and took leave until January 1, 1869. While on leave, he rested in Santa Fe and Albuquerque before going home to Maine. When he returned to active duty, he served in the Department of Texas until his death. For Carleton's career after leaving New Mexico, see Hunt, *Major General James Henry Carleton,* pp. 340-44.

17. Sabin, *Kit Carson Days,* pp. 494-97; Harvey Lewis Carter, *"Dear Old Kit": The Historical Christopher Carson,* pp. 176-78.

18. W. J. Ghent, "Kit Carson," *Dictionary of American Biography* (New York, 1939), 3:530; Sabin, *Kit Carson Days,* p. 503; Carter, *"Dear Old Kit,"* pp. 215-16.

19. James Rusling, *Across America,* pp. 137-38.

20. Ibid.

21. Thompson, *The Army and the Navajo,* p. 158.

22. Ibid., pp. 151-52.

23. Roessel, *Navajo Stories of the Long Walk Period,* pp. 212, 238-39, 244.

24. Martin A. Link, intro., *Treaty Between the United States of America and the Navajo Tribe of Indians, with a Record of the Discussions that led to its Signing* (Las Vegas, Nev., 1968), pp. 1-2.

25. Ibid., p. 4.

26. Ibid., pp. 5-9.

27. Thompson, *The Army and the Navajo,* pp. 140-57.

Bibliography

Documents

Abel, Annie H., comp. and ed. *Official Correspondence of James S. Calhoun While Indian Agent at Santa Fe and Superintendent of Indian Affairs in New Mexico.* Washington, D.C.: Government Printing Office, 1915.

Albert, James W. "Report of Lt. J. W. Albert on his Examination of New Mexico in the Years 1846-47." *Senate Executive Document* 3, 30th Cong., 1st Sess.

Compiled Service Records of Volunteer Union Soldiers Who Served in Organizations from the Territory of New Mexico. National Archives, Microfilm Publications, microcopy M-427.

"Condition of the Indian Tribes." *Senate Executive Document* 156, 39th Cong., 2d Sess., 1866.

Congressional Globe, 1855-56.

Emory, William H. "Notes of a Military Reconnaissance from Fort Leavenworth in Missouri, to San Diego, in California, including parts of the Arkansas, Del Norte, and Gila Rivers." *Senate Executive Document* 7, 30th Cong., 1st Sess.

Executive Orders Relating to Indian Reservations from May 14, 1885, to July 1, 1912. National Archives.

House Executive Document 17, 31st Cong., 2d Sess., 1849.

House Executive Document 1, 32d Cong., 2d Sess., 1852.

House Executive Document 508, 36th Cong., 1st Sess., 1859.

House Executive Document 1, 37th Cong., 3d Sess., 1862-63.

House Executive Document 1, 38th Cong., 1st Sess., 1863.

House Executive Document 1, 38th Cong., 2d Sess., 1863.

House Miscellaneous Document 113, 34th Cong., 1st Sess., 1856.

House Miscellaneous Document 1, 38th Cong., 1st Sess., 1864.

Kappler, Charles Joseph. *Indian Affairs, Laws and Treaties.* 2 vols. Washington, D.C.: Government Printing Office, 1904.

Letterman, Jonathan. "Sketch of the Navajo Tribe of Indians, Territory of New Mexico." *House Miscellaneous Document* 113, 34th Cong., 1st Sess., 1856.

Post Returns, Forts Defiance, Fauntleroy, Lyon, Wingate, and Canby. National Archives, record group 94.

Records of the Adjutant General's Office, Department of New Mexico, Orders and Special Orders, 1862. National Archives, record group 94.

Records of the Adjutant General's Office, Letters Received, 1861-1870. National Archives, Microfilm Publications, microcopy M-619.

Records of the Bureau of Indian Affairs, New Mexico Superintendency. Letters Received. National Archives, record group 75.

Records of United States Army Continental Commands, 1821-1920, Department of New Mexico. Letters Received and Letters Sent. National Archives, record group 393.

Senate Executive Document 1, 32d Cong., 1st Sess., 1851.

Senate Executive Document 1, 33d Cong., 1st Sess., 1853.

Senate Executive Document 1, 35th Cong., 2d Sess., 1858.

Senate Executive Document 1, 37th Cong., 2d Sess., 1862.

Simpson, James H. "Journal of a Military Reconnaissance from Santa Fe, New Mexico, to the Navajo Country in 1849." *Senate Executive Document* 64, 31st Cong., 2d Sess.

"Treaty Between the United States of America and the Navajo Tribe of Indians." Signed by President Andrew Johnson and ratified by the United States Senate, July 25, 1868. In Charles J. Kappler, *Indian Affairs, Laws and Treaties.* Vol. 2. Washington, D.C.: Government Printing Office, 1904.

U.S. Department of War. *War of the Rebellion: A Compilation of the Official Records of Union and Confederate Armies.* Washington, D.C.: Government Printing Office, 1880-1901.

Original Sources

"Annual Report of the Commissioner of Indian Affairs, 1861-68."

House Executive Documents and *Senate Executive Documents.*

Bibo, Nathan. "Reminiscences of Early Days in New Mexico." *Albuquerque Evening Herald,* June 11, 1922.

Bieber, Ralph P., ed., "Letters of William Carr Lane, 1852-1854." *New Mexico Historical Review* 2 (1928): 183-84.

———, ed. Marching with the Army of the West. Glendale, Calif.: Arthur H. Clark, 1936.

Biographical Files, Arizona Historical Society.

Bloom, Lansing, B., ed., "The Rev. Hiram Walter Read, Baptist Missionary." *New Mexico Historical Review* 17 (1942): 113-47.

Brewerton, George D. "A Ride with Kit Carson Through the Great American Desert and the Rocky Mountains." *Harper's New Monthly Magazine,* August, 1853, pp. 306-34.

Brooks, Clinton E., and Frank D. Reeve, eds. "A Dragoon in New Mexico, 1850-1856." *New Mexico Historical Review* 22 (1947): 51-97, 140-76.

Brugge, David M. *Long Ago in Navajoland.* Window Rock, Ariz.: Navajo Tribe, 1965.

———. *Navajos in the Catholic Church Records of New Mexico, 1694-1875.* Window Rock, Ariz.: Navajo Tribe, 1968.

———, and Raymond Wilson. Administrative History, *Canyon de Chelly National Monument.* Washington, D.C.: Government Printing Office, 1976.

———, ed. and trans. "Vizcarra's Navajo Campaign of 1823." *Arizona and the West* 6 (1964): 223-44.

Carson Copybook, Library of Congress, Manuscript Division.

Carson Papers, Bancroft Library.

Connelley, William E. *Doniphan's Expedition and the Conquest of New Mexico and California.* Kansas City, Mo.: Bryant and Douglas Book Co., 1907.

Cooke, Philip St. George. *The Conquest of New Mexico and California, An Historical and Personal Narrative.* New York: G. P. Putnam's Sons, 1878.

Correll, J. Lee. *Through White Men's Eyes: A Contribution to Navajo History.* Window Rock, Ariz.: Navajo Heritage Center, 1976.

Cremony, John C. *Life Among the Apaches.* San Francisco: A. Roman and Co., 1868.

Croix, Teodoro de. "Report." In A. B. Thomas, *Teodoro de Croix and the Northern Frontier of New Spain, 1776-1783.* Norman, University of Oklahoma Press, 1941.

Day, Sam, Sr. "Canyon de Chelly." Printed manuscript. Day Collection. Library of Northern Arizona University, Flagstaff.

Day Collection, Northern Arizona University Library, Special Collections.

DeHarport, David. "An Archaeological Survey of Cañon de Chelly, Northeastern Arizona." Ph.D. dissertation, Harvard University, 1959.

Dillon, Richard H., ed. *A Cannoneer in Navajo Country: The Journal of Josiah M. Rice.* Denver: Old West Publishing Co., 1970.

Dunn, Jacob P. *Massacres of the Mountains: A History of the Indian Wars of the Far West, 1815-1875.* New York: Harper, 1886.

Edwards, Marcellus Ball. "Diary." In Ralph P. Bieber, ed. *Marching with the Army of the West.* Vol. 4. Glendale, Calif.: Arthur H. Clark, 1936.

Espinosa, J. Manuel. *First Expedition of Vargas into New Mexico, 1692.* Albuquerque: University of New Mexico Press, 1940.

Ferguson, Philip G. "Diary." In Ralph P. Bieber, ed. *Marching with the Army of the West.* Vol. 4. Glendale, Calif.: Arthur H. Clark, 1936.

Gibson, George R. *Journal of a Soldier Under Kearny and Doniphan, 1846-47.* Edited by Ralph Bieber. Glendale, Calif.: Arthur H. Clark, 1935.

Heitman, Francis B. *Historical Register and Dictionary of the United States Army, 1789-1903.* 2 vols. Urbana: University of Illinois Press, 1965.

Hodge, Frederick Webb, ed. *Handbook of American Indians North of Mexico.* 2 vols. Washington, D.C.: Smithsonian Institution, 1907.

Hughes, John T. *Doniphan's Expedition; Containing an Account of the Conquest of Mexico.* Cincinnati: U. P. James, 1847.

James, Thomas. *Three Years Among the Indians and Mexicans.* Chicago: Rio Grande Press, 1962.

Jenkins, Myra Ellen, and Ward Allen Minge. "Record of Navajo Activities Affecting the Acoma-Laguna Area, 1746-1910." Typed manuscript, New Mexico State Records Center and Archives.

Jett, Stephen C. "The Destruction of the Navajo Orchards, 1864: John Thompson's Journal." *Arizona and the West* 16 (1974): 365-78.

Letterman, Jonathan. "Sketch of the Navajo Tribe of Indians." *Smith-*

sonian Report, 1855. Washington, D.C.: Government Printing Office, 1855.

Lindgren, Raymond E., ed. "A Diary of Kit Carson's Navajo Campaign 1863-1864." *New Mexico Historical Review* 21 (1946): 226-47.

Magoffin, Susan S. *Down the Santa Fe Trail and into Mexico: The Diary of Susan Shelby Magoffin, 1846-1847.* Edited by Stela Drumm. New Haven, Conn.: Yale University Press, 1962.

Mangiante, Rosal. *History of Fort Defiance, 1841-1900.* M.A. thesis. Tucson: University of Arizona, 1950.

Mansfield, Joseph K. *Mansfield on the Condition of the Western Forts, 1853-1854.* Edited by Robert W. Frazer. Norman: University of Oklahoma Press, 1962.

"Memorandum of Events at Fort Canby, September 9-12, 1863." Records of United States Army Continental Commands, 1821-1920, Department of New Mexico. Letters Received.

"Memorial of the Legislature of New Mexico." *House Miscellaneous Document* 1, 38th Cong., 1st Sess., 1864.

Meriwether, David. *My Life in the Mountains and on the Plains.* Norman: University of Oklahoma Press, 1965.

Navajo Land Claims Files, Land Claims Office, Navajo Tribe.

Oral Interviews: author with Willard Draper, April 17, 1977; sessions with Mike Mitchell, Ruth Roessel, Frank Harvey, Ray Winnie, Milton Chee, and Teddy Draper, March 1-May 1, 1977; sessions with Chancellor and Ella Damon, September, 1976-May, 1977.

Quaife, Milo Milton, ed. *Kit Carson's Autobiography.* Lincoln: University of Nebraska Press, 1966.

Ritch and Kern Collections, Henry E. Huntington Library.

Robinson, Jacob S. *A Journal of the Santa Fe Expedition under Colonel Doniphan.* Princeton, N.J.: Princeton University Press, 1932.

Rodenbough, Theodore F. *From Everglade to Cañon with the Second United States Cavalry: An Authentic Account of Service in Florida, Mexico, Virginia, and the Indian Country, Including the Personal Recollections of Prominent Officers; with an Appendix Containing Orders, Reports and Correspondence, Military Records, etc., etc., etc., 1836-1875.* New York: D. Van Nostrand, 1875.

Roessel, Ruth, ed. *Navajo Stories of the Long Walk Period.* Tsaile, Ariz.: Navajo Community College Press, 1973.

Rowland, Buford, ed. "Report of the Commissioners on the Road From Missouri to New Mexico, October 1827." *New Mexico Historical*

Review 14 (1939): 213-29.

Rusling, James. *Across America.* New York: Sheldon Co., 1874.

Schoolcraft, Henry R. *Information Respecting the History, Condition and Prospects of the Indian Tribes of the United States.* Vol. 4. Philadelphia: Lippincott, Crambo and Co., 1854.

Steck Collection, University of New Mexico Library.

Van Valkenburgh, Richard. "Diné Bikéyah." Mimeograph ed. Window Rock, Ariz.: Navajo Tribe, 1941.

Walker, John G. and Oliver L. Shepherd. *The Navajo Reconnaissance.* Edited by Lynn R. Bailey. Los Angeles: Westernlore Press, 1964.

Ward, John. "Indian Affairs in New Mexico Under the Administration of William Carr Lane: From the Journal of John Ward." Edited by Annie H. Abel. *New Mexico Historical Review* 16 (1941): 206-32, 328-58.

Watson, Editha L. *Navajo Sacred Places.* Window Rock, Ariz.: Navajo Tribe, 1964.

Yazzie, Ethelou. *Navajo History.* Many Farms, Ariz.: Navajo Community College Press, 1971.

Newspapers

Albuquerque Rio Abajo Press
Gallup Independent
Navajo Times
New York Daily Tribune
New York Tribune
Salt Lake City Deseret News
Santa Fe Gazette
Santa Fe New Mexican
Santa Fe Weekly Gazette
Santa Fe Weekly New Mexican
Santa Fe Republican

Secondary Sources

Amsden, Charles. "The Navajo Exile at Bosque Redondo." *New Mexico Historical Review* 8 (1933): 31-50.

Bailey, Lynn R. *Indian Slave Trade in the Southwest.* Los Angeles: Westernlore Press, 1973.

————. *The Long Walk: A History of the Navajo Wars, 1846-1868.* Los Angeles: Westernlore Press, 1964.

Bancroft, Hubert H. *History of Arizona and New Mexico.* San Francisco: History Co., 1889.

Barber, Ruth K. "Indian Labor in the Spanish Colonies." *New Mexico Historical Review* 7 (1932): 105-43, 233-73, 311-49.

Bennett, James A. "A Dragoon in New Mexico: 1850-1856." *New Mexico Historical Review* 22 (1947): 51-97, 140-76.

Bolton, Herbert Eugene. *Coronado: Knight of Pueblos and Plains.* Albuquerque: University of New Mexico Press, 1949.

————, ed. *Spanish Exploration in the Southwest, 1542-1706.* New York: Charles Scribner's Sons, 1916.

Brugge, David M. *Zarcillos Largos: Courageous Advocate of Peace.* Window Rick, Ariz.: Navajo Tribe, 1970.

Carter, Harvey L. *"Dear Old Kit": The Historical Christopher Carson.* Norman: University of Oklahoma Press, 1968.

Clark, Laverne H. *They Sang for Horses: The Impact of the Horse on Navajo and Apache Folklore.* Tucson: University of Arizona Press, 1966.

Colton, Ray C. *The Civil War in the Western Territories.* Norman: University of Oklahoma Press, 1959.

Correll, J. Lee, *Sandoval—Traitor or Patriot?* Window Rock, Ariz.: Navajo Tribe, 1970.

Estergreen, M. Morgan. *Kit Carson: A Portrait in Courage.* Norman: University of Oklahoma Press, 1962.

Fisher, Kathy. "The Forgotten Dodge." *Annals of Iowa* 40 (1970): 296-305.

Forbes, Jack D. *Apache, Navajo, and Spaniard.* Norman: University of Oklahoma Press, 1960.

Frink, Maurice. *Fort Defiance and the Navajos.* Boulder, Colo.: Pruett Press, 1968.

Ganaway, Loomis, M. "New Mexico and the Sectional Controversy, 1846-1861." *New Mexico Historical Review* 18 (1943-44): 113-47, 205-46, 325-48.

Ghent, W. J. "Kit Carson." *Dictionary of American Biography.* Vol. 3. New York: Scribner's, 1939.

Heyman, Max L., Jr. "On the Navajo Trail: The Campaign of 1860-1861." *New Mexico Historical Review* 26 (1951): 44-64.

————. *Prudent Soldier: A Biography of Major General E. R. S. Canby, 1817-1873.* Glendale, Calif.: Arthur H. Clark, 1959.

Hill, W. W. *Navajo Warfare.* Yale University Publications in Anthropology, no. 5. New Haven, Conn.: Yale University Press, 1936.

Hunt, Aurora. *Major General James H. Carleton.* Glendale, Calif.: Arthur H. Clark, 1958.

Jennings, Francis. *The Invasion of America: Indians, Colonialism, and the Cant of Conquest.* Chapel Hill: University of North Carolina Press, 1975

Keleher, William A. *Turmoil in New Mexico, 1846-1868.* Santa Fe, N.Mex.: Rydal Press, 1952.

————. *Violence in Lincoln County.* Albuquerque: University of New Mexico Press, 1957.

Kelly, Lawrence C. *Navajo Roundup.* Boulder, Colo.: Pruett Press, 1970.

————. "Where Was Fort Canby?" *New Mexico Historical Review* 42 (1967): 49-62.

Kerby, Robert L. *The Confederate Invasion of New Mexico and Arizona, 1861-1862.* Los Angeles: Westernlore Press, 1958.

McNitt, Frank. *Navajo Wars: Military Campaigns, Slave Raids, and Reprisals.* Albuquerque: University of New Mexico Press, 1972.

————, ed. *Navajo Expedition: Journal of a Military Reconnaissance from Santa Fe, New Mexico, to the Navaho Country Made in 1849 by Lieutenant James H. Simpson.* Norman: University of Oklahoma Press, 1964.

Moody, Marshall D. "Kit Carson, Agent to the Indians in New Mexico, 1853-1861." *New Mexico Historical Review* 28 (1953): 1-20.

Moorhead, Max L. *The Apache Frontier: Jacob Ugarte and Spanish-Indian Relations in Northern New Spain, 1769-1791.* Norman: University of Oklahoma Press, 1968.

Morris, Earl H. "Exploring in the Canyon of Death." *National Geographic Magazine* 48 (1925): 263-300.

Prucha, Francis P. *A Guide to the Military Posts of the United States, 1789-1895.* Madison: State Historical Society of Wisconsin, 1964.

Reeve, Frank D. "The Federal Indian Policy in New Mexico." *New Mexico Historical Review* 13 (1938): 14-49.

————. "The Federal Indian Policy in New Mexico, 1858-1880." *New Mexico Historical Review* 12 (1937): 218-69.

——. "The Government and the Navaho, 1846-1858." *New Mexico Historical Review* 14 (1939): 82-115.

——. "Navajo Foreign Affairs, 1795-1864." Edited by Eleanor B. Adams and John L. Kessell. *New Mexico Historical Review* 46 (1971): 101-32, 223-51.

——. "Navaho-Spanish Wars, 1860-1720." *New Mexico Historical Review,* 33 (1958): 205-31.

Reichard, Gladys A. *Navajo Religion.* New York: Bollingen Foundation, 1950.

Sabin, Edwin L. *Kit Carson Days, 1809-1868: Adventures in the Path of Empire.* New York: Press of the Pioneers, 1935.

Simmons, Marc. "Horse Race at Fort Fauntleroy: An Incident of the Navajo Wars." *La Gaceta* 5 (1970).

——. *The Little Lion of the Southwest: A Life of Manuel Chaves.* Chicago: Sage Books, 1973.

Spicer, Edward H. *Cycles of Conquest: The Impact of Spain, Mexico, and the United States on the Indians of the Southwest.* Tucson: University of Arizona Press, 1962.

Taylor, Morris F. "Ka-ni-ache." *Colorado Magazine* 43 (1966-67): 275-302.

Thompson, Gerald. *The Army and the Navajo.* Tucson: University of Arizona Press, 1976.

Trafzer, Clifford E. *Anglo Expansionists and Navajo Raiders: A Conflict of Interests.* Tsaile, Ariz.: Navajo Community College Press, 1978.

——. "Defeat of the Lords of New Mexico: The Navajo-Apache Wars." *Military History of Texas and the Southwest* 9 (1971): 215-25.

——. *Diné and Bilagáana: The Navajos and the First Anglos.* Tsaile, Ariz., 1978.

——. "Mr. Lincoln's Army Fights the Navajos, 1863-1864." *Lincoln Herald,* 77 (1975): 148-58.

——. *Navajos and Spaniards.* Tsaile, Ariz., 1978.

——. "Politicos and Navajos." *Journal of the West* 13 (1974): 3-16.

Twitchell, Ralph Emerson. *History of the Military Occupation of the Territory of New Mexico from 1846 to 1851.* Chicago: Rio Grande Press, 1963.

————. *The Leading Facts of New Mexican History.* 2 vols. Cedar Rapids, Iowa: Torch Press, 1912.

Tyler, Lyman. *A History of Indian Policy.* Washington, D.C.: Government Printing Office, 1973.

Underhill, Ruth. *The Navajos.* Norman: University of Oklahoma Press, 1956.

Utley, Robert M. *Frontiersmen in Blue: The United States Army and the Indian, 1848-1865.* New York: Macmillan, 1967.

Van Valkenburgh, Richard. "Captain Red Shirt." *New Mexico Magazine* (July 1941): 44-45.

Waldrip, William I. "New Mexico During the Civil War." *New Mexico Historical Review* 28 (1953): 163-82, 251-90.

Westphall, Victor. *The Public Domain in New Mexico, 1854-1891.* Albuquerque: University of New Mexico Press, 1965.

Wilson, John P. *Military Campaigns in the Navajo Country, Northwestern New Mexico, 1800-1846.* Santa Fe: Museum of New Mexico, 1967.

Woodward, Arthur. "The First American Through Cañon de Chelly, Arizona." *Masterkey* 13 (1939): 136-38.

Worcester, Donald E. "The Navaho During the Spanish Regime in New Mexico." *New Mexico Historical Review* 26 (1951): 101-18.

Young, Robert W. *The Role of the Navajo in the Southwestern Drama.* Gallup, N.Mex.: *Gallup Independent,* 1968.

Index

271